VOL. 7

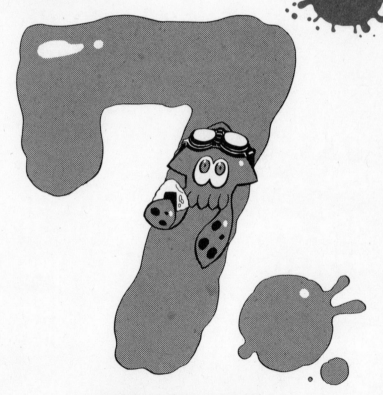

STORY AND ART BY
Sankichi Hinodeya

CONTENTS

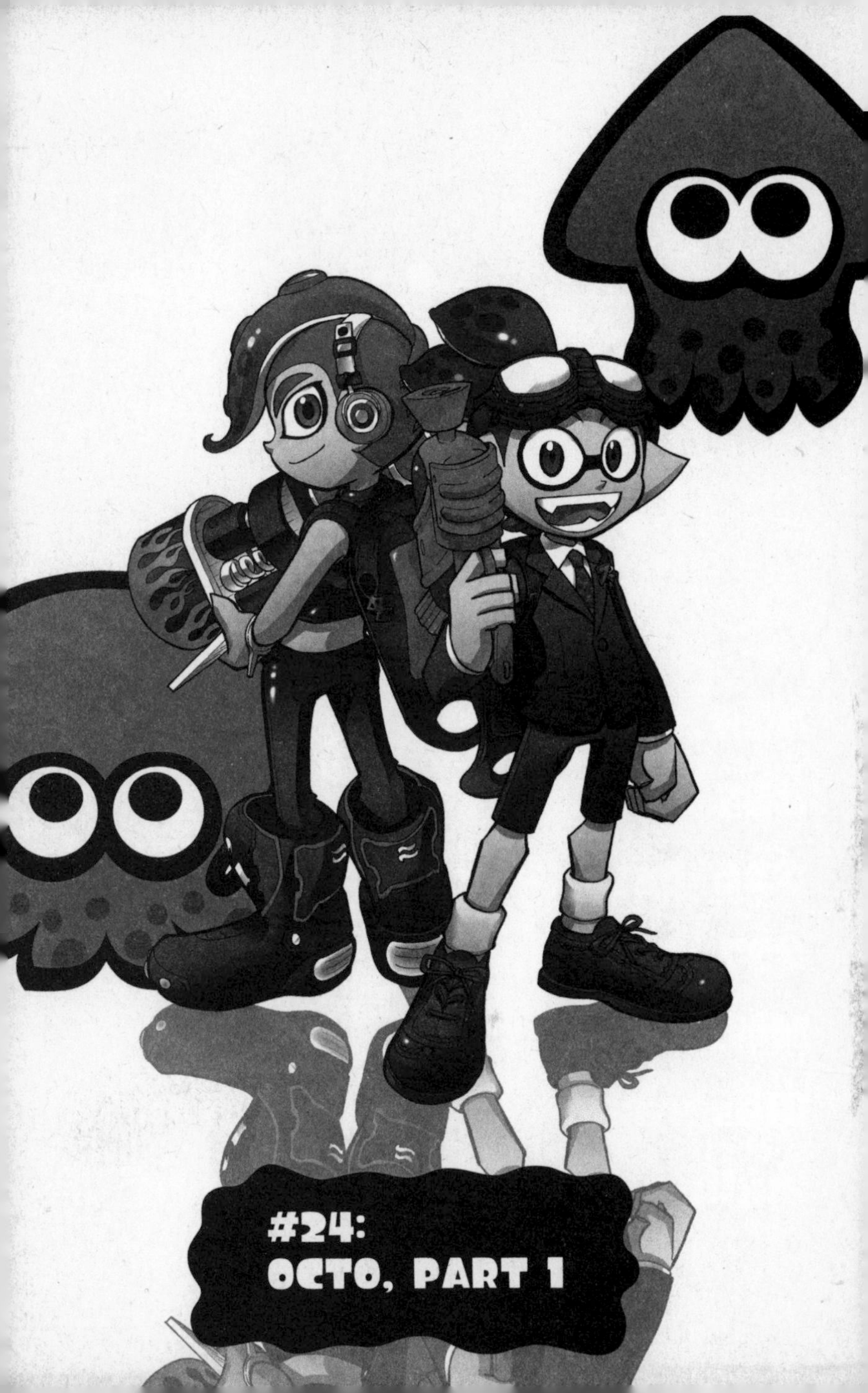
#24:
OCTO, PART 1

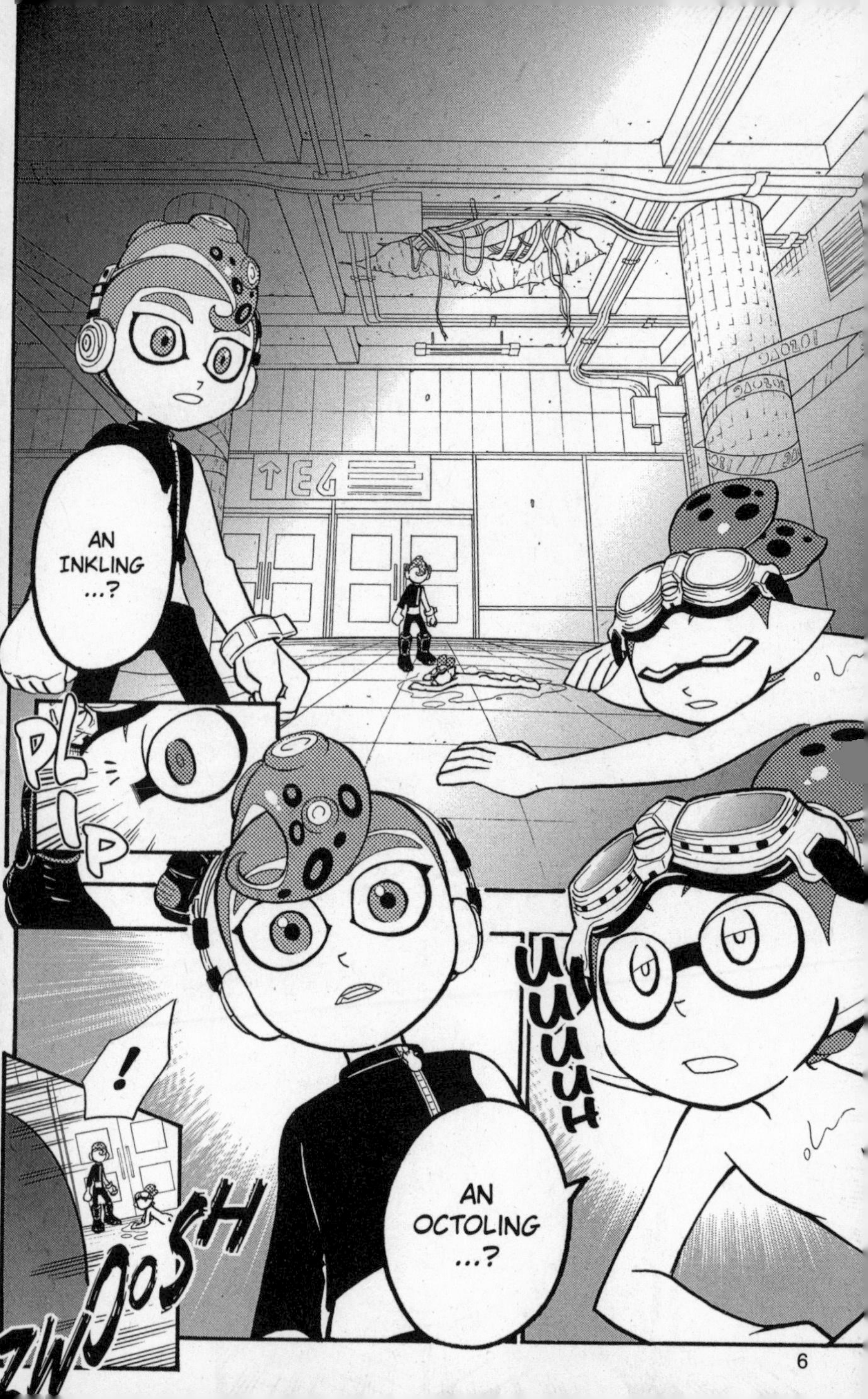
AN INKLING ...?
PLIP
UUUUUH
AN OCTOLING ...?
!
ZWOOSH

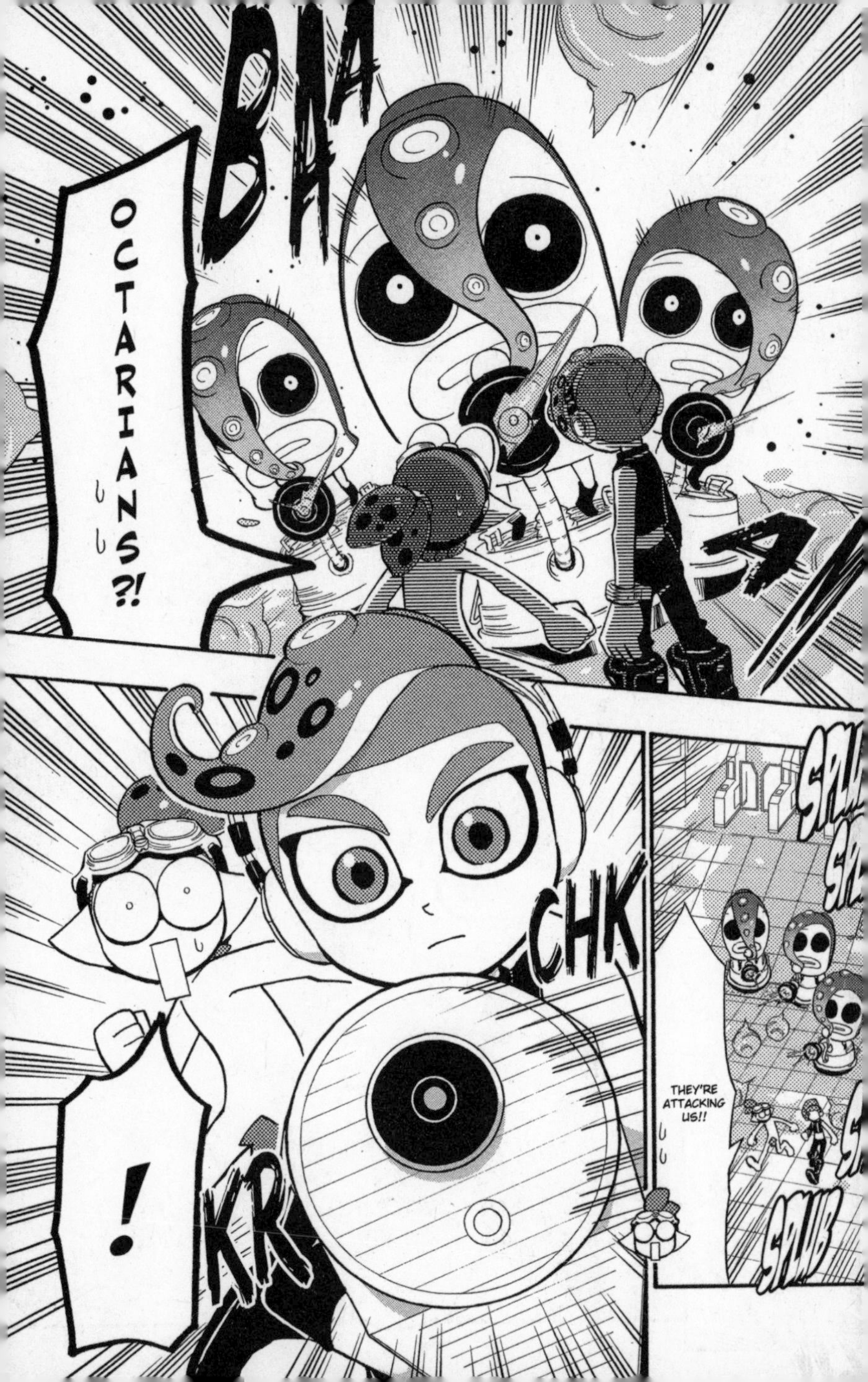
BHA
OCTARIANS?!
THEY'RE ATTACKING US!!
CHK
!
KR

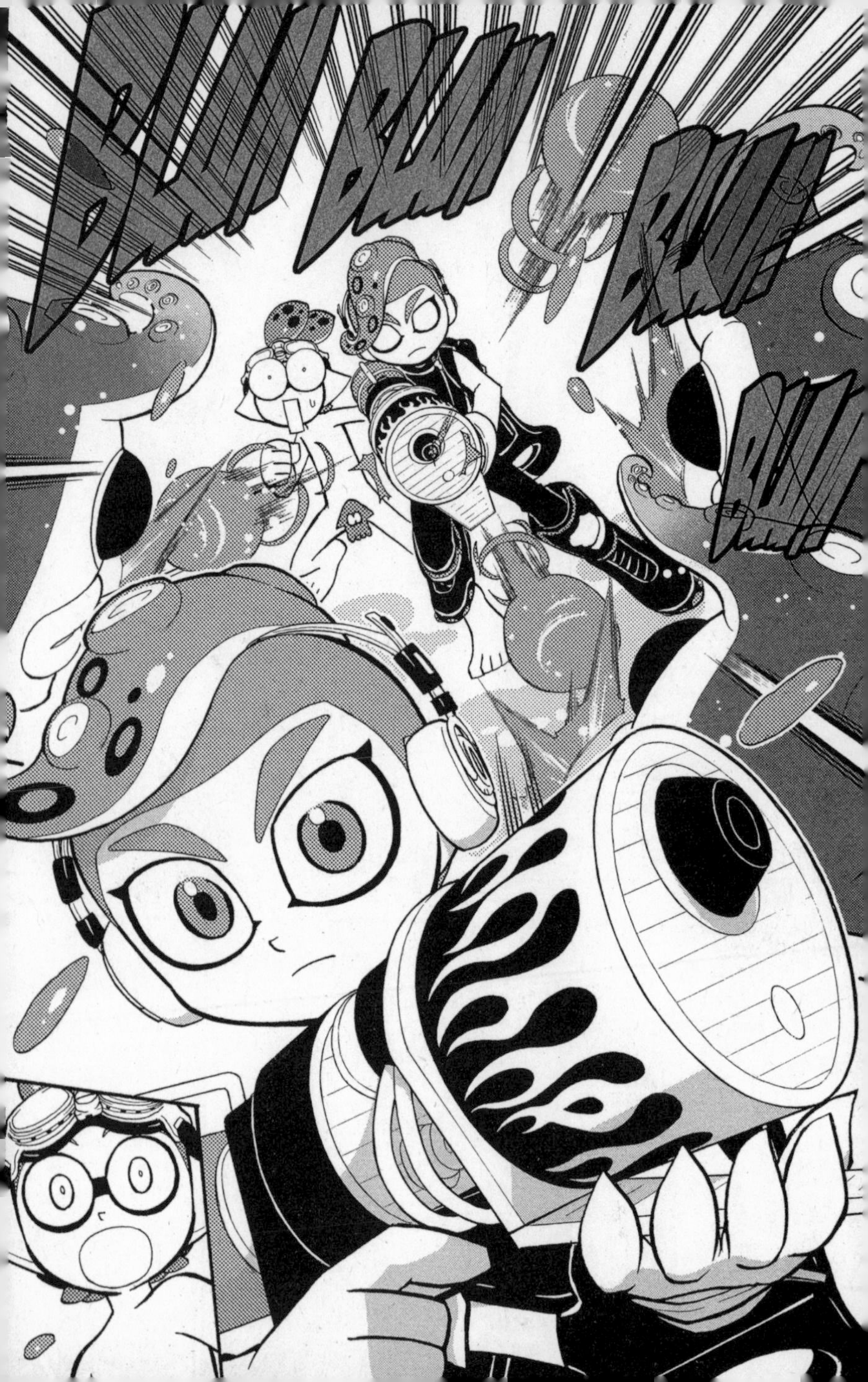

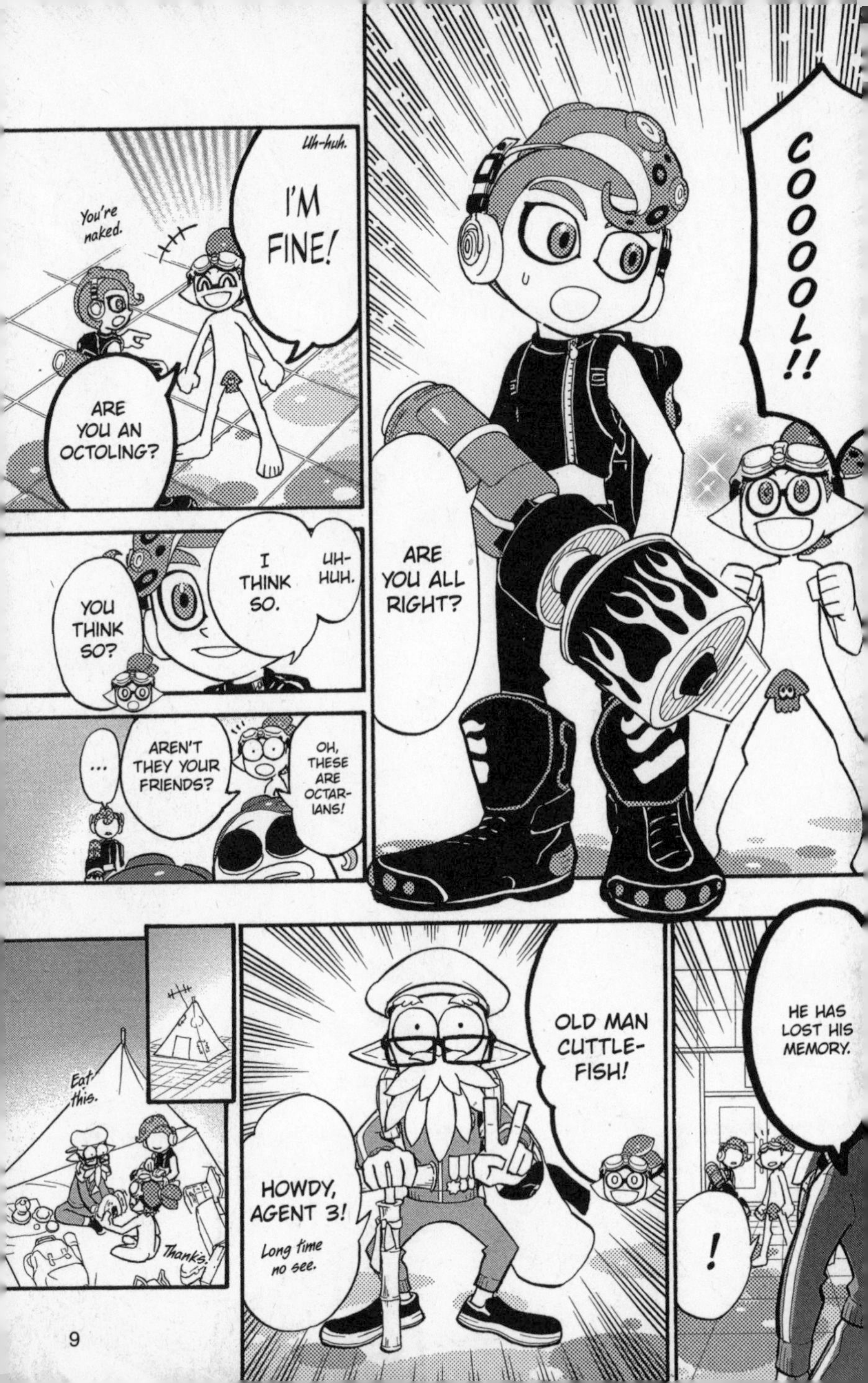
COOOOOL!!
ARE YOU ALL RIGHT?
Uh-huh.
I'M FINE!
You're naked.
ARE YOU AN OCTOLING?
UH-HUH.
I THINK SO.
YOU THINK SO?
OH, THESE ARE OCTARIANS!
AREN'T THEY YOUR FRIENDS?
...
HE HAS LOST HIS MEMORY.
!
OLD MAN CUTTLEFISH!
HOWDY, AGENT 3!
Long time no see.
Eat this.
Thanks.

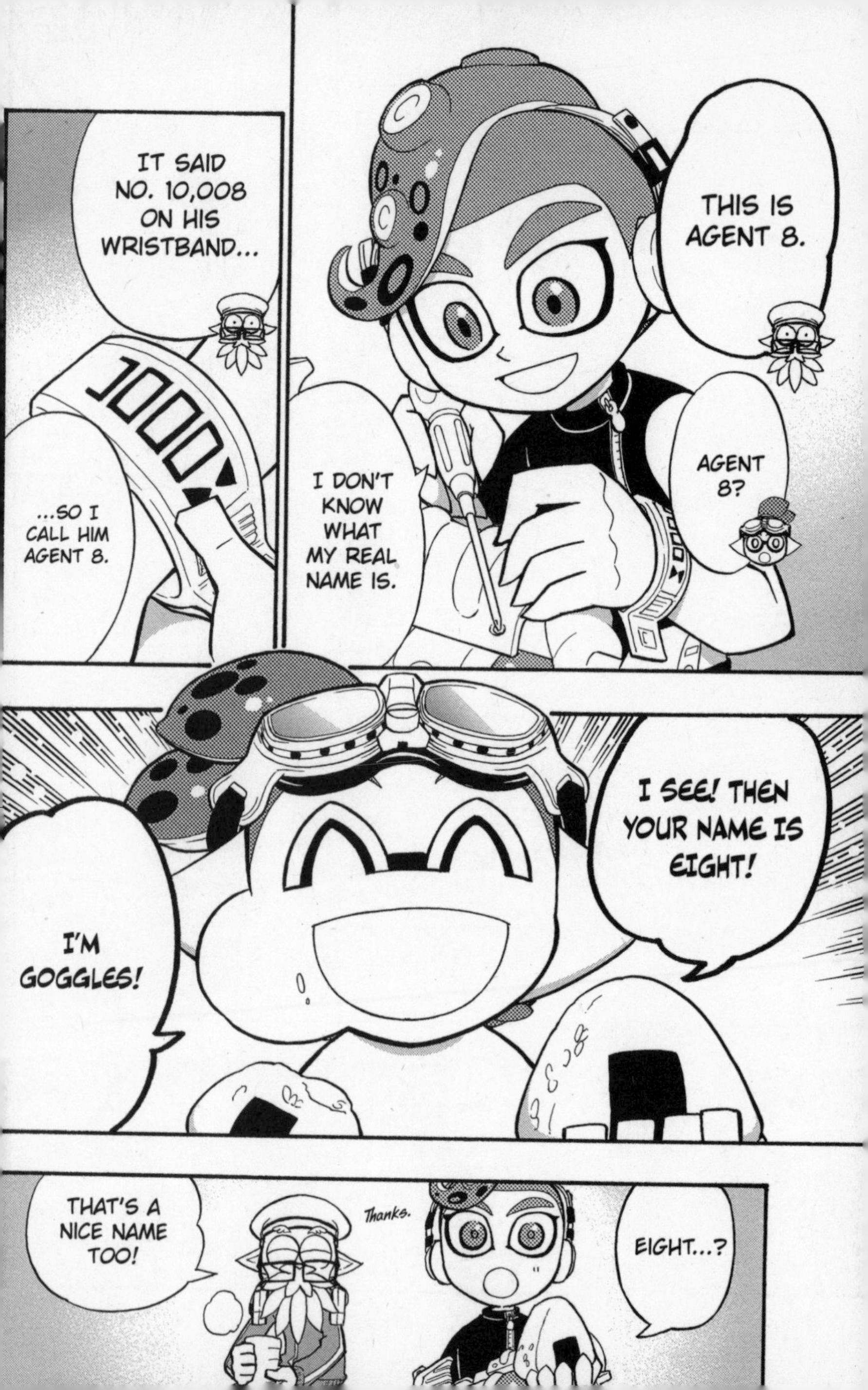
THIS IS AGENT 8.
AGENT 8?
I DON'T KNOW WHAT MY REAL NAME IS.
IT SAID NO. 10,008 ON HIS WRISTBAND...
...SO I CALL HIM AGENT 8.
I SEE! THEN YOUR NAME IS EIGHT!
I'M GOGGLES!
EIGHT...?
Thanks.
THAT'S A NICE NAME TOO!

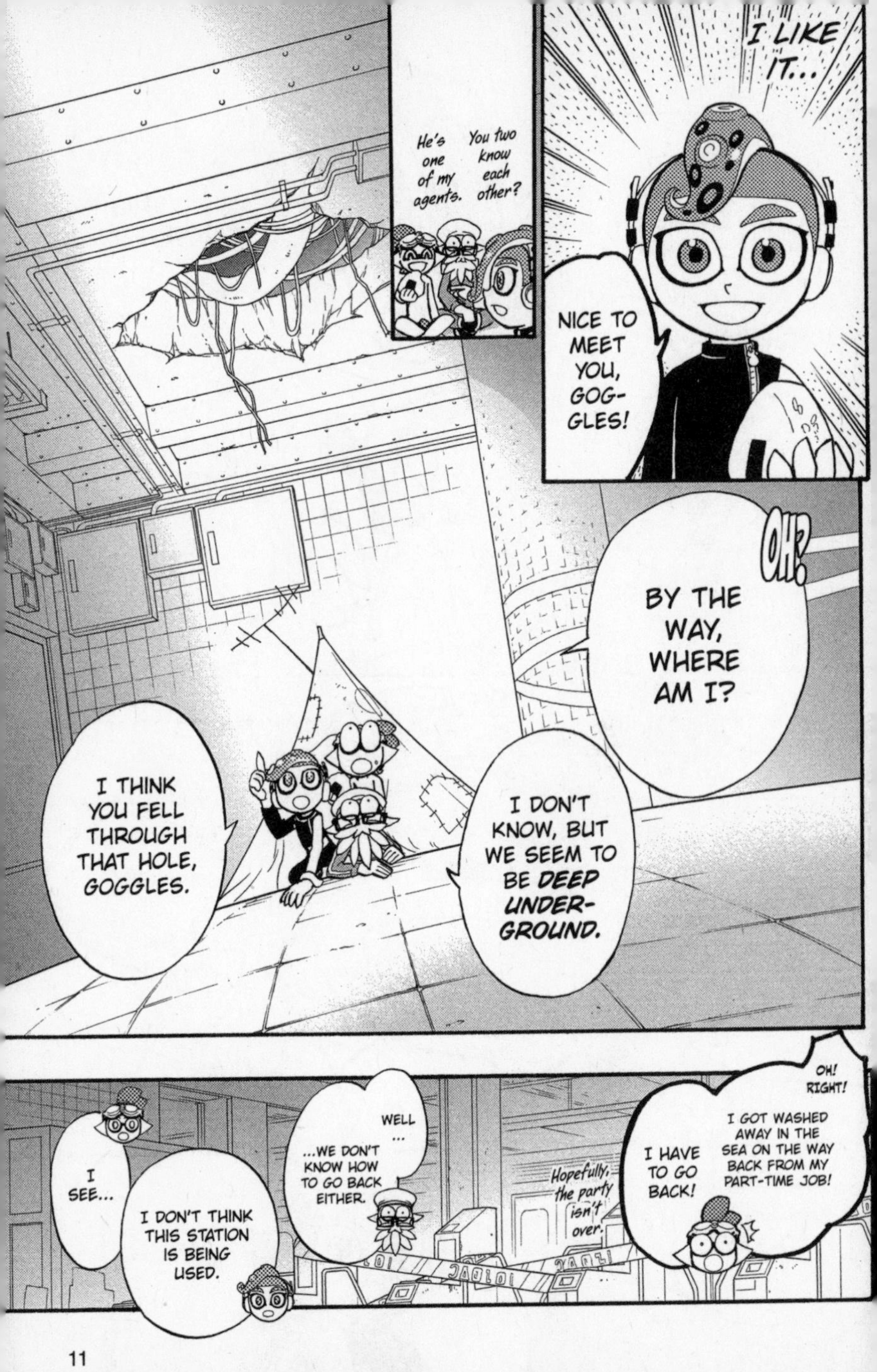
I LIKE IT...
NICE TO MEET YOU, GOG-GLES!
You two know each other?
He's one of my agents.
OH?
BY THE WAY, WHERE AM I?
I DON'T KNOW, BUT WE SEEM TO BE *DEEP UNDER-GROUND.*
I THINK YOU FELL THROUGH THAT HOLE, GOGGLES.
OH! RIGHT!
I GOT WASHED AWAY IN THE SEA ON THE WAY BACK FROM MY PART-TIME JOB!
I HAVE TO GO BACK!
Hopefully, the party isn't over.
WELL...
...WE DON'T KNOW HOW TO GO BACK EITHER.
I SEE...
I DON'T THINK THIS STATION IS BEING USED.

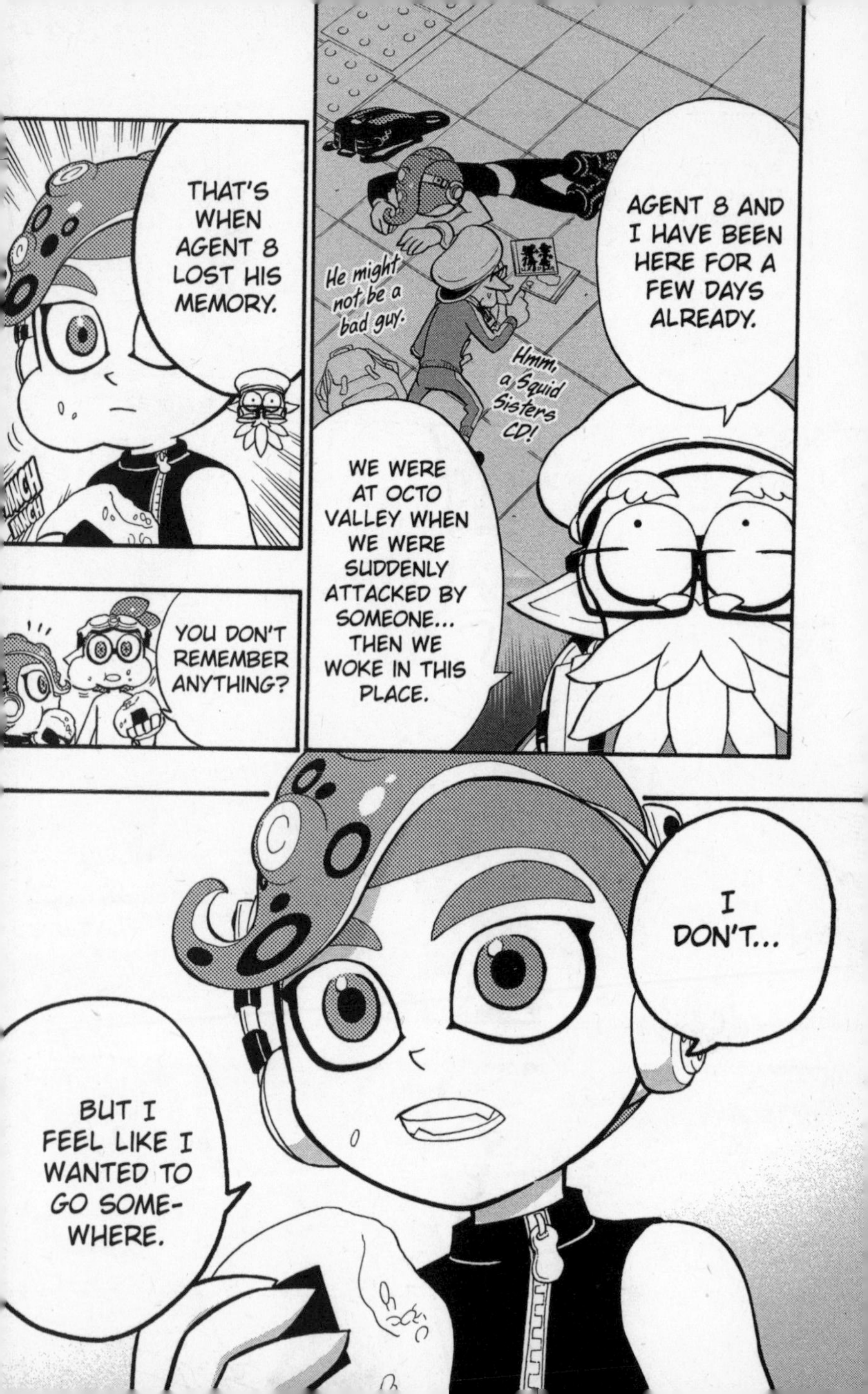
AGENT 8 AND I HAVE BEEN HERE FOR A FEW DAYS ALREADY.
Hmm, a Squid Sisters CD!
He might not be a bad guy.
WE WERE AT OCTO VALLEY WHEN WE WERE SUDDENLY ATTACKED BY SOMEONE... THEN WE WOKE IN THIS PLACE.
THAT'S WHEN AGENT 8 LOST HIS MEMORY.
YOU DON'T REMEMBER ANYTHING?
I DON'T...
BUT I FEEL LIKE I WANTED TO GO SOME-WHERE.

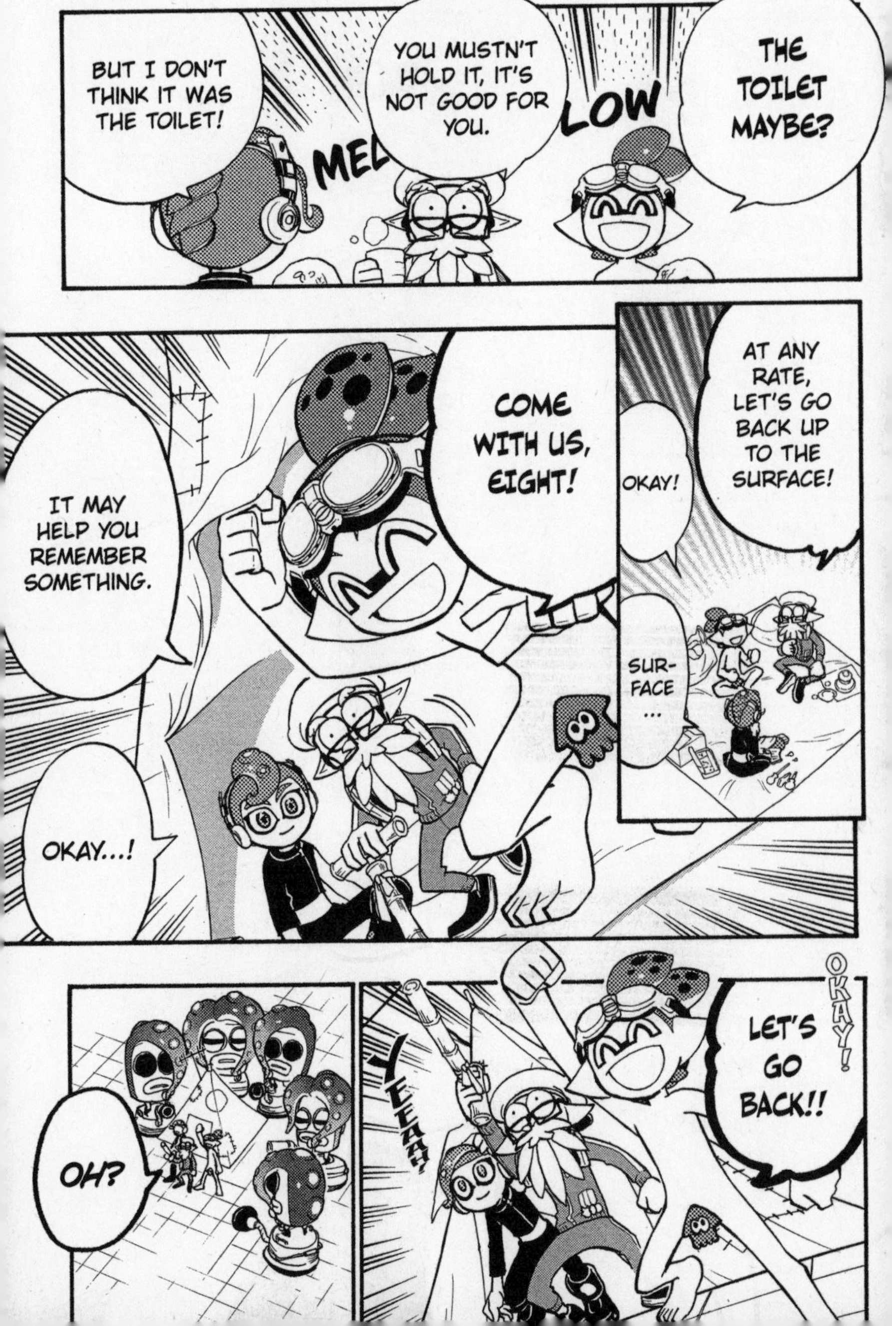
THE TOILET MAYBE?
LOW
YOU MUSTN'T HOLD IT, IT'S NOT GOOD FOR YOU.
MEL
BUT I DON'T THINK IT WAS THE TOILET!
AT ANY RATE, LET'S GO BACK UP TO THE SURFACE!
OKAY!
SUR-FACE ...
COME WITH US, EIGHT!
IT MAY HELP YOU REMEMBER SOMETHING.
OKAY...!
OKAY!
LET'S GO BACK!!
YEAAAH!
OH?

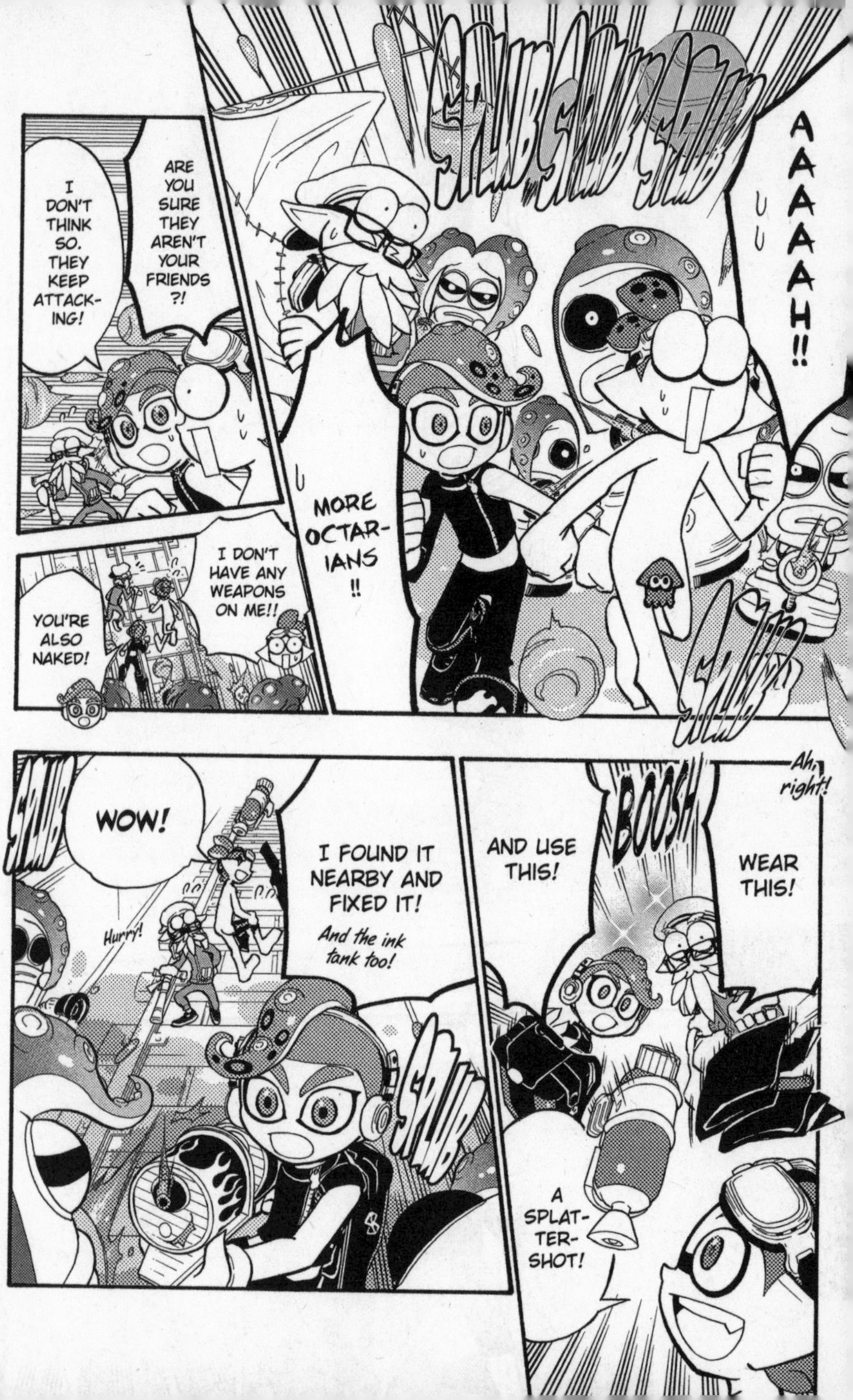
AAAAAH!!
MORE OCTAR-IANS!!
ARE YOU SURE THEY AREN'T YOUR FRIENDS?!
I DON'T THINK SO. THEY KEEP ATTACK-ING!
I DON'T HAVE ANY WEAPONS ON ME!!
YOU'RE ALSO NAKED!
Ah, right!
WEAR THIS!
BOOSH
AND USE THIS!
A SPLAT-TER-SHOT!
I FOUND IT NEARBY AND FIXED IT!
And the ink tank too!
WOW!
Hurry!

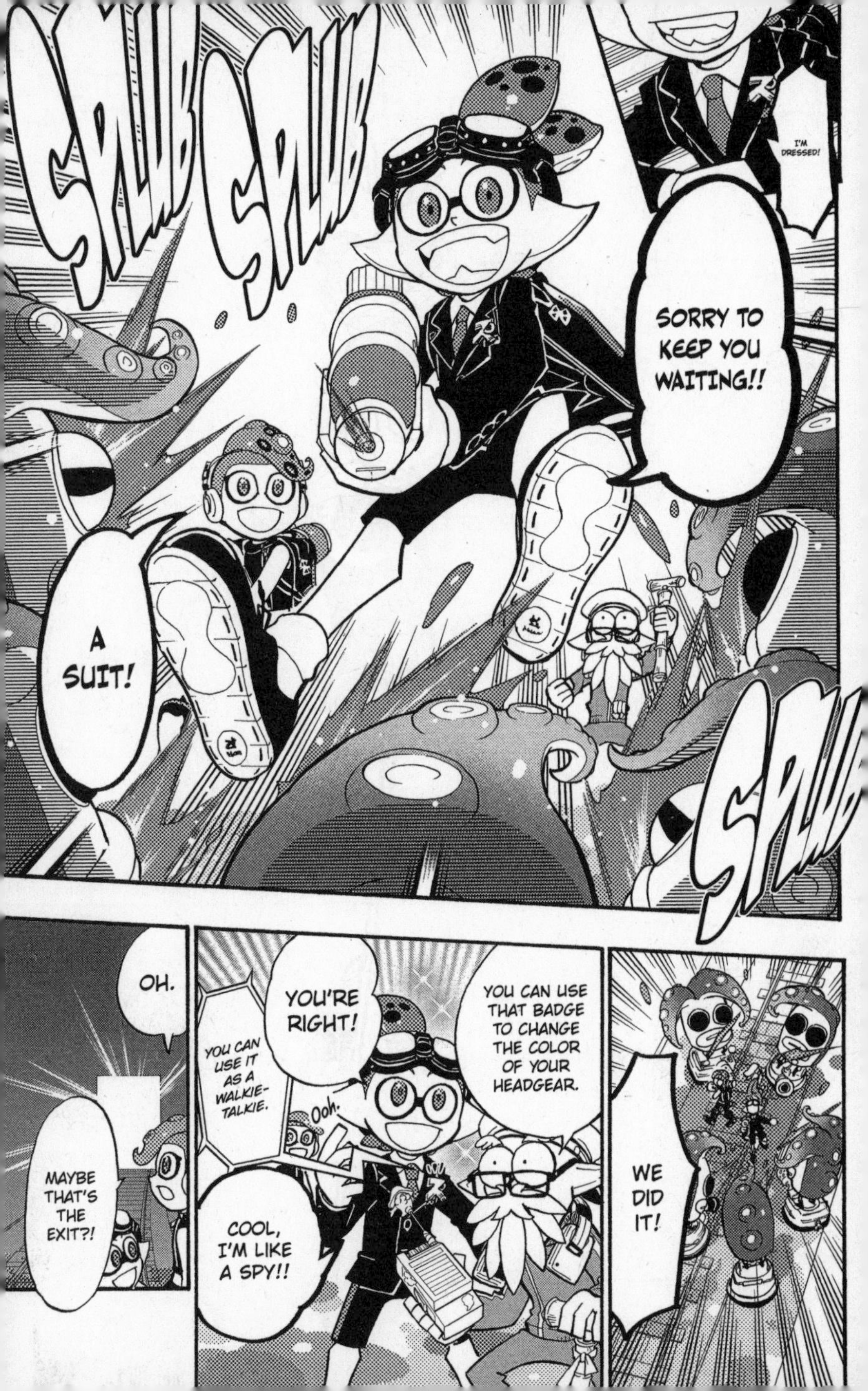
I'M DRESSED!
SORRY TO KEEP YOU WAITING!!
SPLUB! SPLUB!
A SUIT!
SPLUB!
WE DID IT!
YOU CAN USE THAT BADGE TO CHANGE THE COLOR OF YOUR HEADGEAR.
YOU'RE RIGHT!
YOU CAN USE IT AS A WALKIE-TALKIE.
Ooh.
COOL, I'M LIKE A SPY!!
OH.
MAYBE THAT'S THE EXIT?!

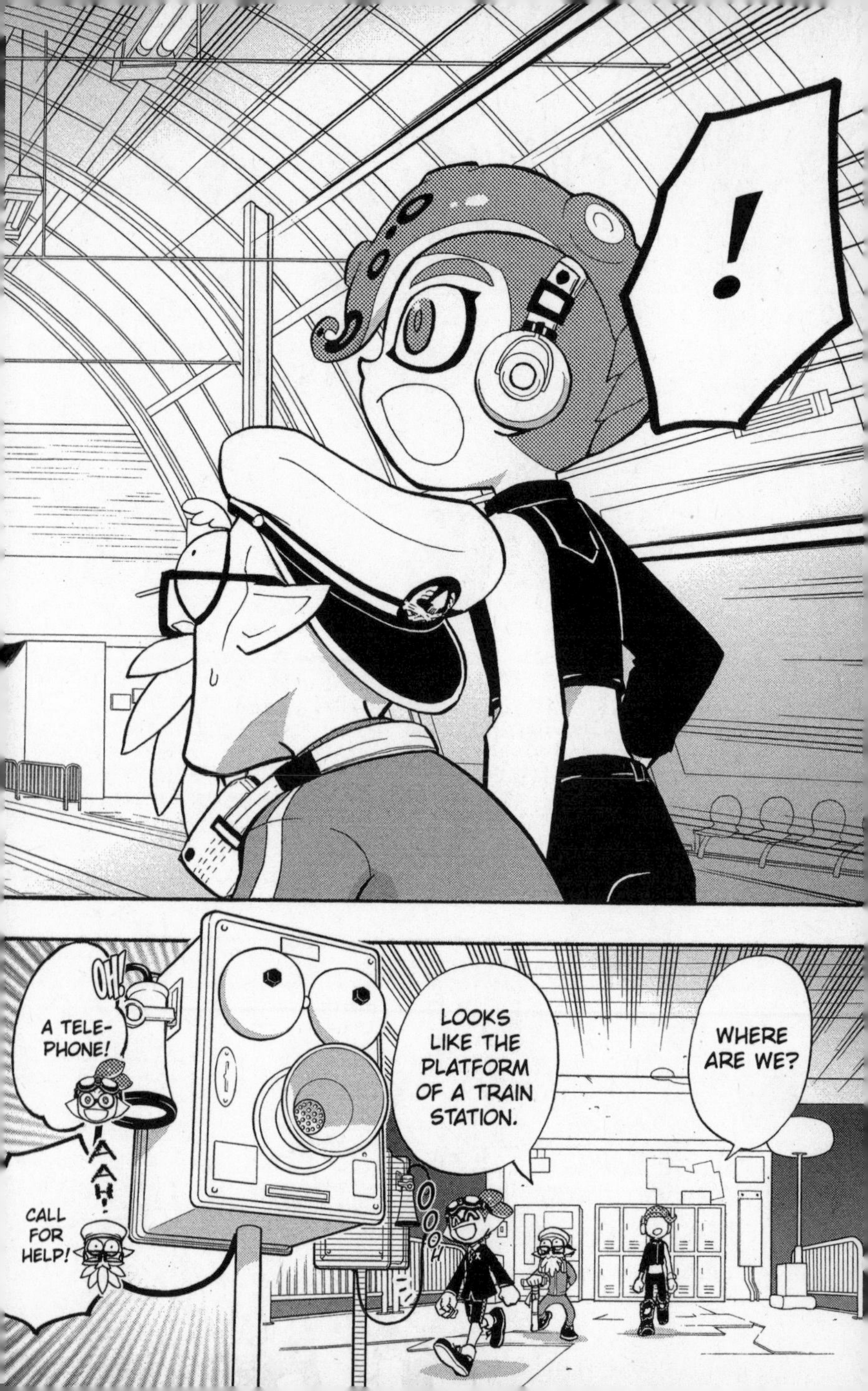
!
WHERE ARE WE?
LOOKS LIKE THE PLATFORM OF A TRAIN STATION.
OH!
A TELEPHONE!
AAH!
CALL FOR HELP!

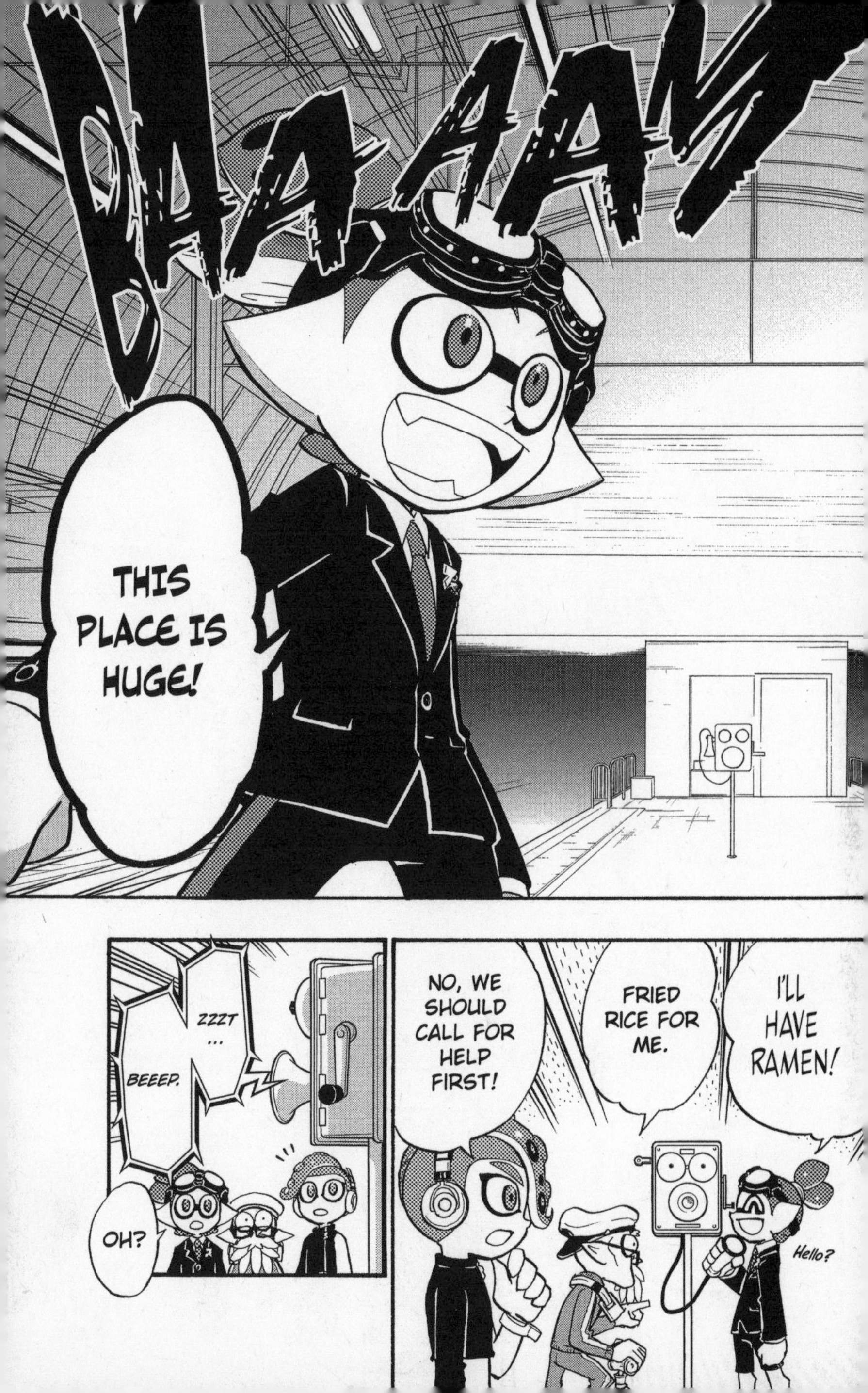
BAAAAM
THIS PLACE IS HUGE!
I'LL HAVE RAMEN!
Hello?
FRIED RICE FOR ME.
NO, WE SHOULD CALL FOR HELP FIRST!
ZZZT ...
BEEEP.
OH?

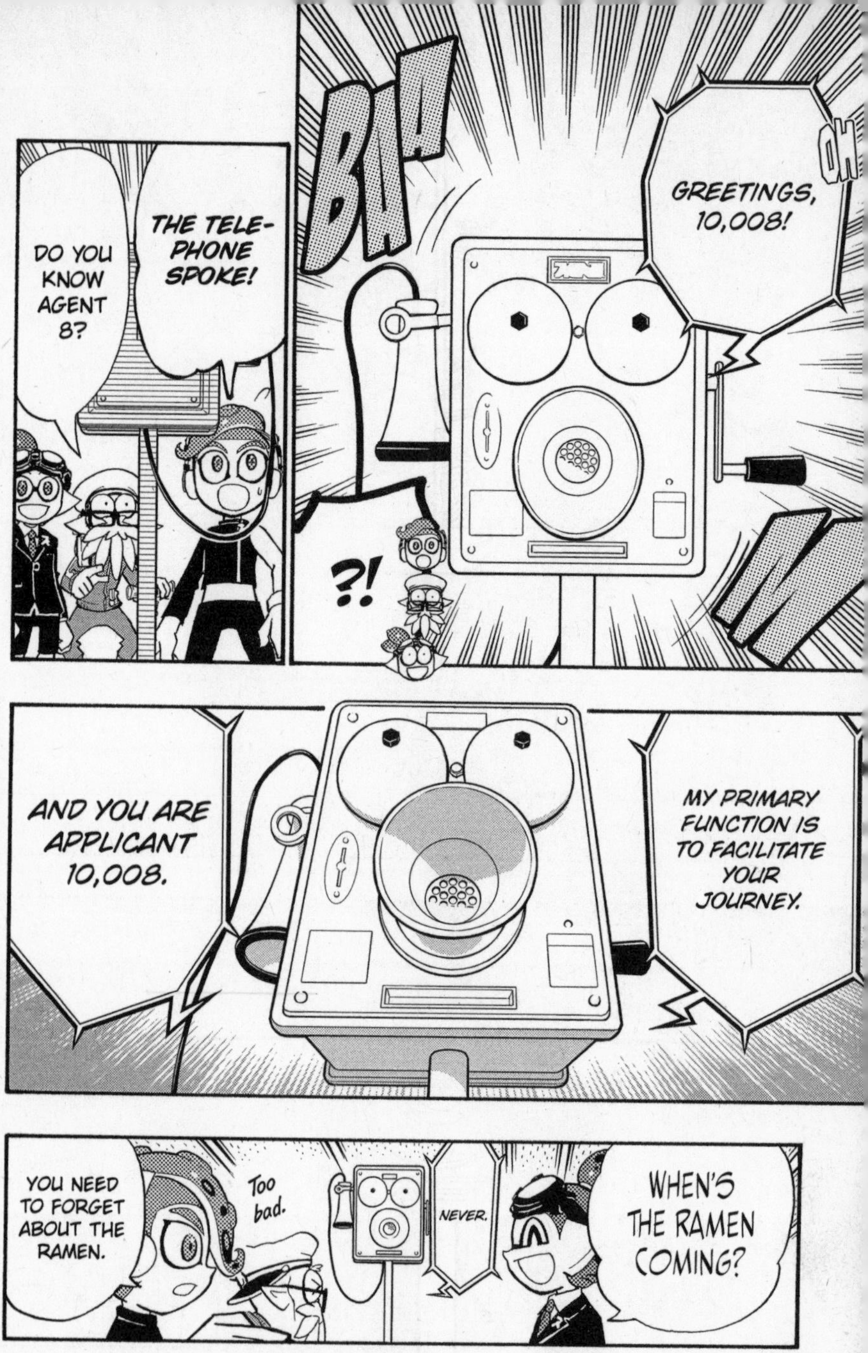
BAA
GREETINGS, 10,008!
OH
?!
THE TELE-PHONE SPOKE!
DO YOU KNOW AGENT 8?
MY PRIMARY FUNCTION IS TO FACILITATE YOUR JOURNEY.
AND YOU ARE APPLICANT 10,008.
WHEN'S THE RAMEN COMING?
NEVER.
Too bad.
YOU NEED TO FORGET ABOUT THE RAMEN.

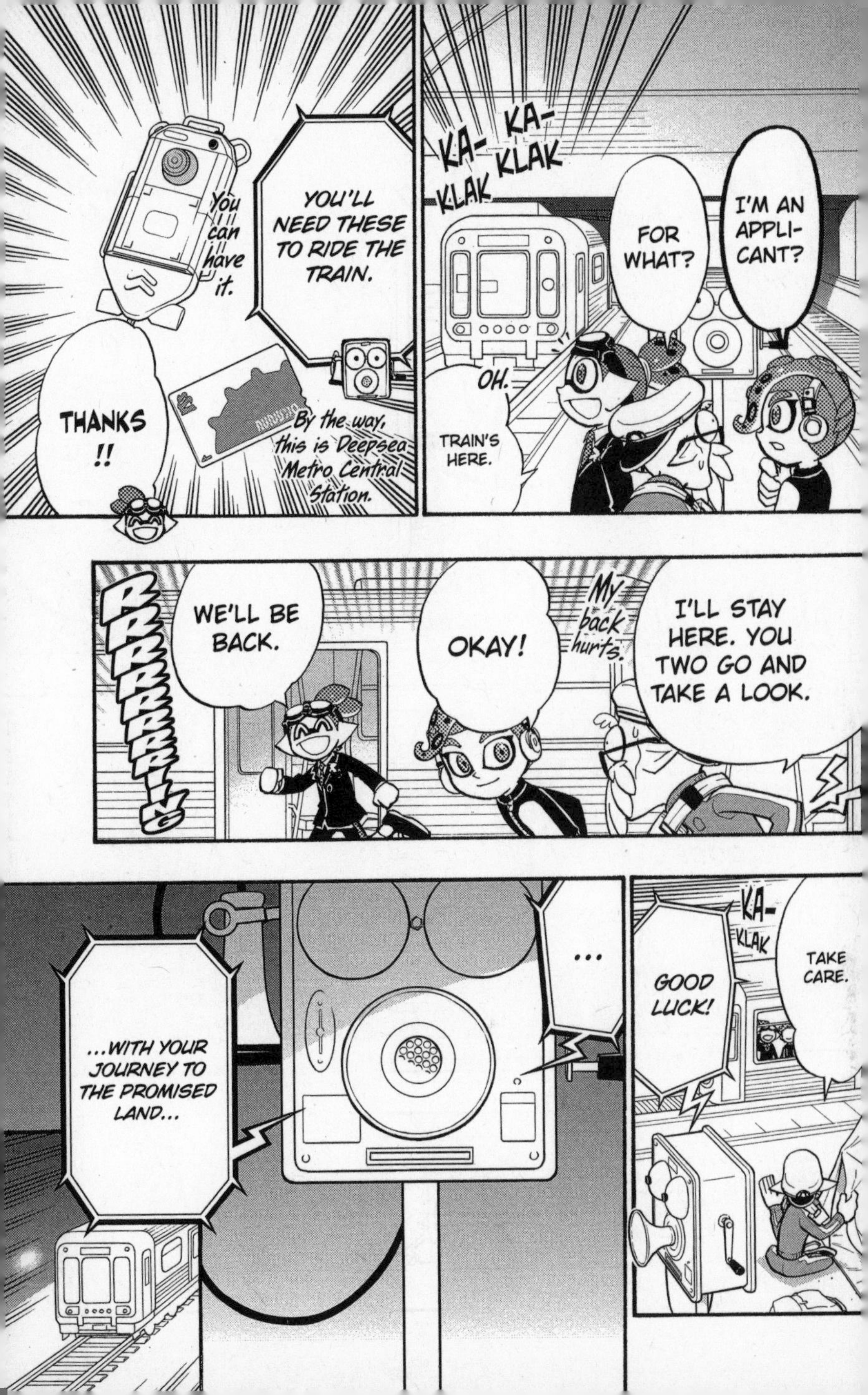
KA-KLAK
KA-KLAK
I'M AN APPLICANT?
FOR WHAT?
OH.
TRAIN'S HERE.
YOU'LL NEED THESE TO RIDE THE TRAIN.
You can have it.
By the way, this is Deepsea Metro Central Station.
THANKS!!
I'LL STAY HERE. YOU TWO GO AND TAKE A LOOK.
My back hurts.
OKAY!
WE'LL BE BACK.
BRRRRRRRING
KA-KLAK
TAKE CARE.
GOOD LUCK!
...
...WITH YOUR JOURNEY TO THE PROMISED LAND...

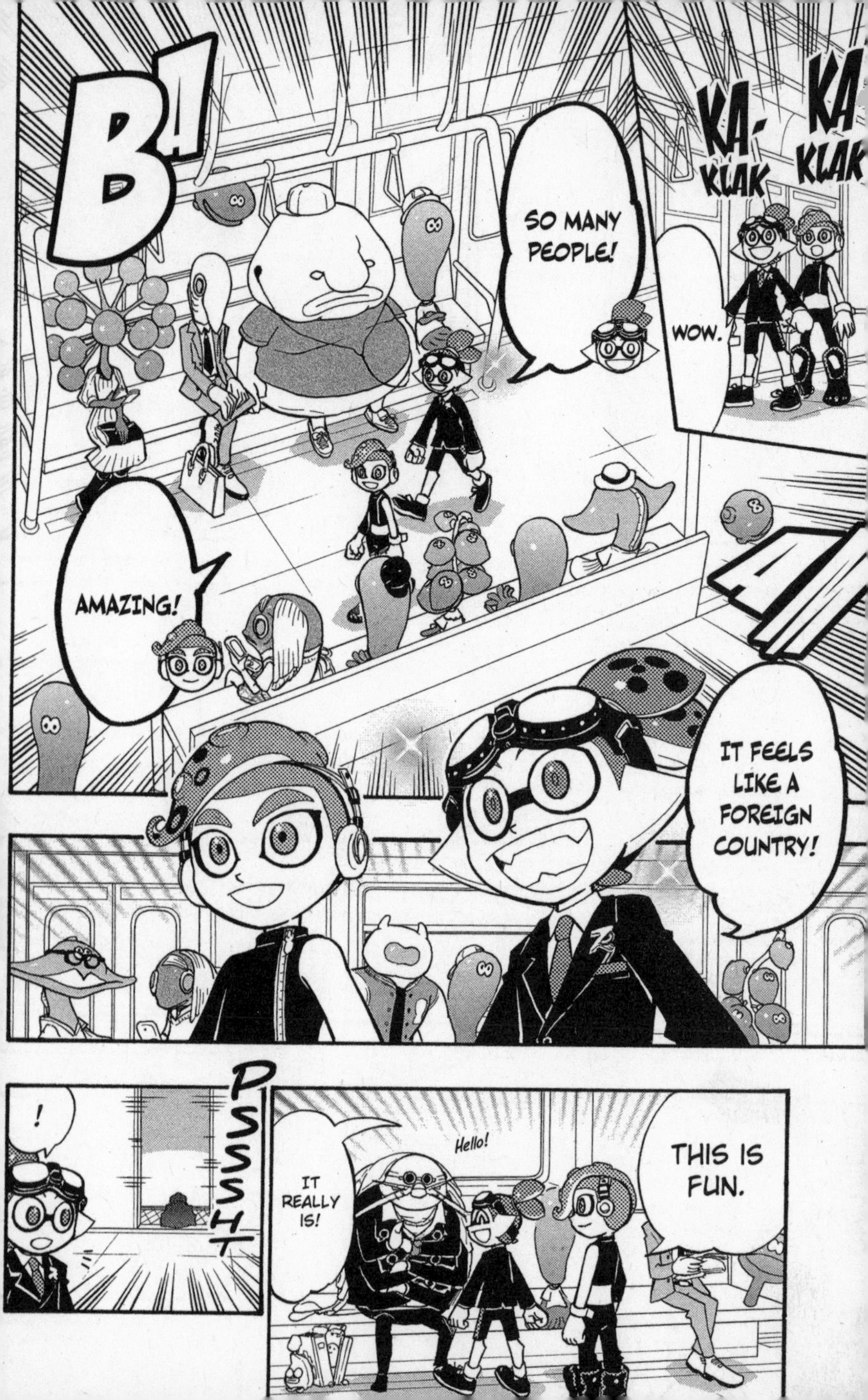

KA-KLAK
KA-KLAK
WOW.
SO MANY PEOPLE!
BA!
AMAZING!
IT FEELS LIKE A FOREIGN COUNTRY!
THIS IS FUN.
Hello!
IT REALLY IS!
PSSSHT
!

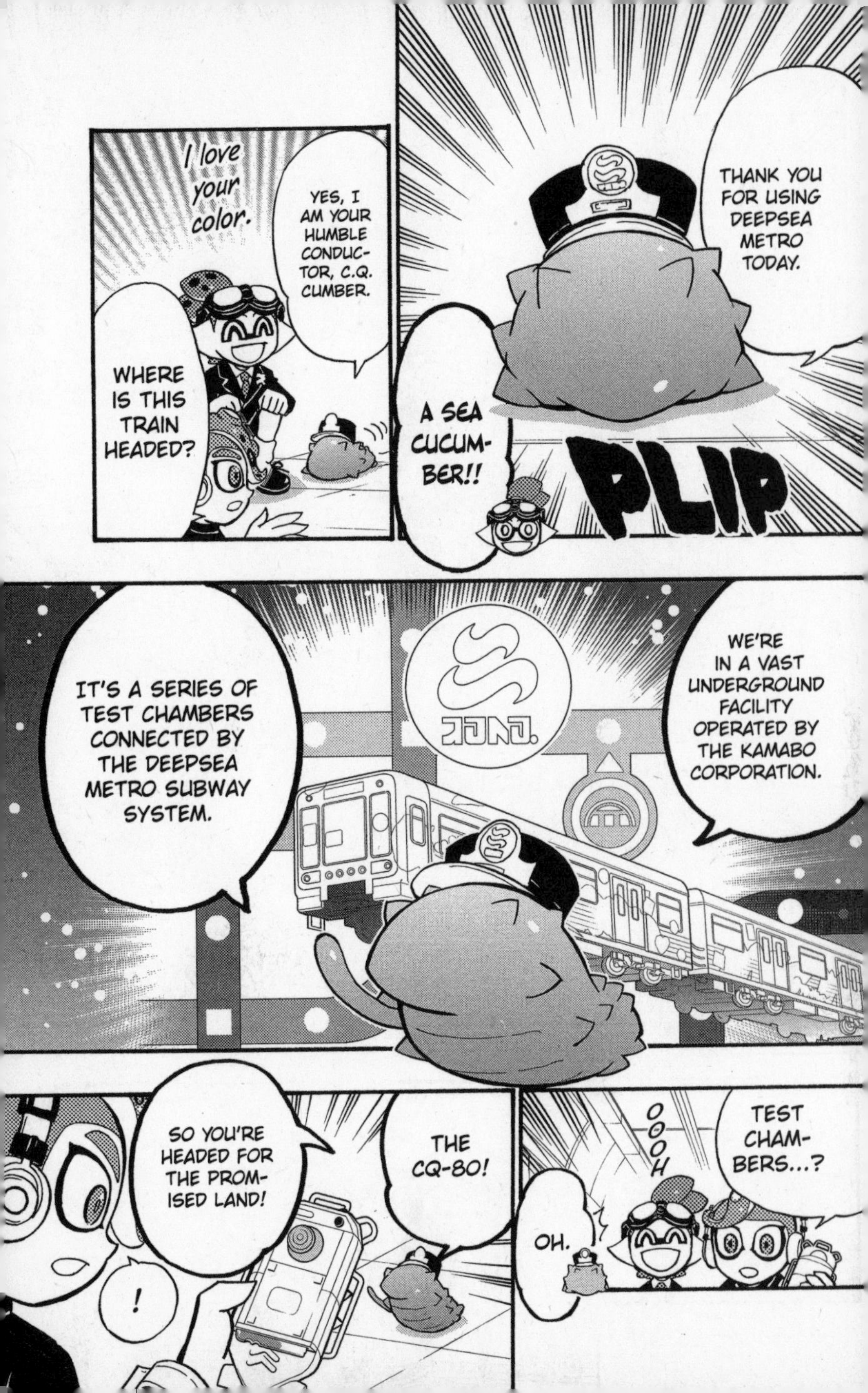

THANK YOU FOR USING DEEPSEA METRO TODAY.
PLIP
A SEA CUCUMBER!!
YES, I AM YOUR HUMBLE CONDUCTOR, C.Q. CUMBER.
I love your color.
WHERE IS THIS TRAIN HEADED?
WE'RE IN A VAST UNDERGROUND FACILITY OPERATED BY THE KAMABO CORPORATION.
IT'S A SERIES OF TEST CHAMBERS CONNECTED BY THE DEEPSEA METRO SUBWAY SYSTEM.
TEST CHAMBERS...?
OOOOH
OH.
THE CQ-80!
SO YOU'RE HEADED FOR THE PROMISED LAND!
!

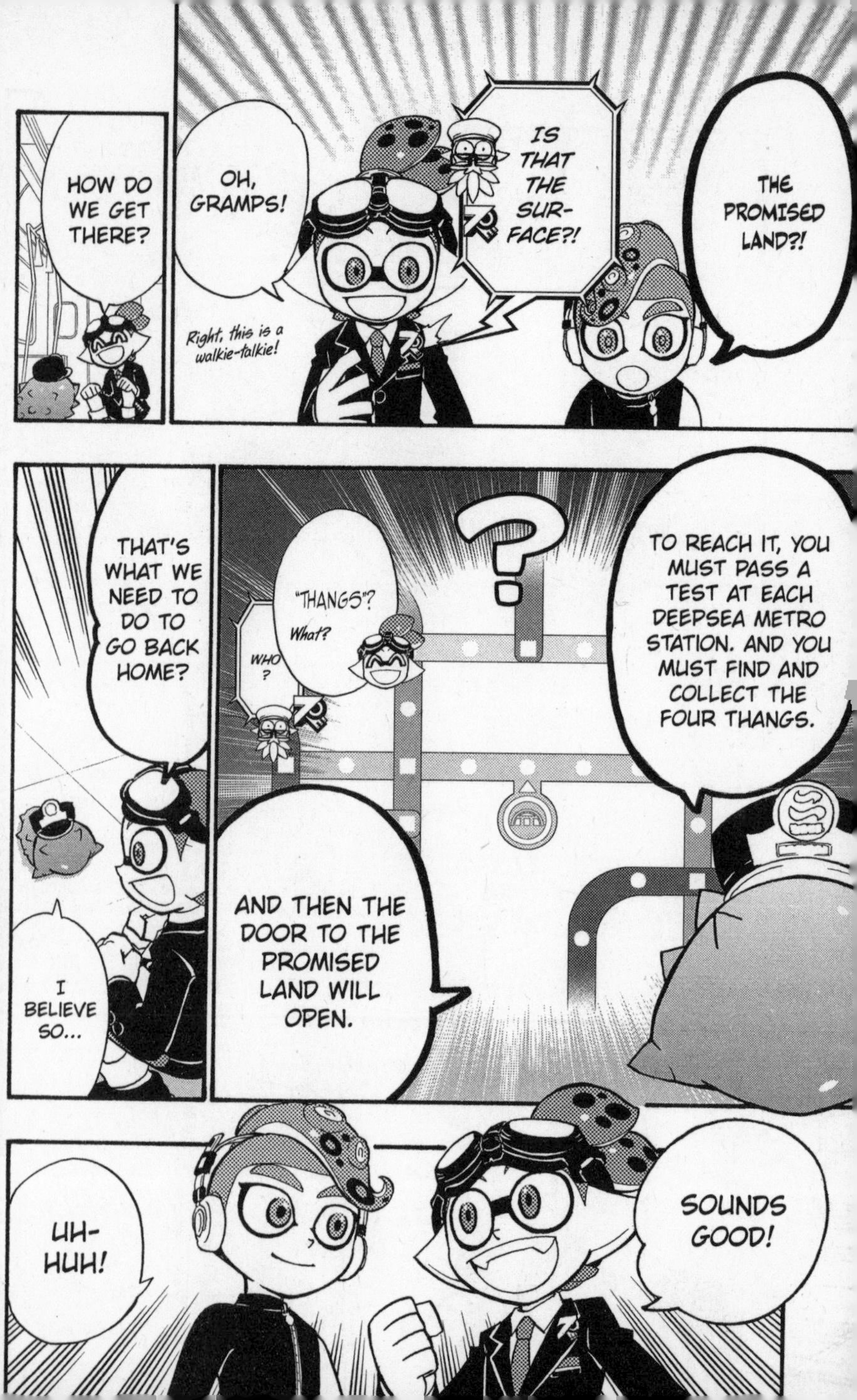
THE PROMISED LAND?!
IS THAT THE SUR-FACE?!
OH, GRAMPS!
Right, this is a walkie-talkie!
HOW DO WE GET THERE?
TO REACH IT, YOU MUST PASS A TEST AT EACH DEEPSEA METRO STATION. AND YOU MUST FIND AND COLLECT THE FOUR THANGS.
?
"THANGS"? What?
WHO ?
AND THEN THE DOOR TO THE PROMISED LAND WILL OPEN.
THAT'S WHAT WE NEED TO DO TO GO BACK HOME?
I BELIEVE SO...
SOUNDS GOOD!
UH-HUH!

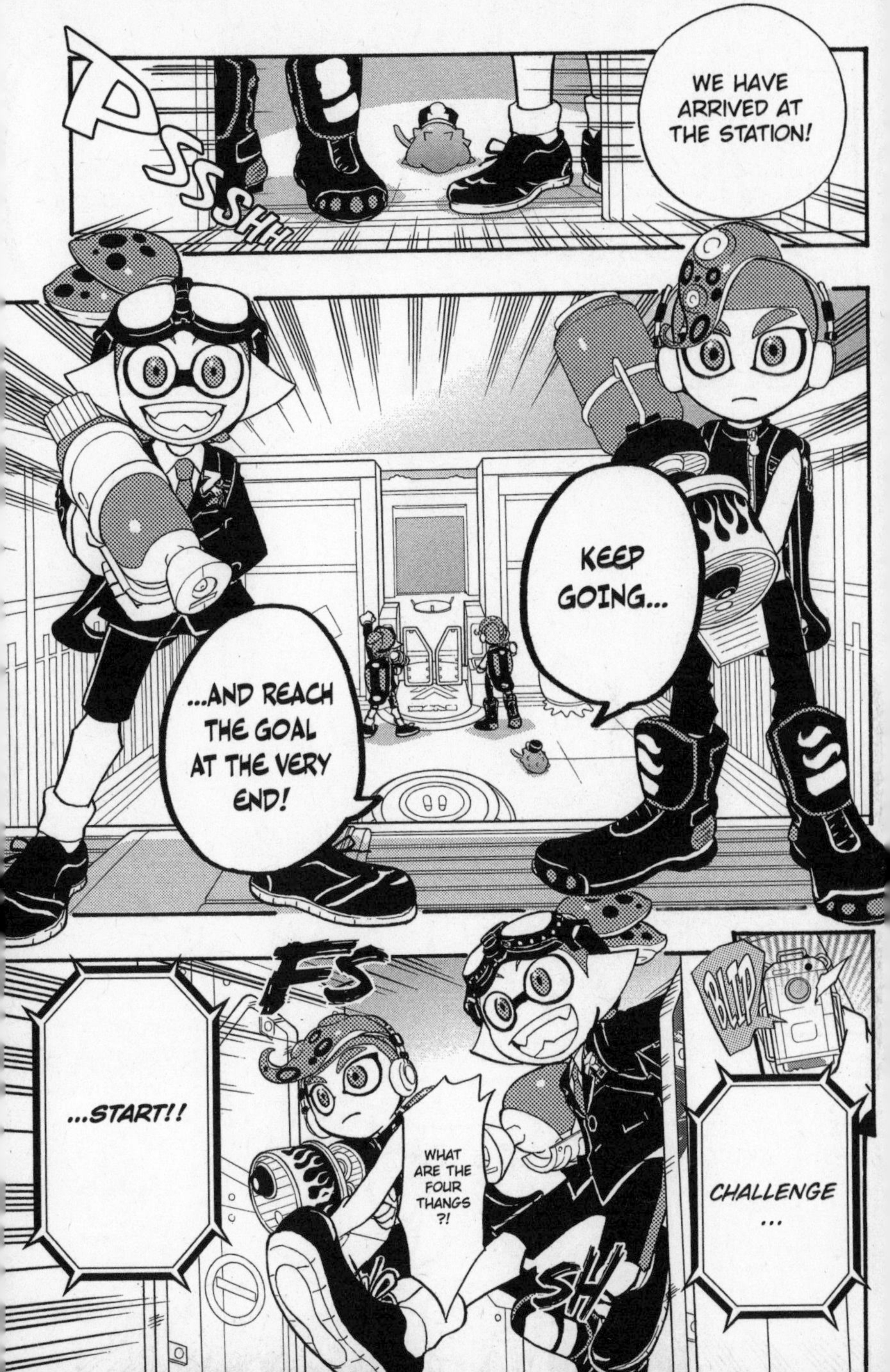
WE HAVE ARRIVED AT THE STATION!
PSSSHH
KEEP GOING...
...AND REACH THE GOAL AT THE VERY END!
BLIP
CHALLENGE ...
FS
WHAT ARE THE FOUR THANGS?!
SH
...START!!

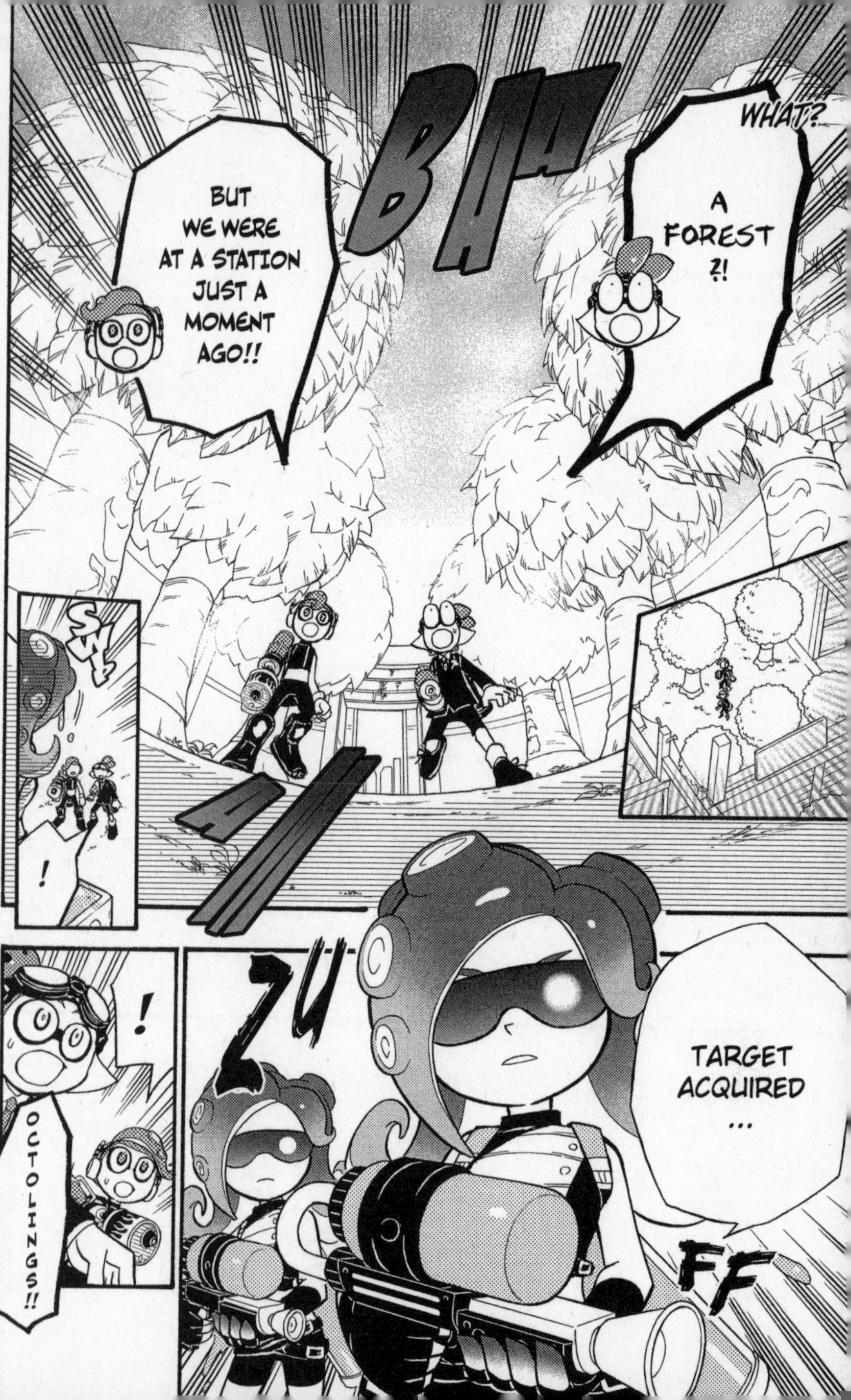

WHAT? A FOREST ?!
BUT WE WERE AT A STATION JUST A MOMENT AGO!!
!
ZU
TARGET ACQUIRED ...
FF
!
OCTOLINGS!!

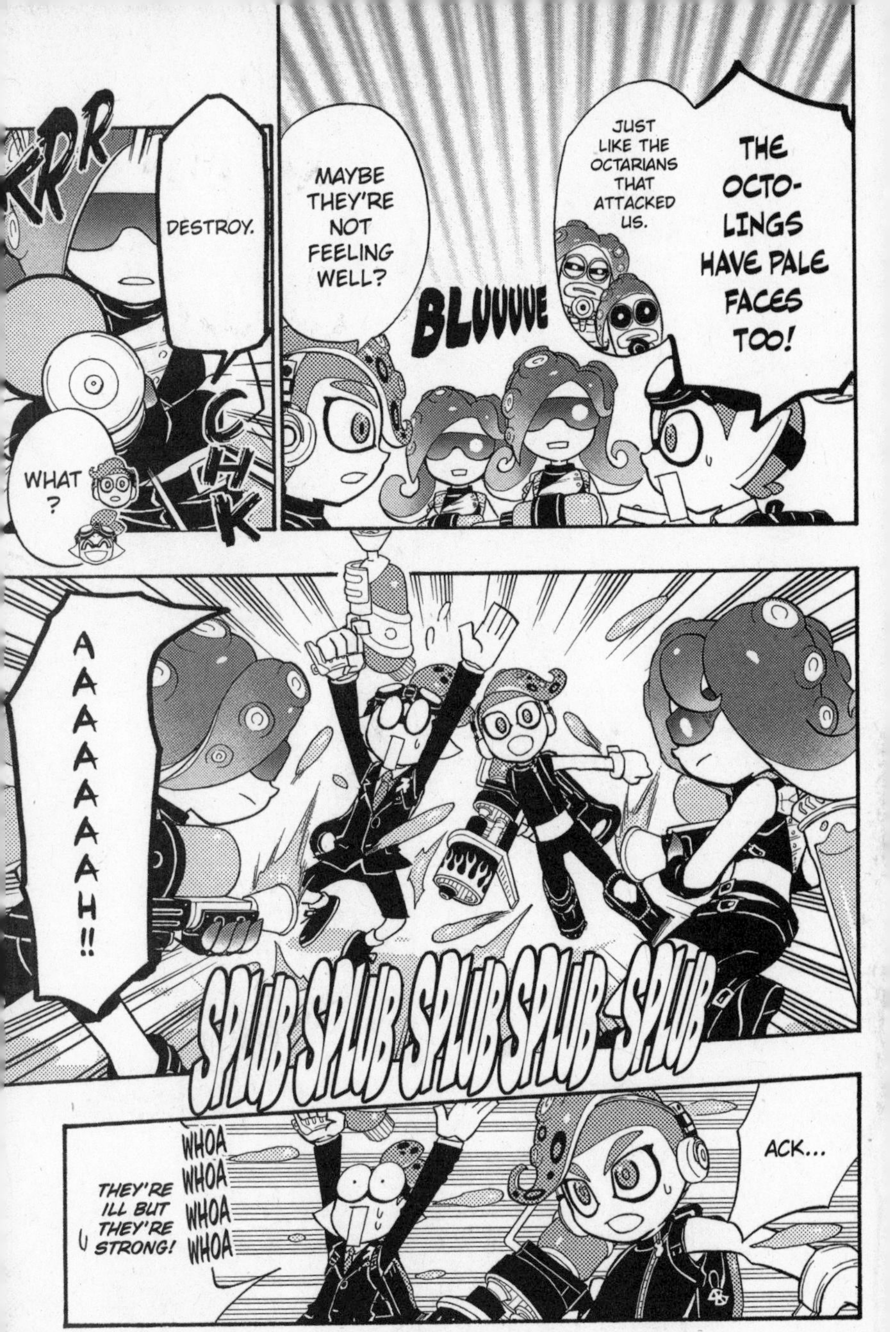
THE OCTO-LINGS HAVE PALE FACES TOO!
JUST LIKE THE OCTARIANS THAT ATTACKED US.
BLUUUVE
MAYBE THEY'RE NOT FEELING WELL?
DESTROY.
CHK
WHAT?
AAAAAAAH!!
SPLUB SPLUB SPLUB SPLUB SPLUB
ACK...
WHOA WHOA WHOA WHOA
THEY'RE ILL BUT THEY'RE STRONG!

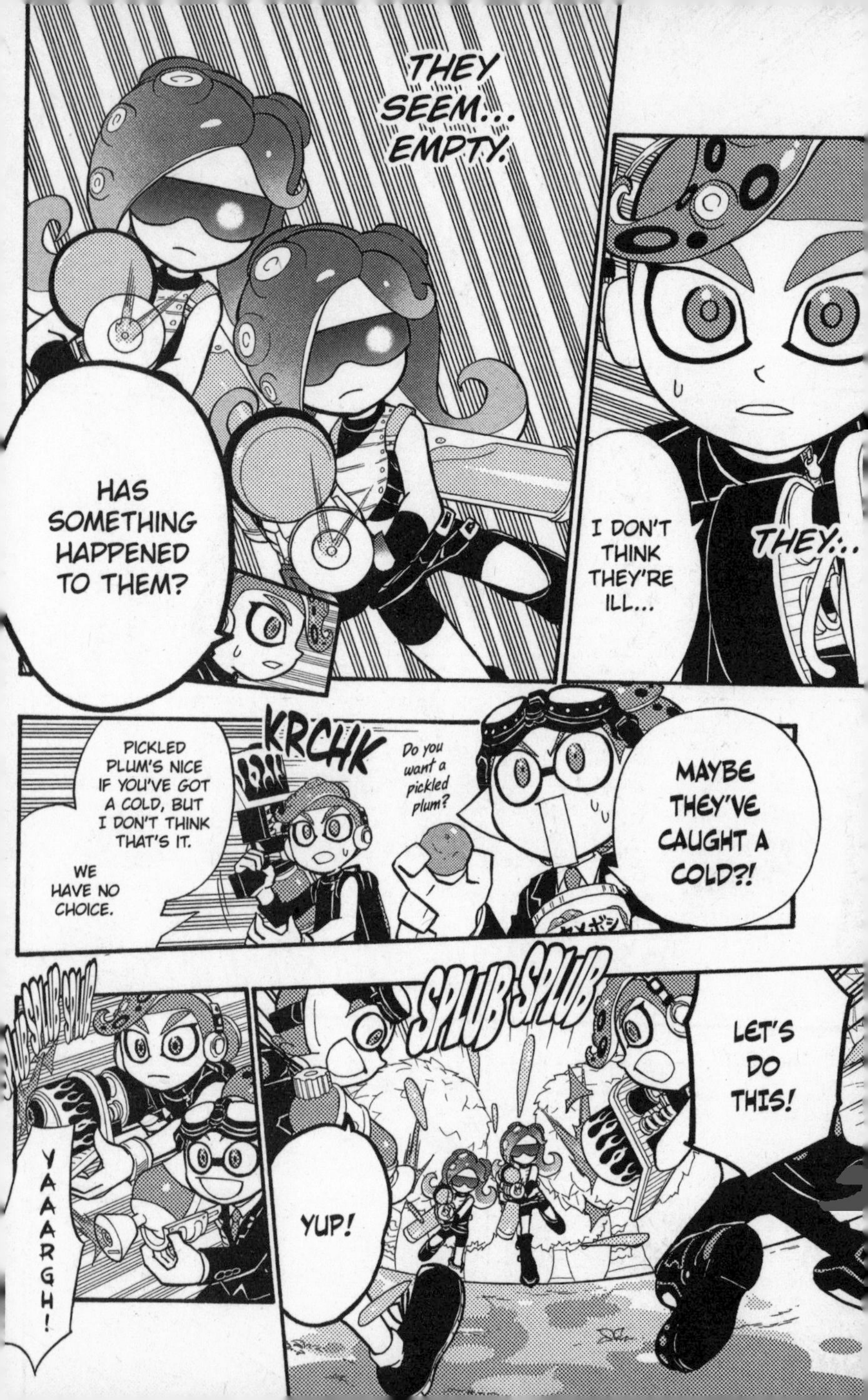
THEY...
I DON'T THINK THEY'RE ILL...
THEY SEEM... EMPTY.
HAS SOMETHING HAPPENED TO THEM?
MAYBE THEY'VE CAUGHT A COLD?!
Do you want a pickled plum?
KRCHK
PICKLED PLUM'S NICE IF YOU'VE GOT A COLD, BUT I DON'T THINK THAT'S IT.
WE HAVE NO CHOICE.
LET'S DO THIS!
SPLUB-SPLUB
YUP!
YAAAARGH!

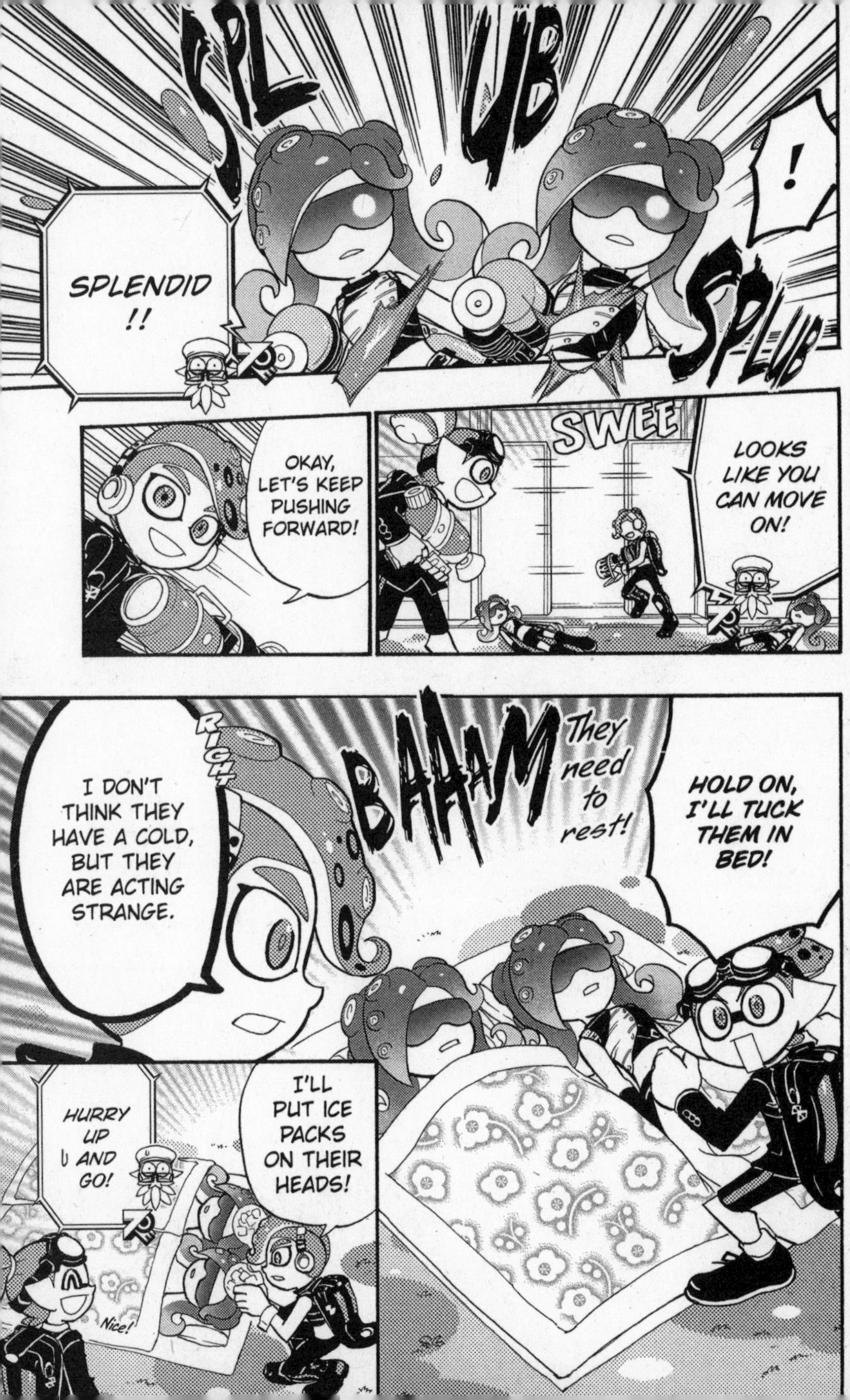
SPL UB
!
SPLUB
SPLENDID !!
SWEE
LOOKS LIKE YOU CAN MOVE ON!
OKAY, LET'S KEEP PUSHING FORWARD!
HOLD ON, I'LL TUCK THEM IN BED!
They need to rest!
BAAAM
RIGHT
I DON'T THINK THEY HAVE A COLD, BUT THEY ARE ACTING STRANGE.
I'LL PUT ICE PACKS ON THEIR HEADS!
HURRY UP AND GO!
Nice!

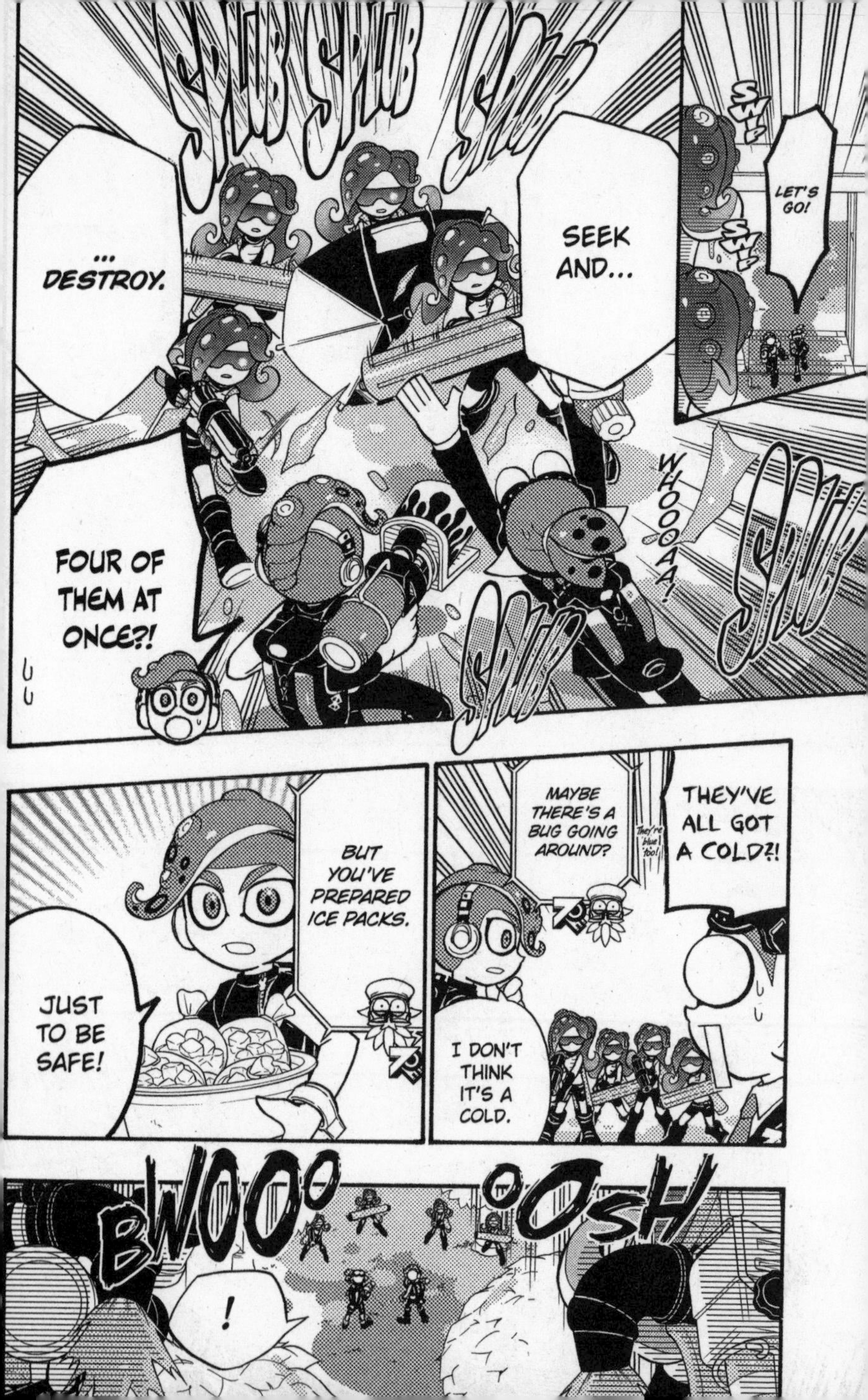
SWIP
LET'S GO!
SWIP
SEEK AND...
... DESTROY.
WHOOOAAA!
FOUR OF THEM AT ONCE?!
THEY'VE ALL GOT A COLD?!
MAYBE THERE'S A BUG GOING AROUND?
They're blue, too!
I DON'T THINK IT'S A COLD.
BUT YOU'VE PREPARED ICE PACKS.
JUST TO BE SAFE!
BWOOOOOSH
!

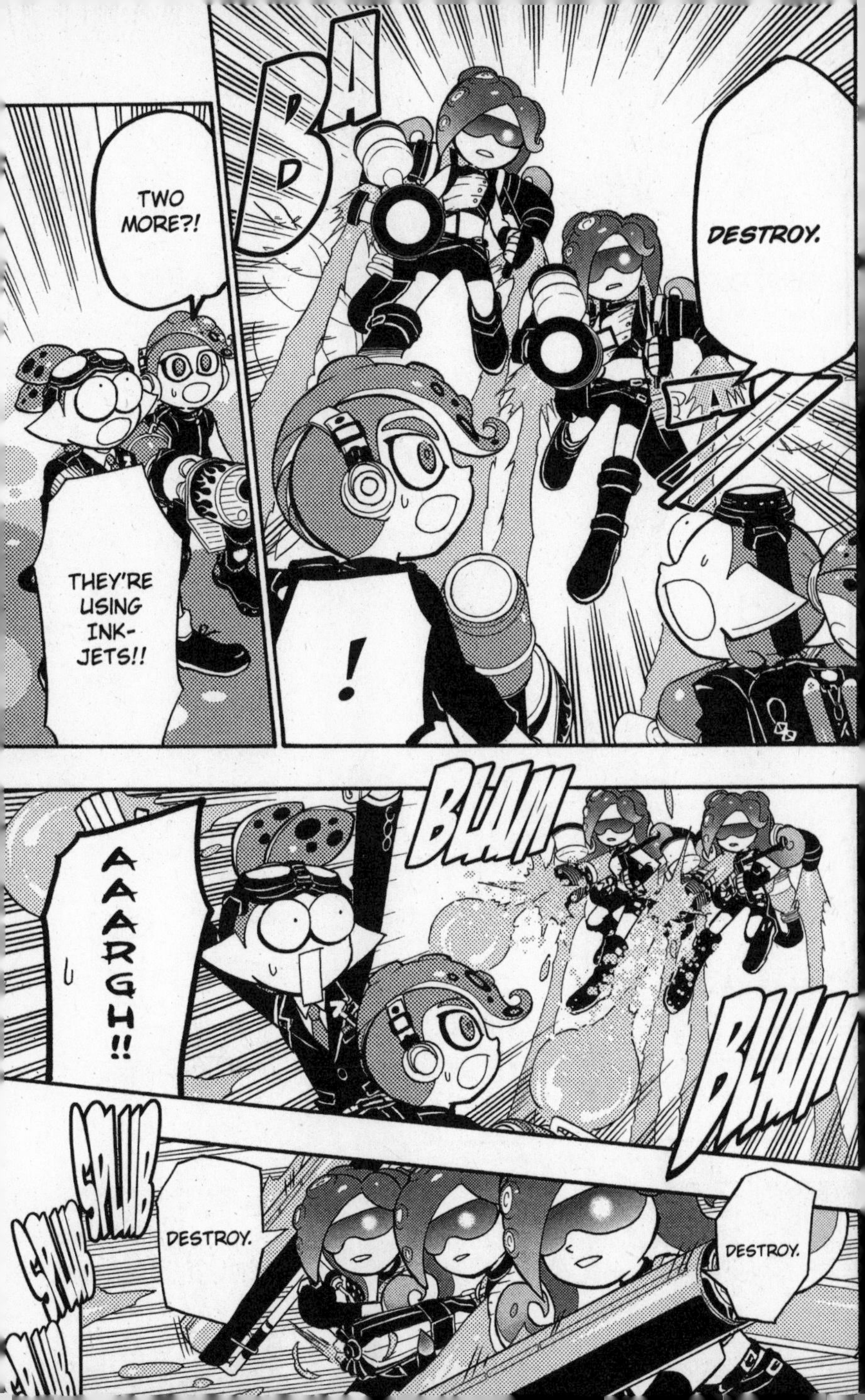

BADD
DESTROY.
!
TWO MORE?!
THEY'RE USING INK-JETS!!
BLAM
BLAM
AAAARGH!!
DESTROY.
DESTROY.
SPLUB
SPLUB

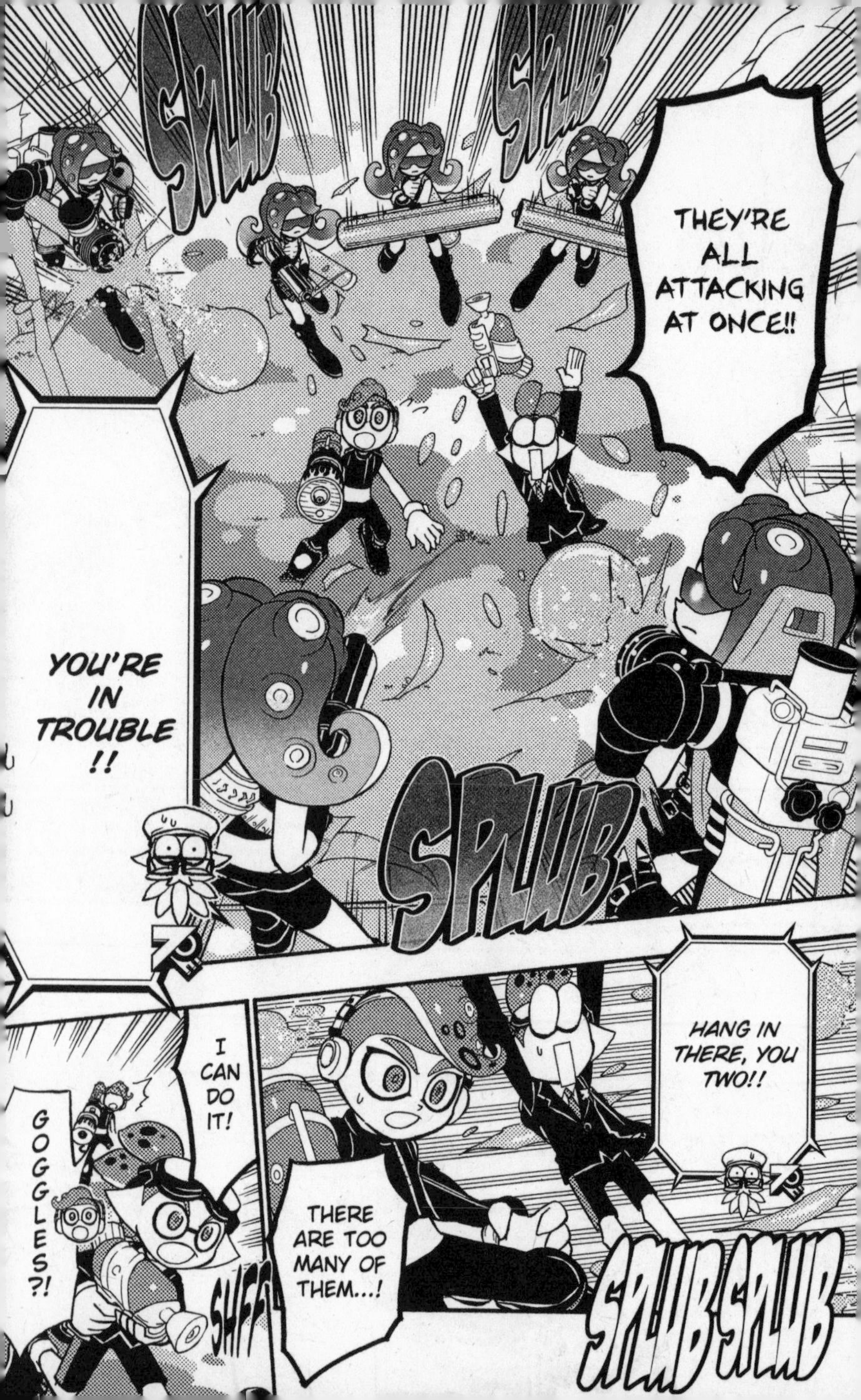
SPLUB
SPLUB
THEY'RE ALL ATTACKING AT ONCE!!
YOU'RE IN TROUBLE!!
SPLUB
HANG IN THERE, YOU TWO!!
SPLUB SPLUB
THERE ARE TOO MANY OF THEM...!
I CAN DO IT!
GOGGLES?!

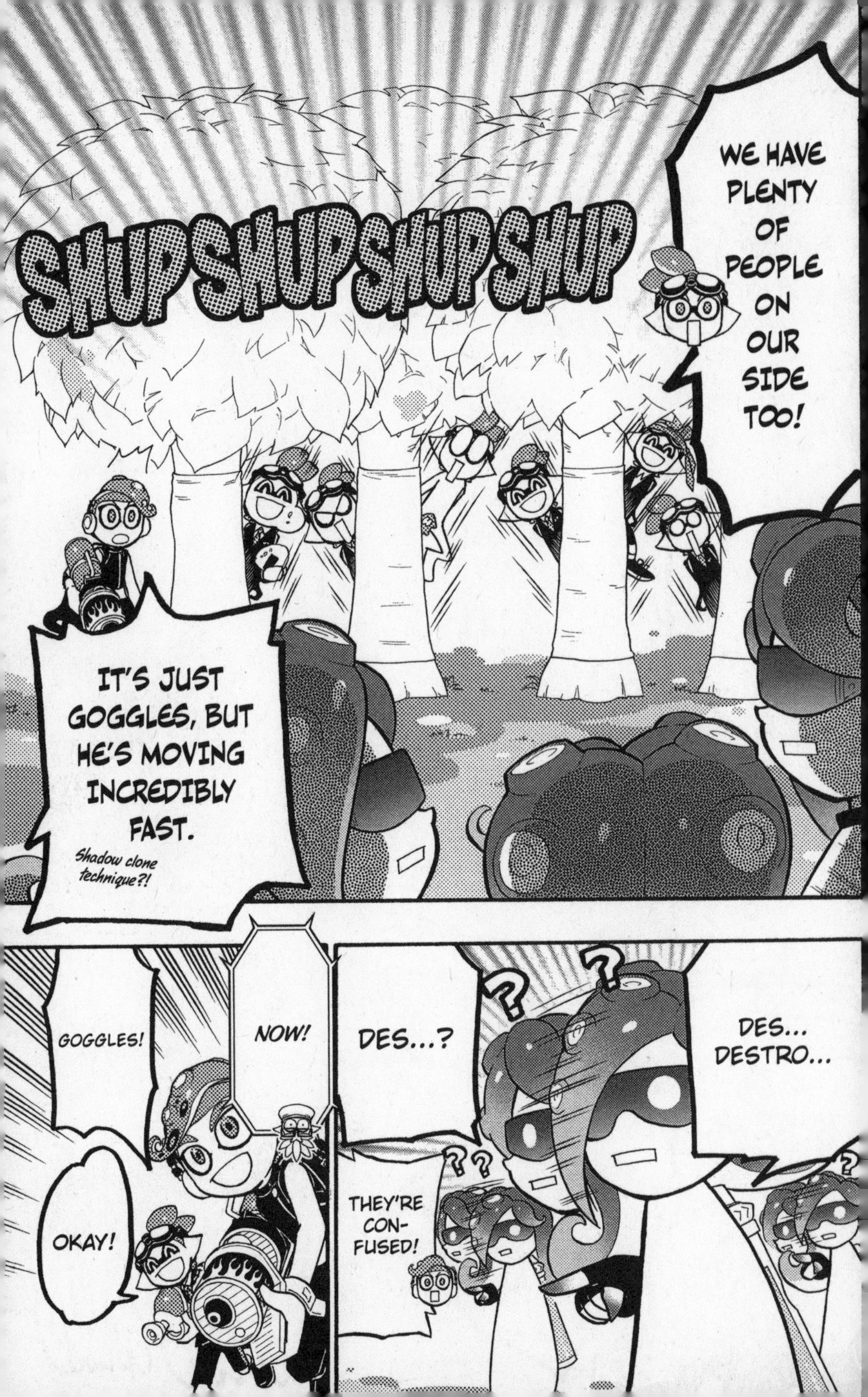
WE HAVE PLENTY OF PEOPLE ON OUR SIDE TOO!
SHUP SHUP SHUP SHUP
IT'S JUST GOGGLES, BUT HE'S MOVING INCREDIBLY FAST.
Shadow clone technique?!
DES... DESTRO...
DES...?
THEY'RE CON-FUSED!
NOW!
GOGGLES!
OKAY!

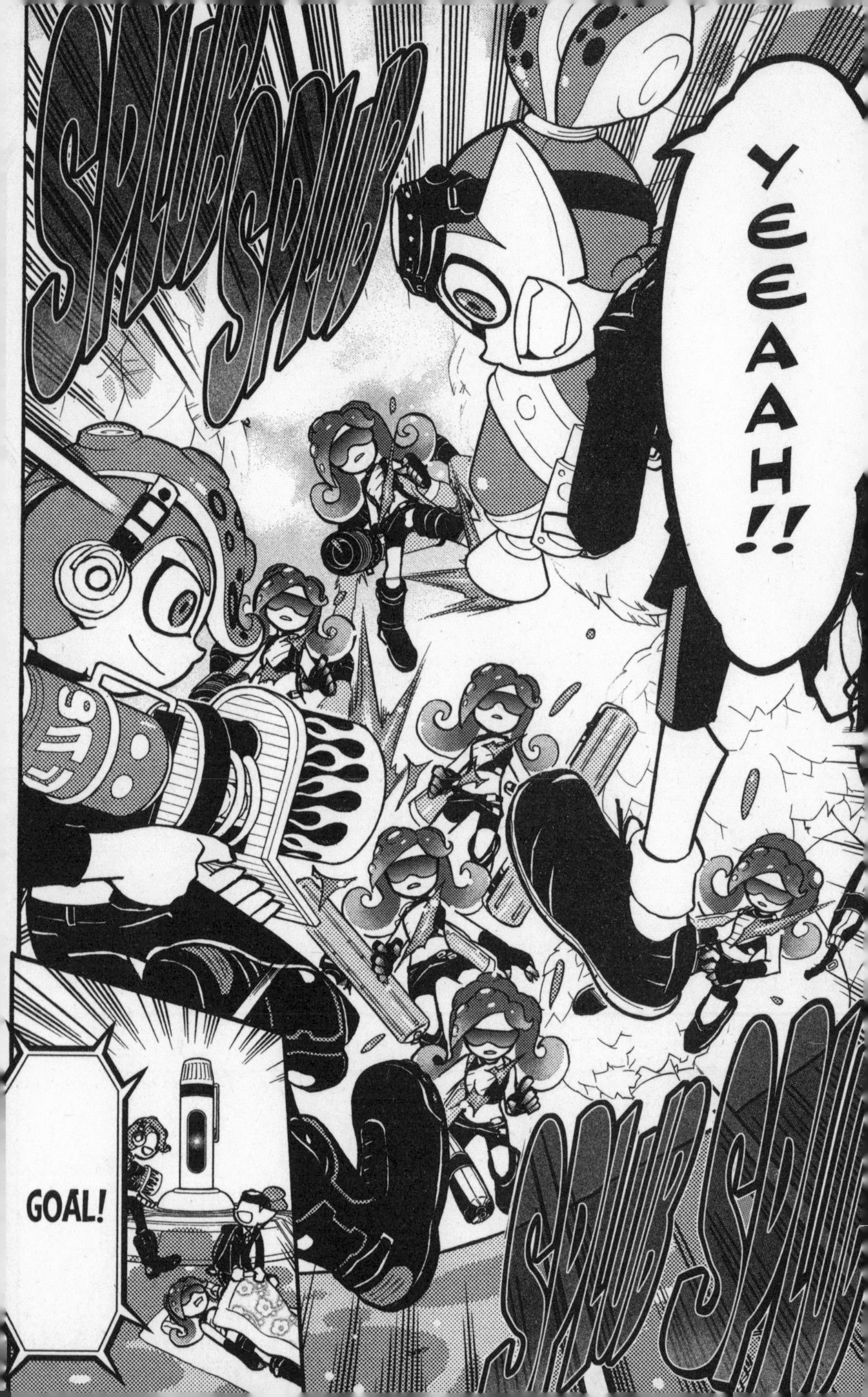
YEEAAH!!
GOAL!

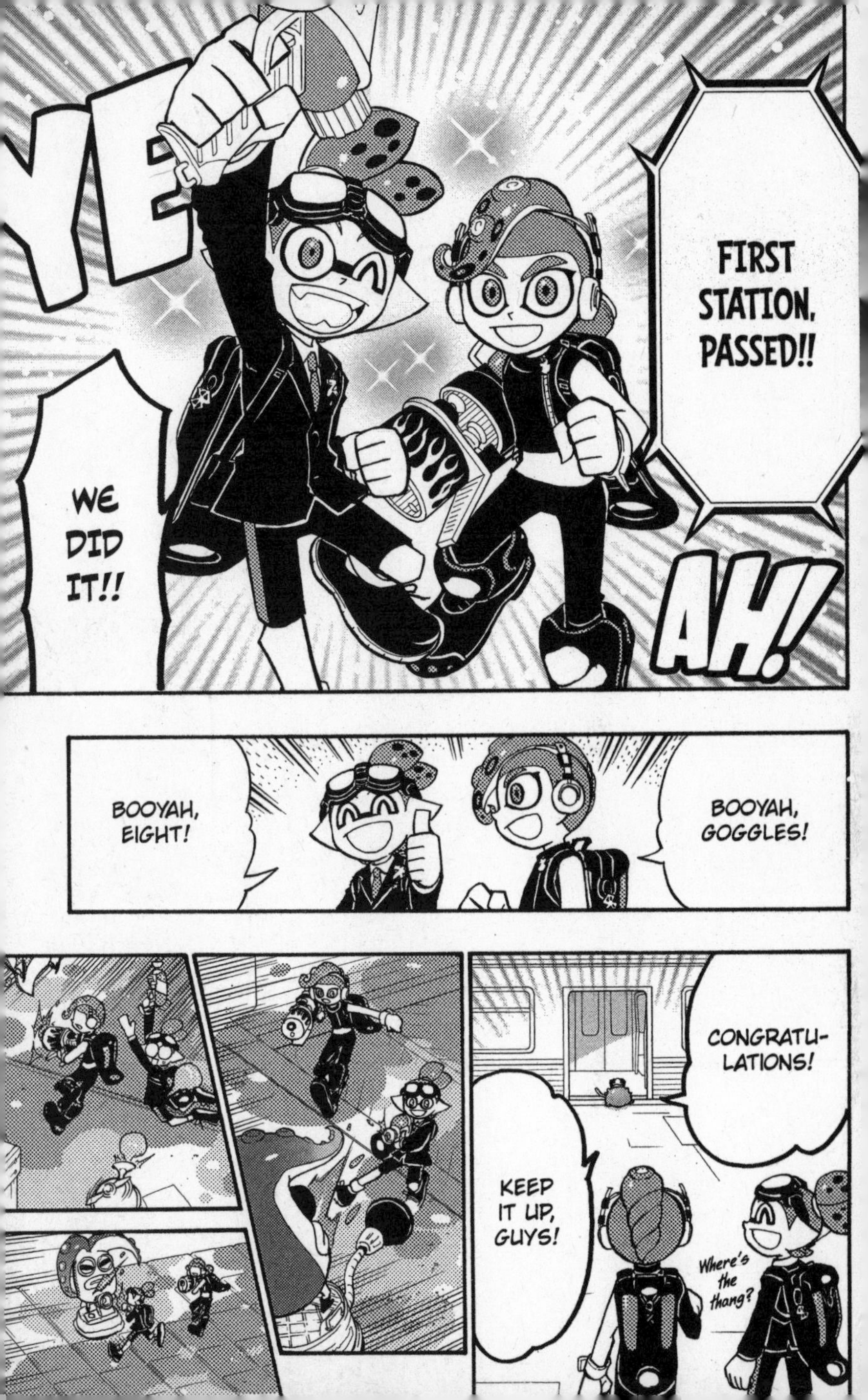
FIRST STATION, PASSED!!
WE DID IT!!
YE
AH!!
BOOYAH, GOGGLES!
BOOYAH, EIGHT!
CONGRATU- LATIONS!
KEEP IT UP, GUYS!
Where's the thang?

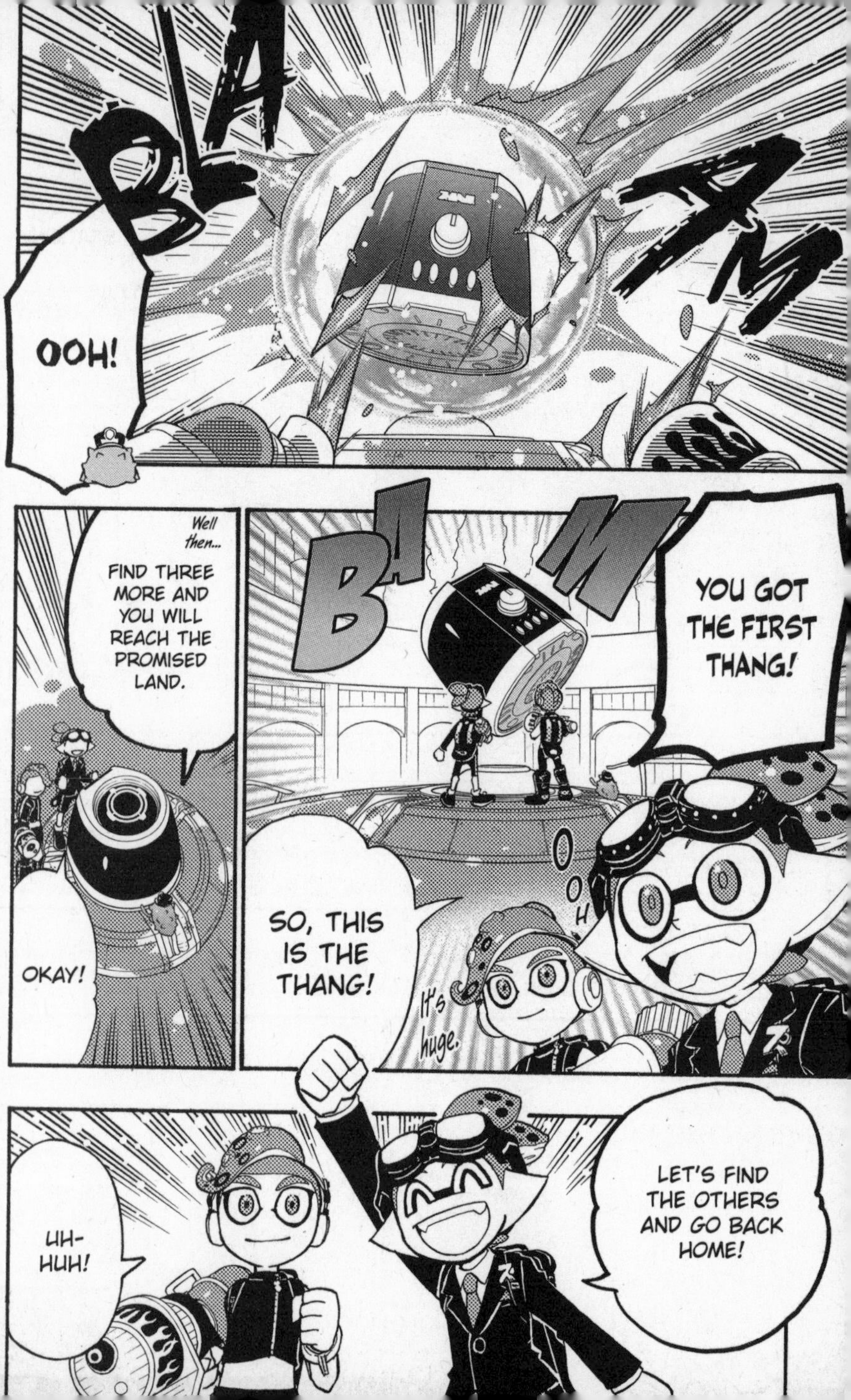
BLAM
OOH!
YOU GOT THE FIRST THANG!
BAM
OOH
SO, THIS IS THE THANG!
It's huge.
Well then... FIND THREE MORE AND YOU WILL REACH THE PROMISED LAND.
OKAY!
LET'S FIND THE OTHERS AND GO BACK HOME!
UH-HUH!

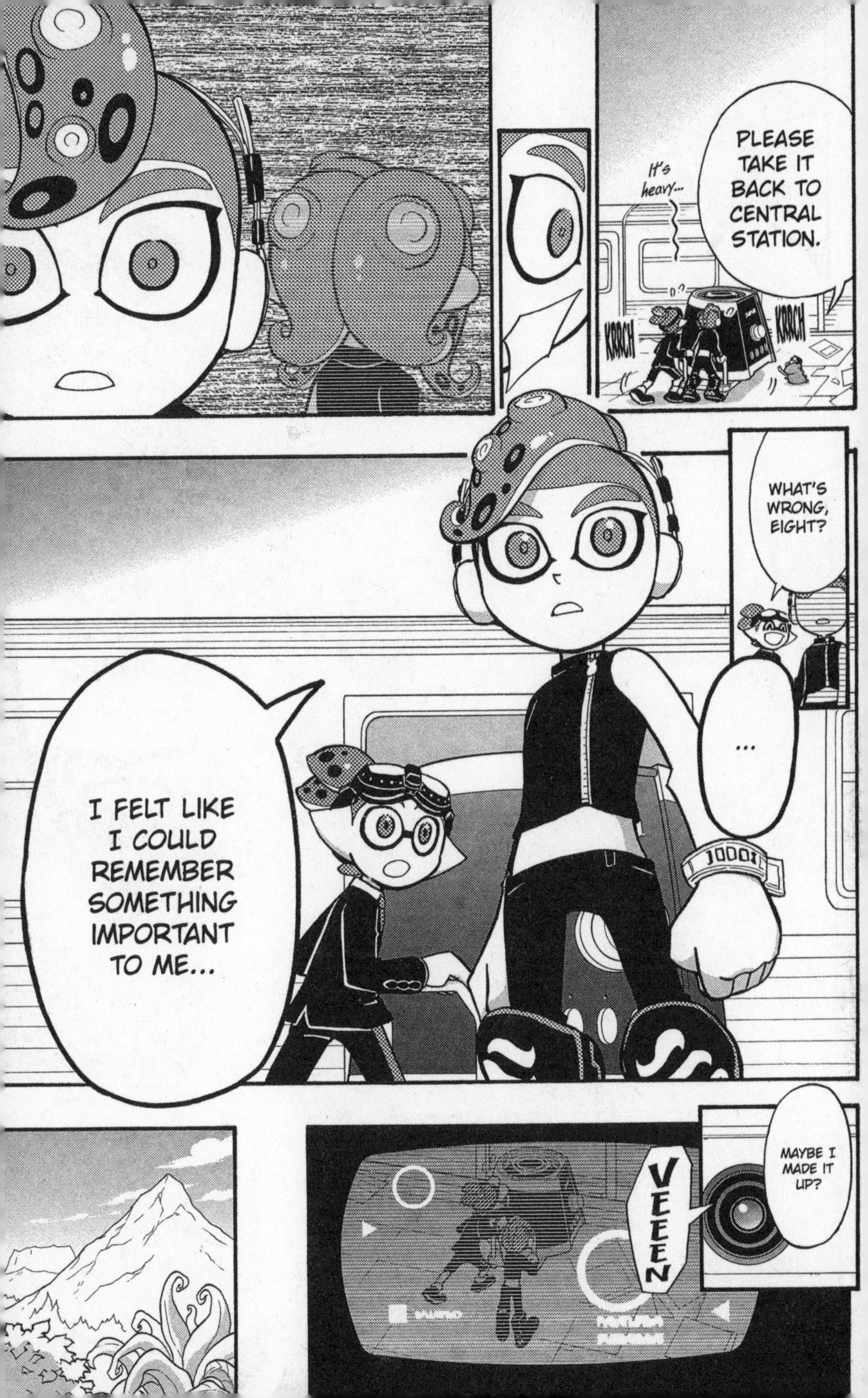
PLEASE TAKE IT BACK TO CENTRAL STATION.
It's heavy...
KRRCH
KRRCH
WHAT'S WRONG, EIGHT?
...
I FELT LIKE I COULD REMEMBER SOMETHING IMPORTANT TO ME...
MAYBE I MADE IT UP?
VEEEN

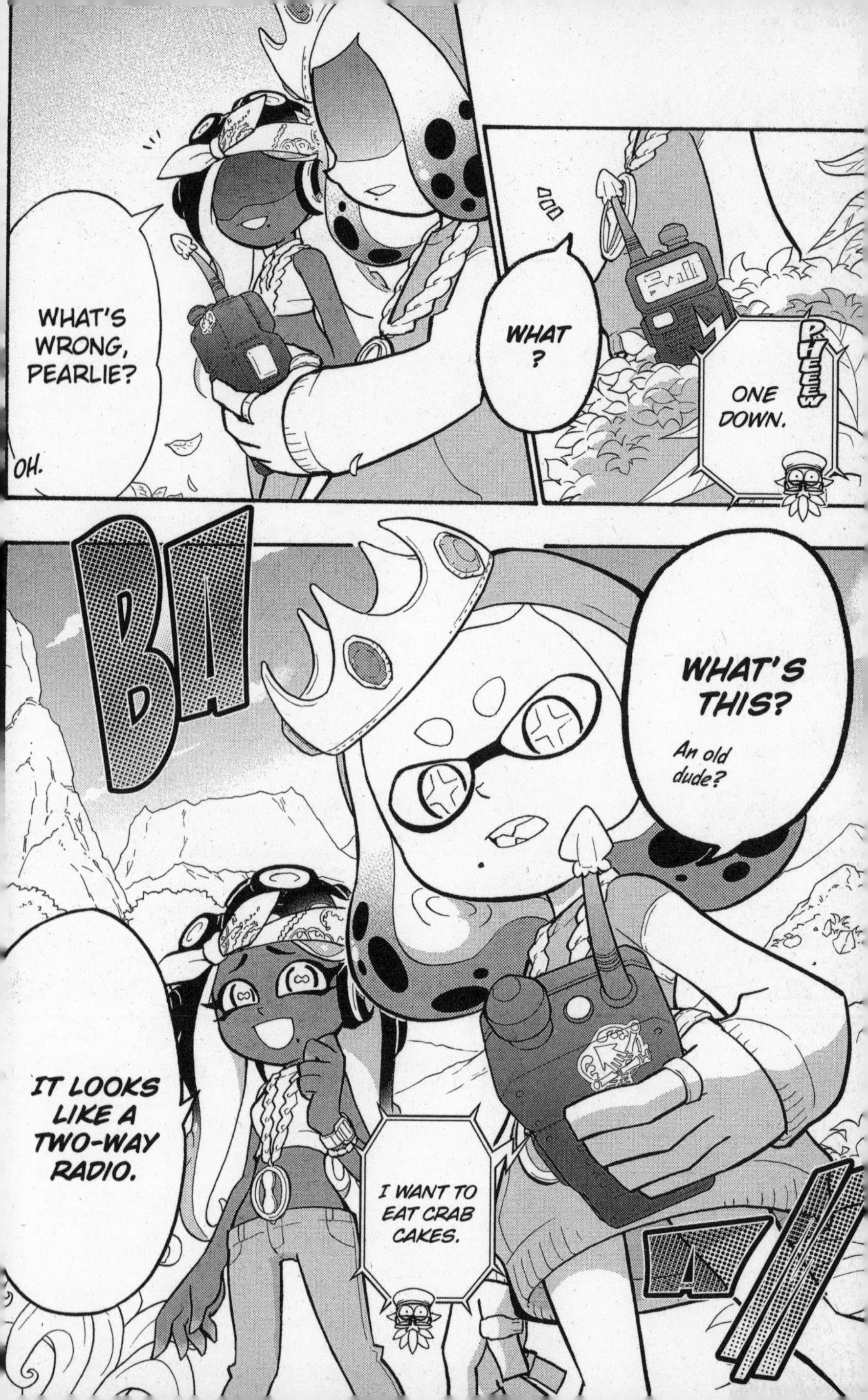
PHEEW
ONE DOWN.
WHAT ?
WHAT'S WRONG, PEARLIE?
OH.
WHAT'S THIS?
An old dude?
BA
I WANT TO EAT CRAB CAKES.
IT LOOKS LIKE A TWO-WAY RADIO.

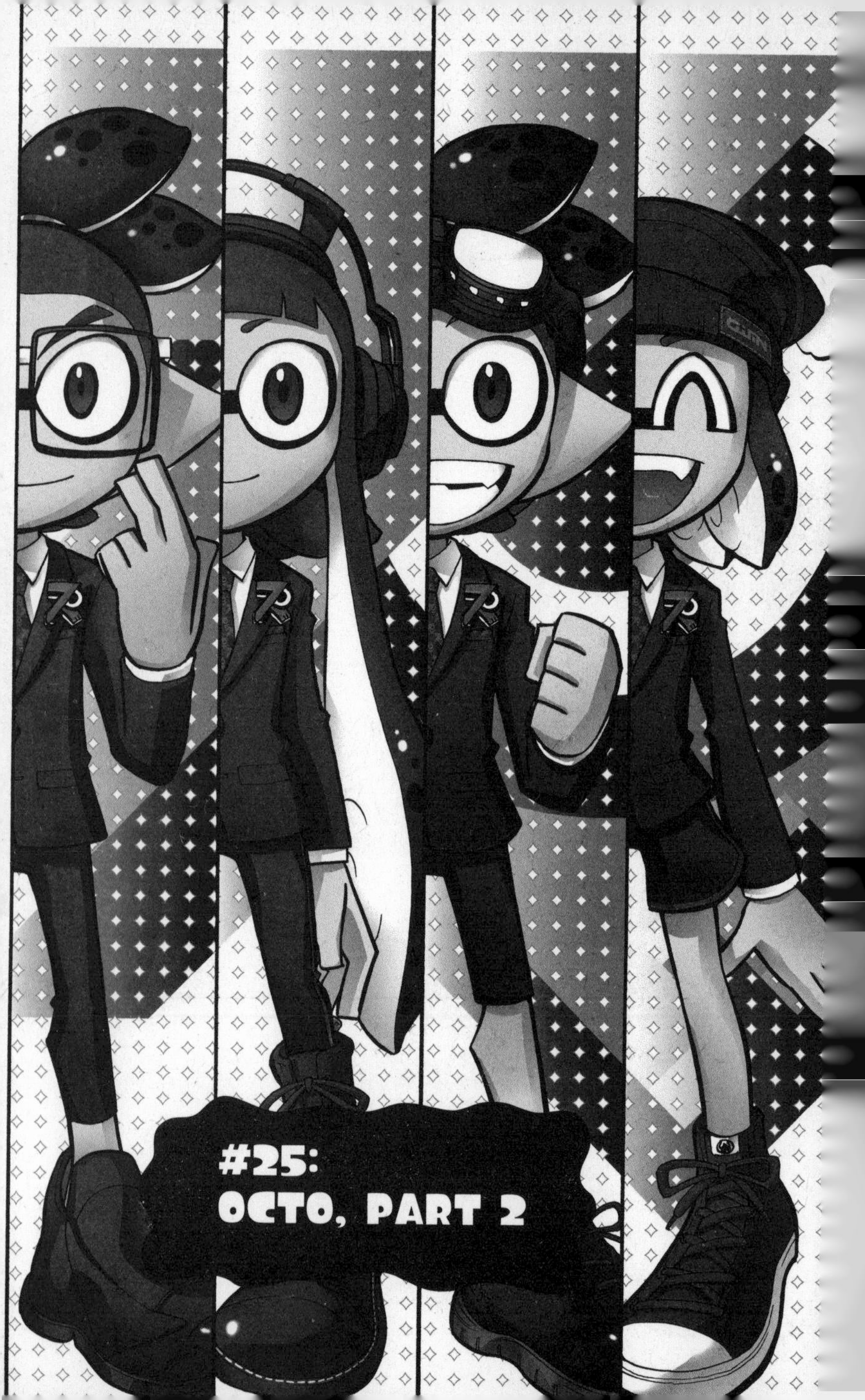
#25:
OCTO, PART 2

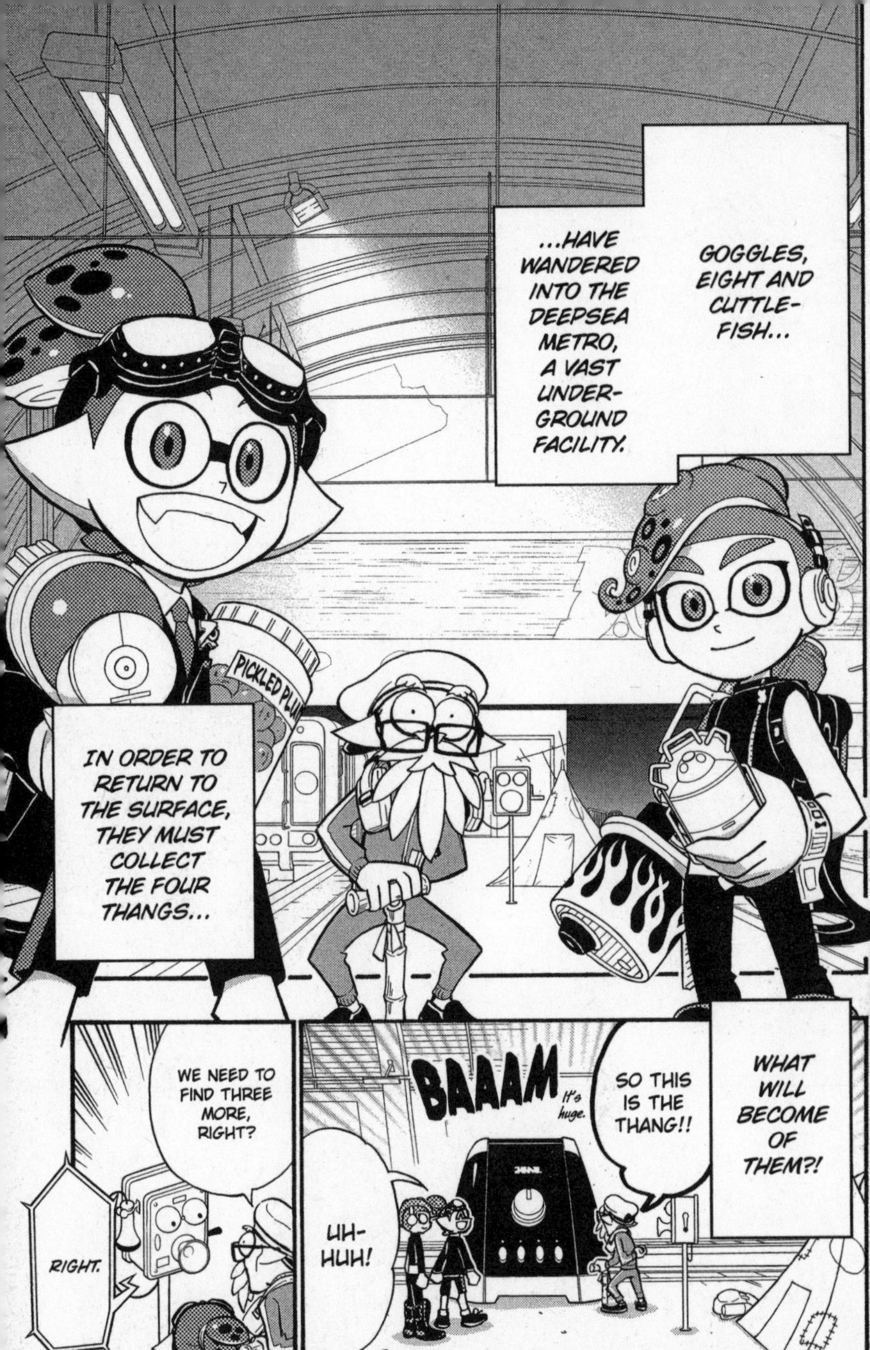
GOGGLES, EIGHT AND CUTTLE-FISH...
...HAVE WANDERED INTO THE DEEPSEA METRO, A VAST UNDER-GROUND FACILITY.
IN ORDER TO RETURN TO THE SURFACE, THEY MUST COLLECT THE FOUR THANGS...
WHAT WILL BECOME OF THEM?!
SO THIS IS THE THANG!!
It's huge.
BAAAM
UH-HUH!
WE NEED TO FIND THREE MORE, RIGHT?
RIGHT.

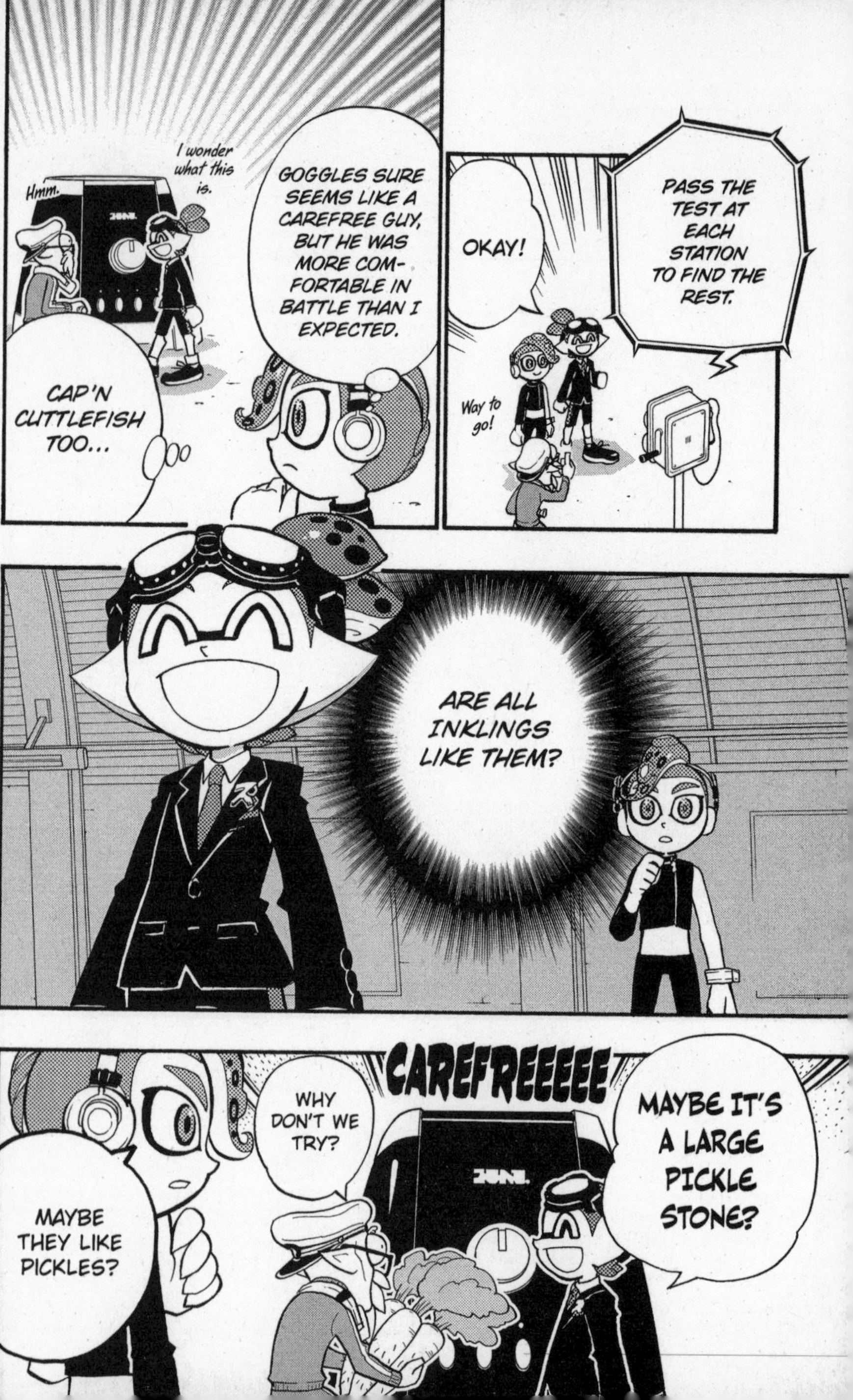
PASS THE TEST AT EACH STATION TO FIND THE REST.
OKAY!
Way to go!
GOGGLES SURE SEEMS LIKE A CAREFREE GUY, BUT HE WAS MORE COM-FORTABLE IN BATTLE THAN I EXPECTED.
I wonder what this is.
Hmm.
CAP'N CUTTLEFISH TOO...
ARE ALL INKLINGS LIKE THEM?
MAYBE IT'S A LARGE PICKLE STONE?
CAREFREEEEEE
WHY DON'T WE TRY?
MAYBE THEY LIKE PICKLES?

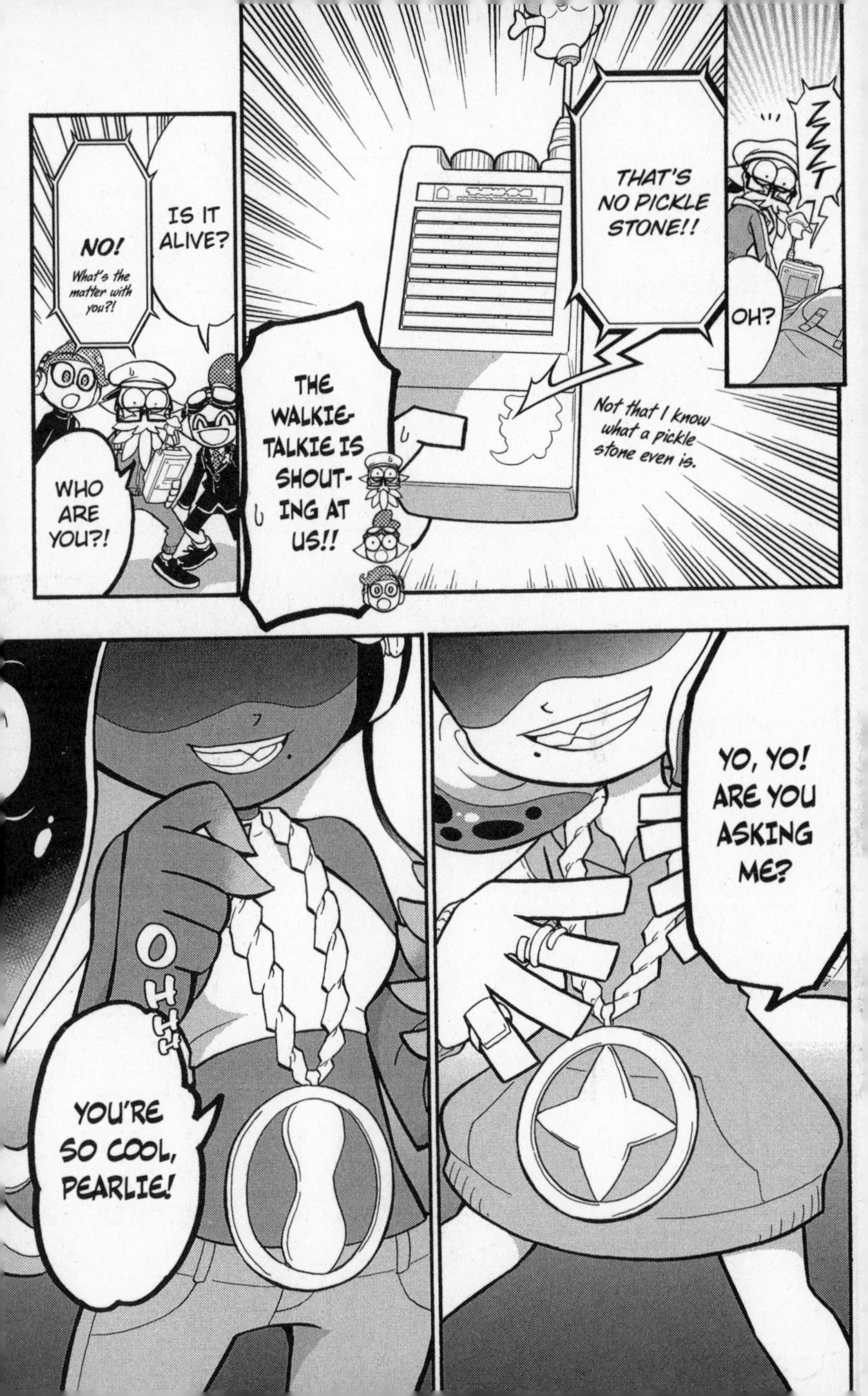
ZZZT
OH?
THAT'S NO PICKLE STONE!!
Not that I know what a pickle stone even is.
THE WALKIE-TALKIE IS SHOUTING AT US!!
IS IT ALIVE?
NO! What's the matter with you?!
WHO ARE YOU?!
YO, YO! ARE YOU ASKING ME?
OHHH
YOU'RE SO COOL, PEARLIE!

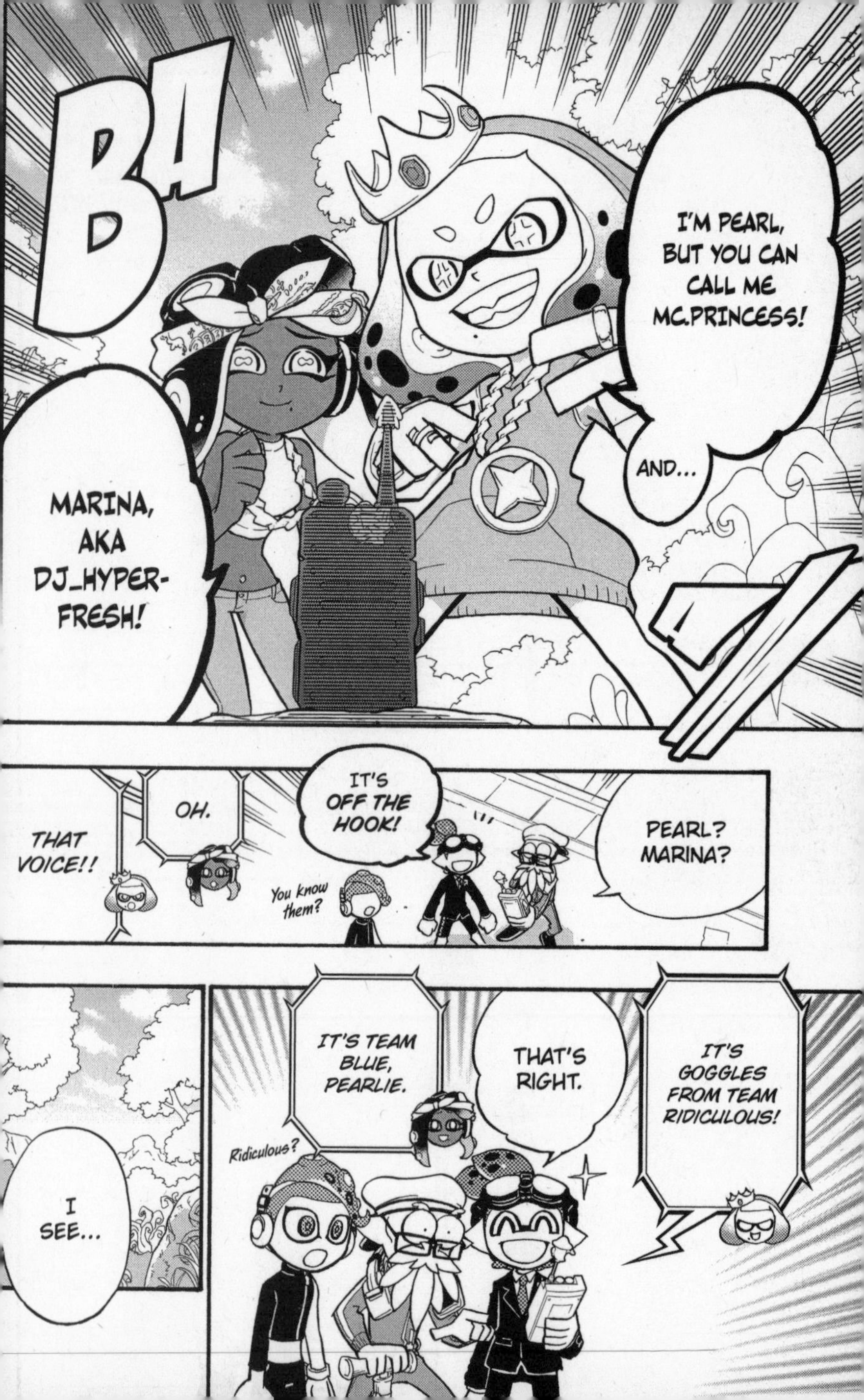
I'M PEARL, BUT YOU CAN CALL ME MC.PRINCESS!
AND...
BA
MARINA, AKA DJ_HYPER-FRESH!
PEARL? MARINA?
IT'S OFF THE HOOK!
You know them?
OH.
THAT VOICE!!
IT'S GOGGLES FROM TEAM RIDICULOUS!
THAT'S RIGHT.
IT'S TEAM BLUE, PEARLIE.
Ridiculous?
I SEE...

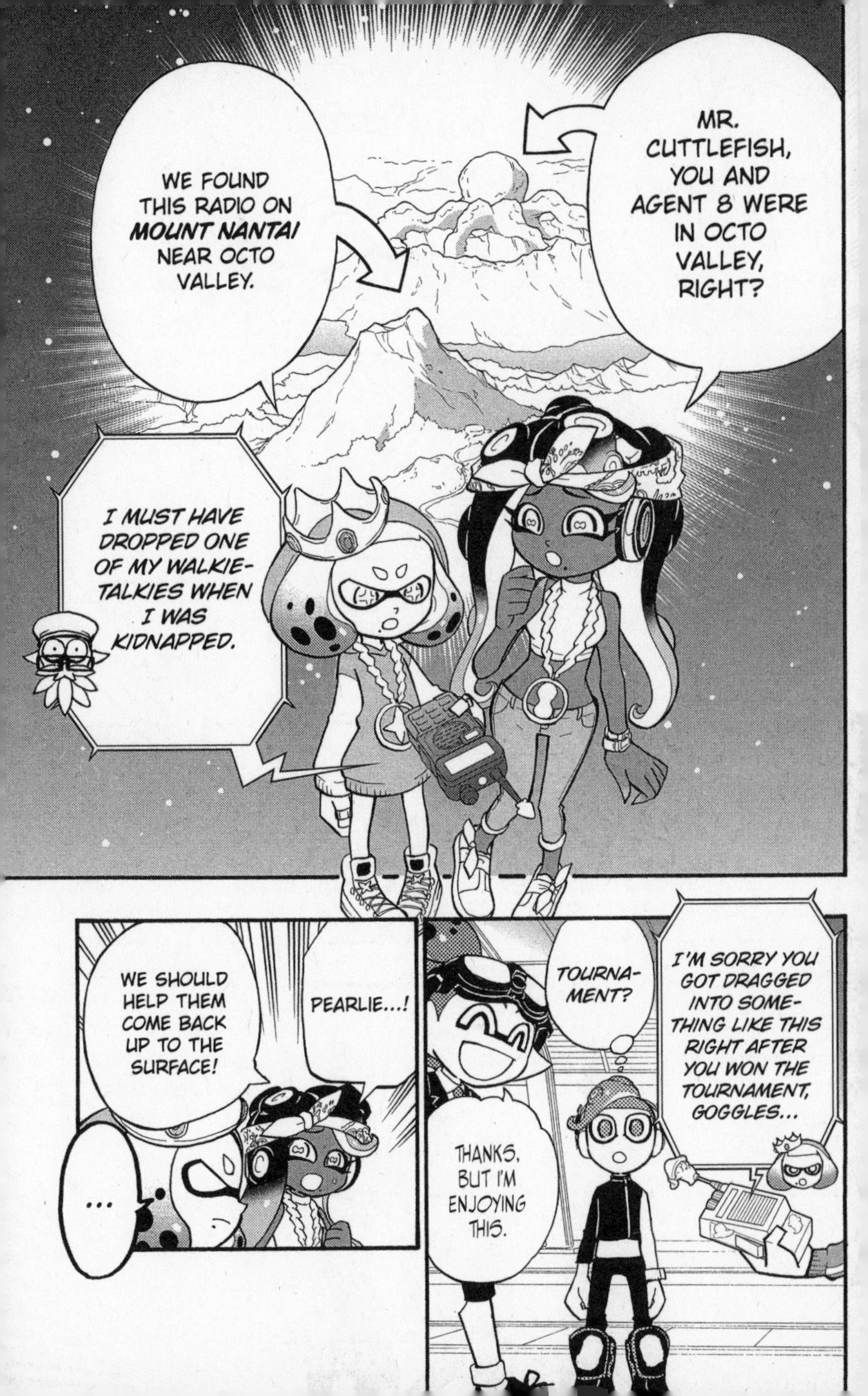
MR. CUTTLEFISH, YOU AND AGENT 8 WERE IN OCTO VALLEY, RIGHT?
WE FOUND THIS RADIO ON *MOUNT NANTAI* NEAR OCTO VALLEY.
I MUST HAVE DROPPED ONE OF MY WALKIE-TALKIES WHEN I WAS KIDNAPPED.
I'M SORRY YOU GOT DRAGGED INTO SOME-THING LIKE THIS RIGHT AFTER YOU WON THE TOURNAMENT, GOGGLES...
TOURNA-MENT?
THANKS, BUT I'M ENJOYING THIS.
PEARLIE...!
WE SHOULD HELP THEM COME BACK UP TO THE SURFACE!
...

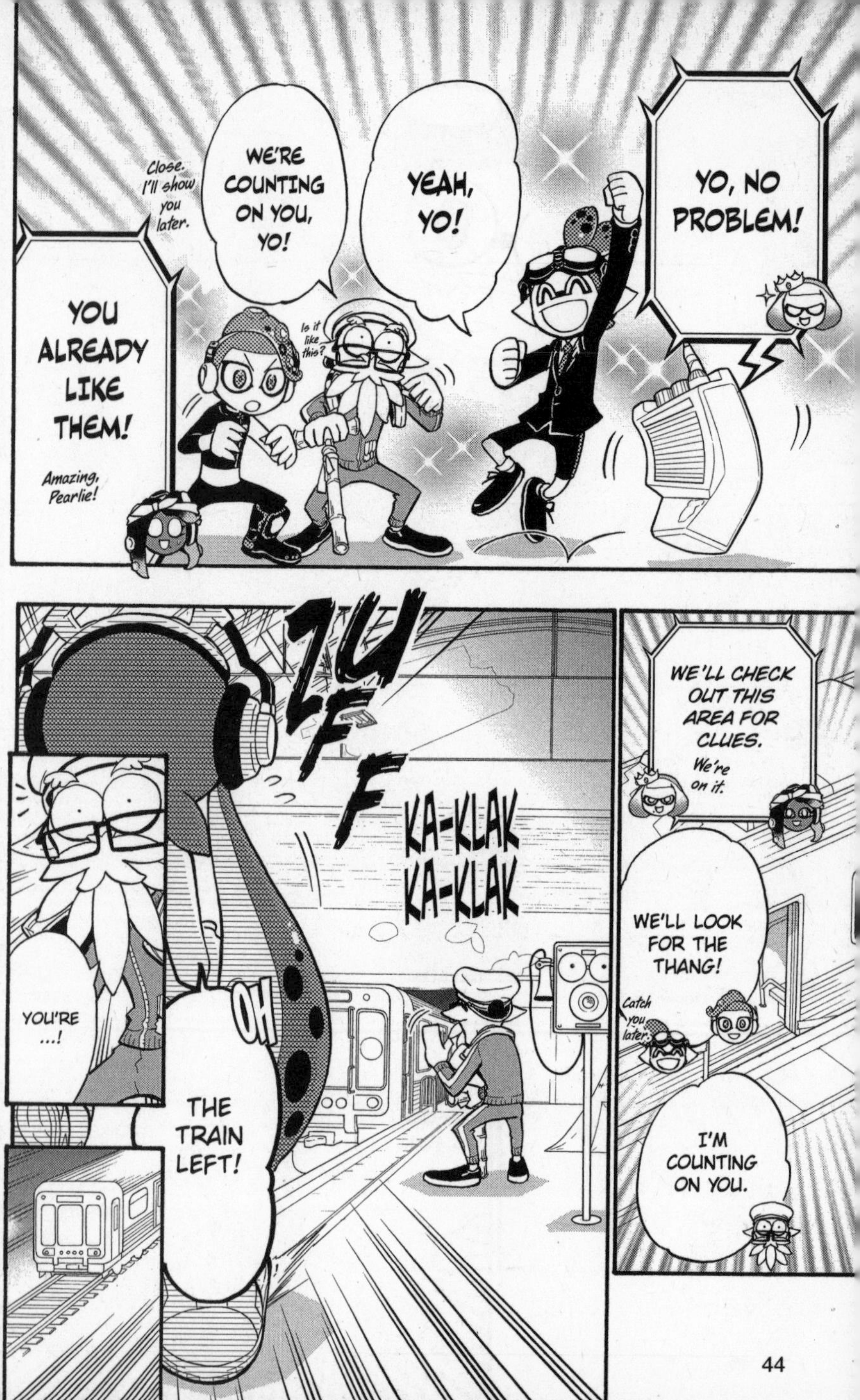
YO, NO PROBLEM!
YEAH, YO!
WE'RE COUNTING ON YOU, YO!
Close. I'll show you later.
Is it like this?
YOU ALREADY LIKE THEM!
Amazing, Pearlie!
WE'LL CHECK OUT THIS AREA FOR CLUES.
We're on it.
WE'LL LOOK FOR THE THANG!
Catch you later.
I'M COUNTING ON YOU.
ZUFF F
KA-KLAK KA-KLAK
OH
THE TRAIN LEFT!
YOU'RE ...!

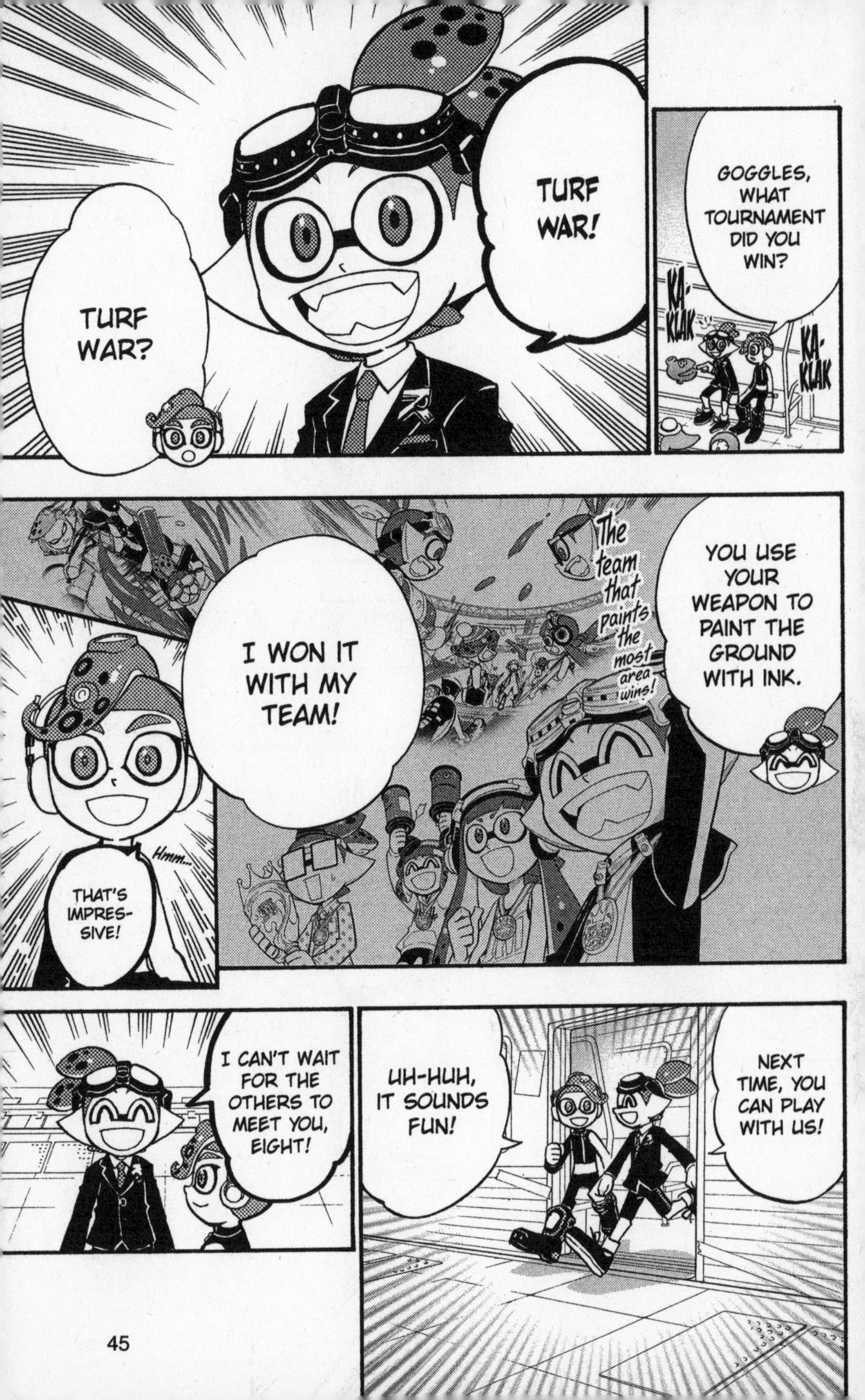
GOGGLES, WHAT TOURNAMENT DID YOU WIN?
KA-KLAK
KA-KLAK
TURF WAR!
TURF WAR?
YOU USE YOUR WEAPON TO PAINT THE GROUND WITH INK.
The team that paints the most area wins!
I WON IT WITH MY TEAM!
Hmm...
THAT'S IMPRES-SIVE!
NEXT TIME, YOU CAN PLAY WITH US!
UH-HUH, IT SOUNDS FUN!
I CAN'T WAIT FOR THE OTHERS TO MEET YOU, EIGHT!

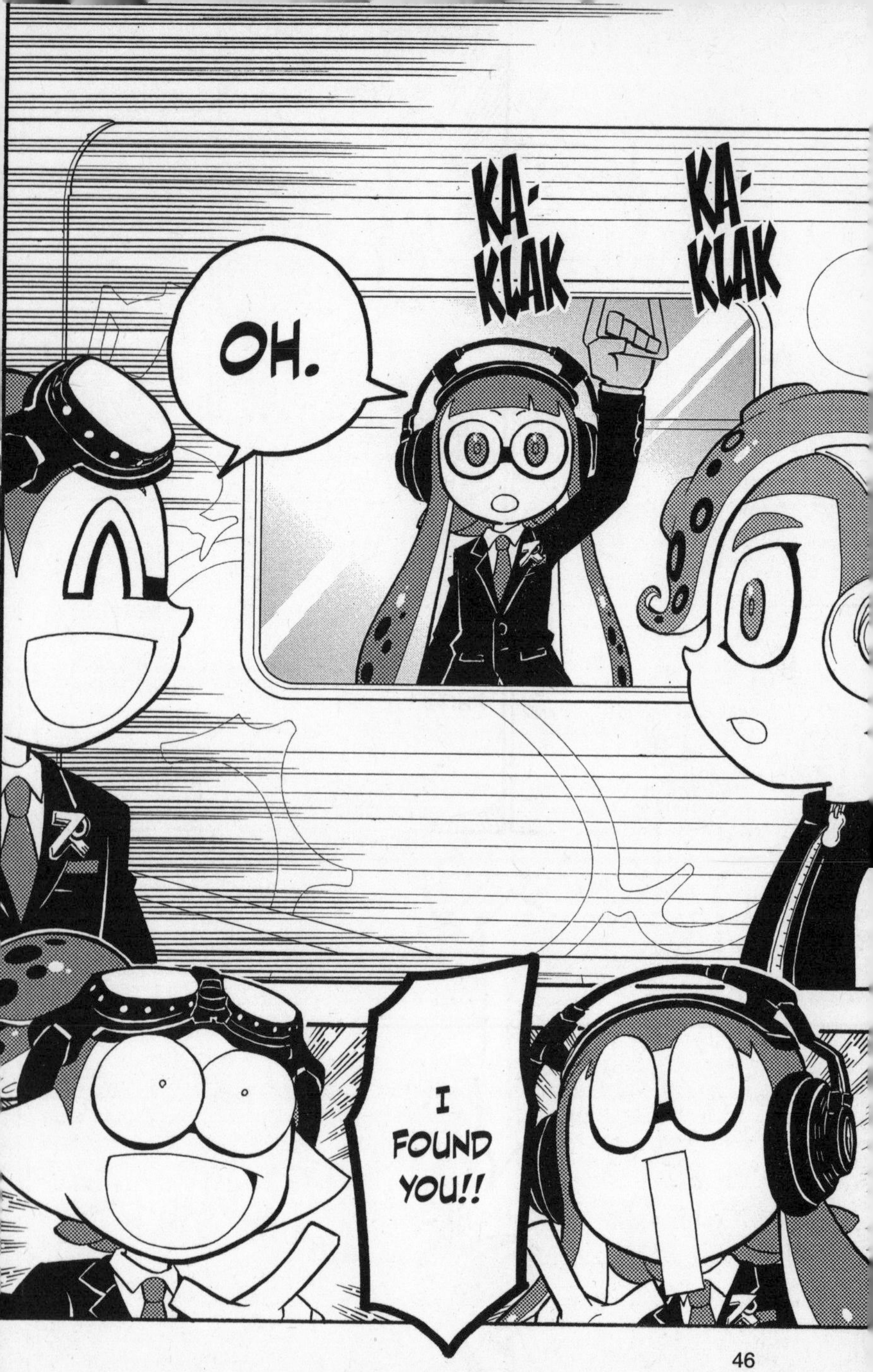
KA-KLAK
KA-KLAK
OH.
I FOUND YOU!!

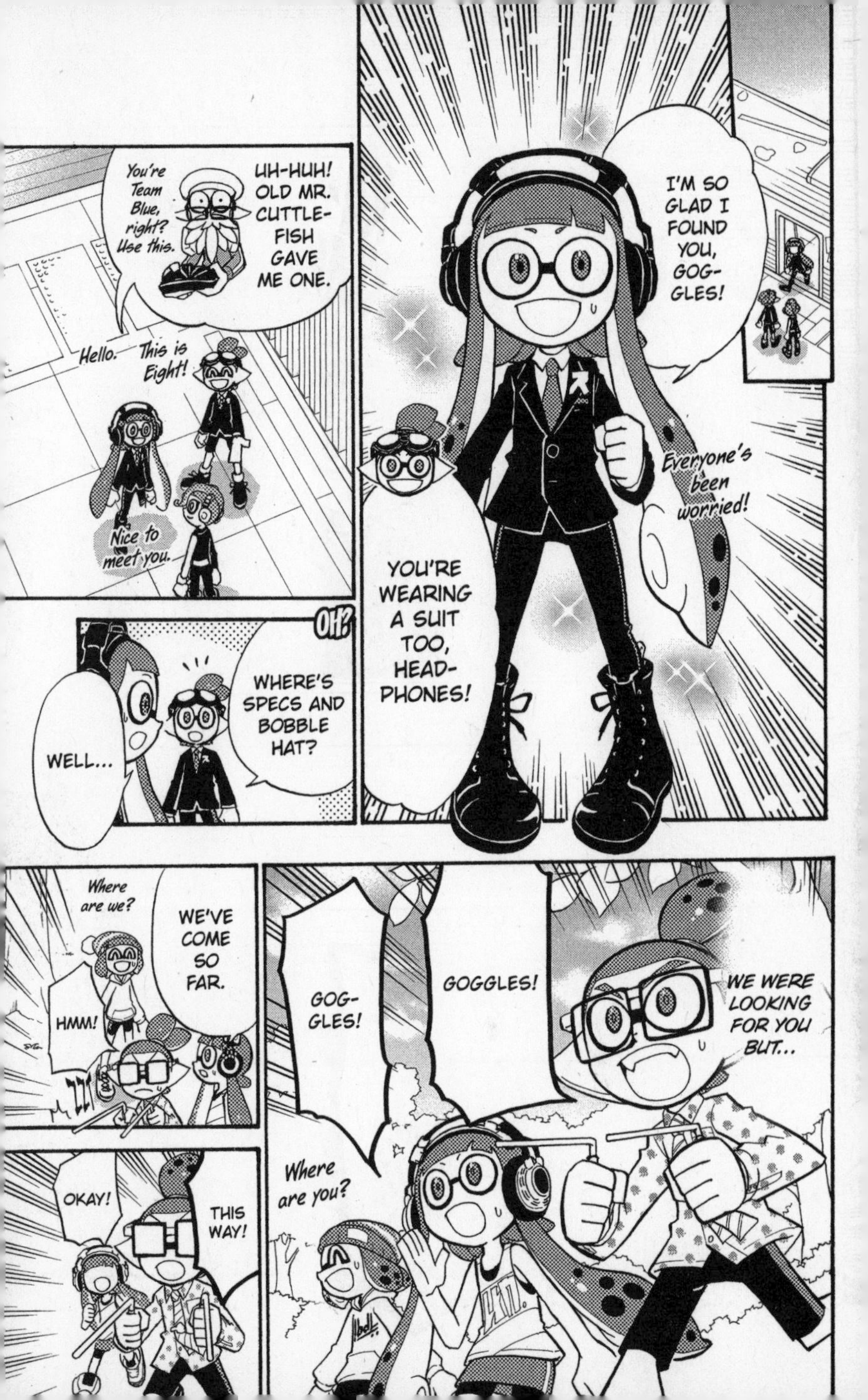
I'M SO GLAD I FOUND YOU, GOGGLES!
Everyone's been worried!
YOU'RE WEARING A SUIT TOO, HEADPHONES!
You're Team Blue, right? Use this.
UH-HUH! OLD MR. CUTTLEFISH GAVE ME ONE.
This is Eight!
Hello.
Nice to meet you.
OH?
WHERE'S SPECS AND BOBBLE HAT?
WELL...
WE WERE LOOKING FOR YOU BUT...
GOGGLES!
GOGGLES!
Where are you?
WE'VE COME SO FAR.
Where are we?
HMM!
THIS WAY!
OKAY!

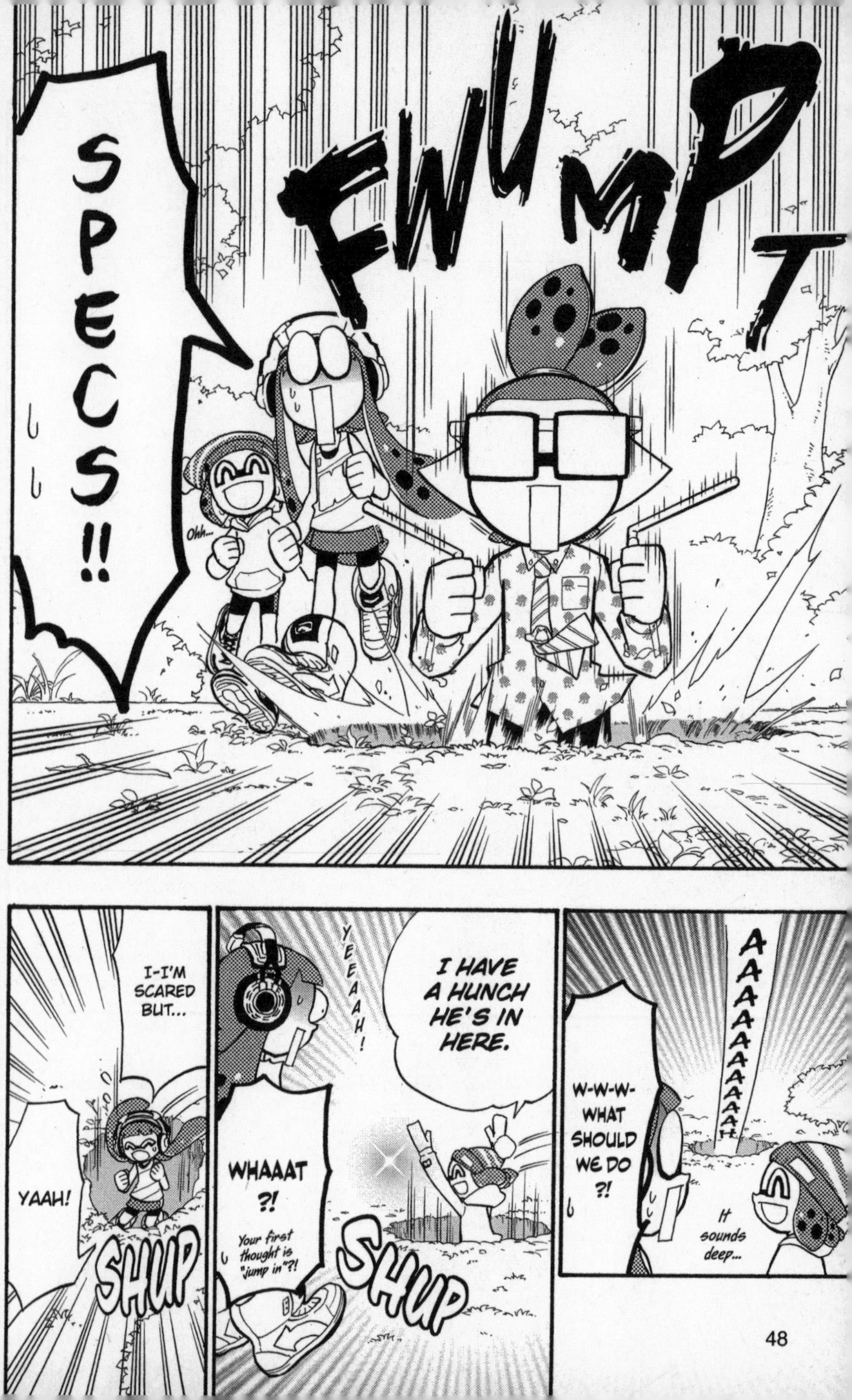
FWUMP
SPECS!!
Ohh...
AAAAAAAAAAAH
W-W-W-WHAT SHOULD WE DO?!
It sounds deep...
I HAVE A HUNCH HE'S IN HERE.
YEEAAAH!
WHAAAT?!
Your first thought is "jump in"?!
SHUP
I-I'M SCARED BUT...
YAAH!
SHUP

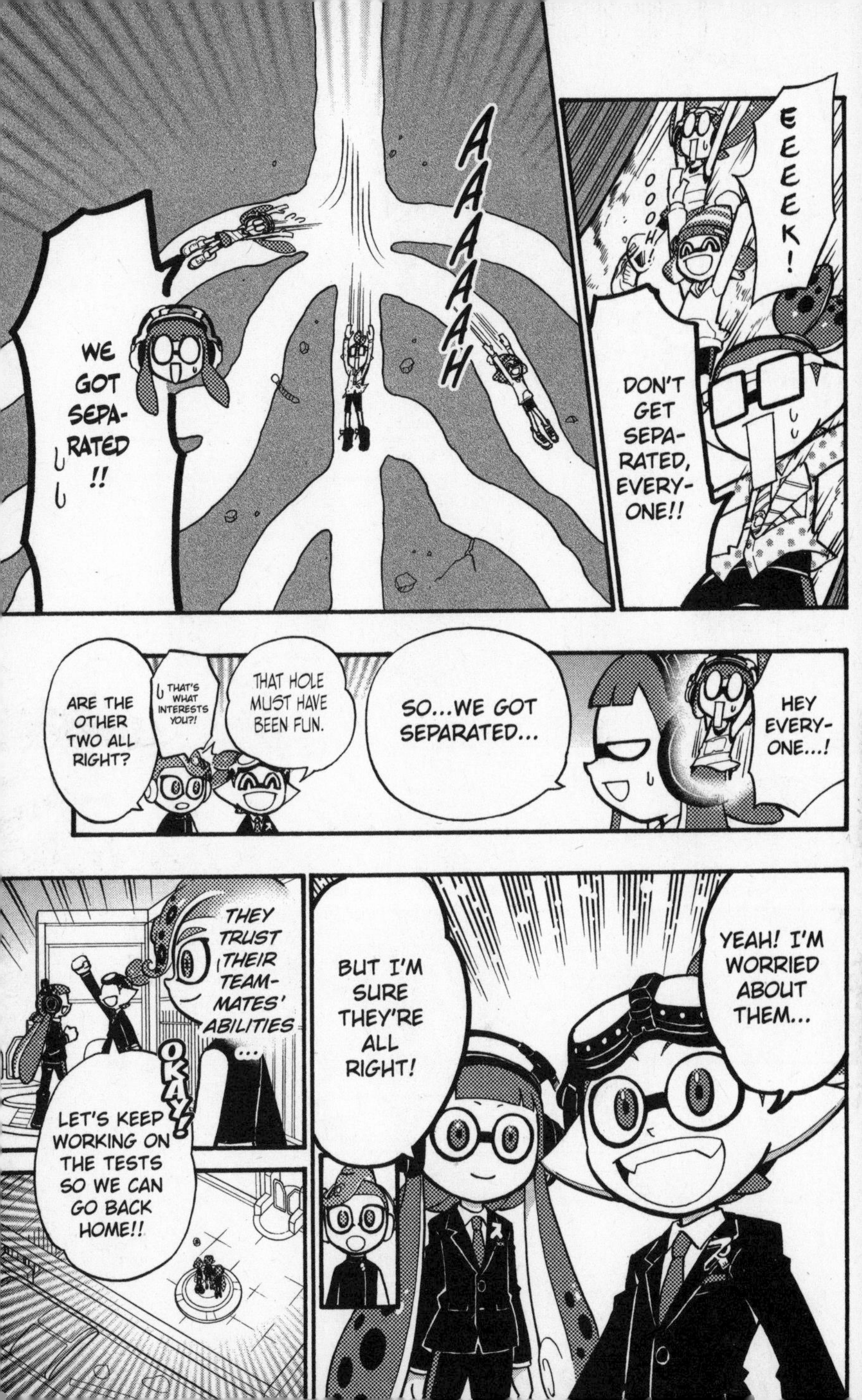
EEEEK!
OOOOH!
DON'T GET SEPARATED, EVERYONE!!
AAAAAAH
WE GOT SEPARATED!!
HEY EVERYONE...!
SO...WE GOT SEPARATED...
THAT HOLE MUST HAVE BEEN FUN.
THAT'S WHAT INTERESTS YOU?!
ARE THE OTHER TWO ALL RIGHT?
YEAH! I'M WORRIED ABOUT THEM...
BUT I'M SURE THEY'RE ALL RIGHT!
THEY TRUST THEIR TEAMMATES' ABILITIES...
OKAY!
LET'S KEEP WORKING ON THE TESTS SO WE CAN GO BACK HOME!!

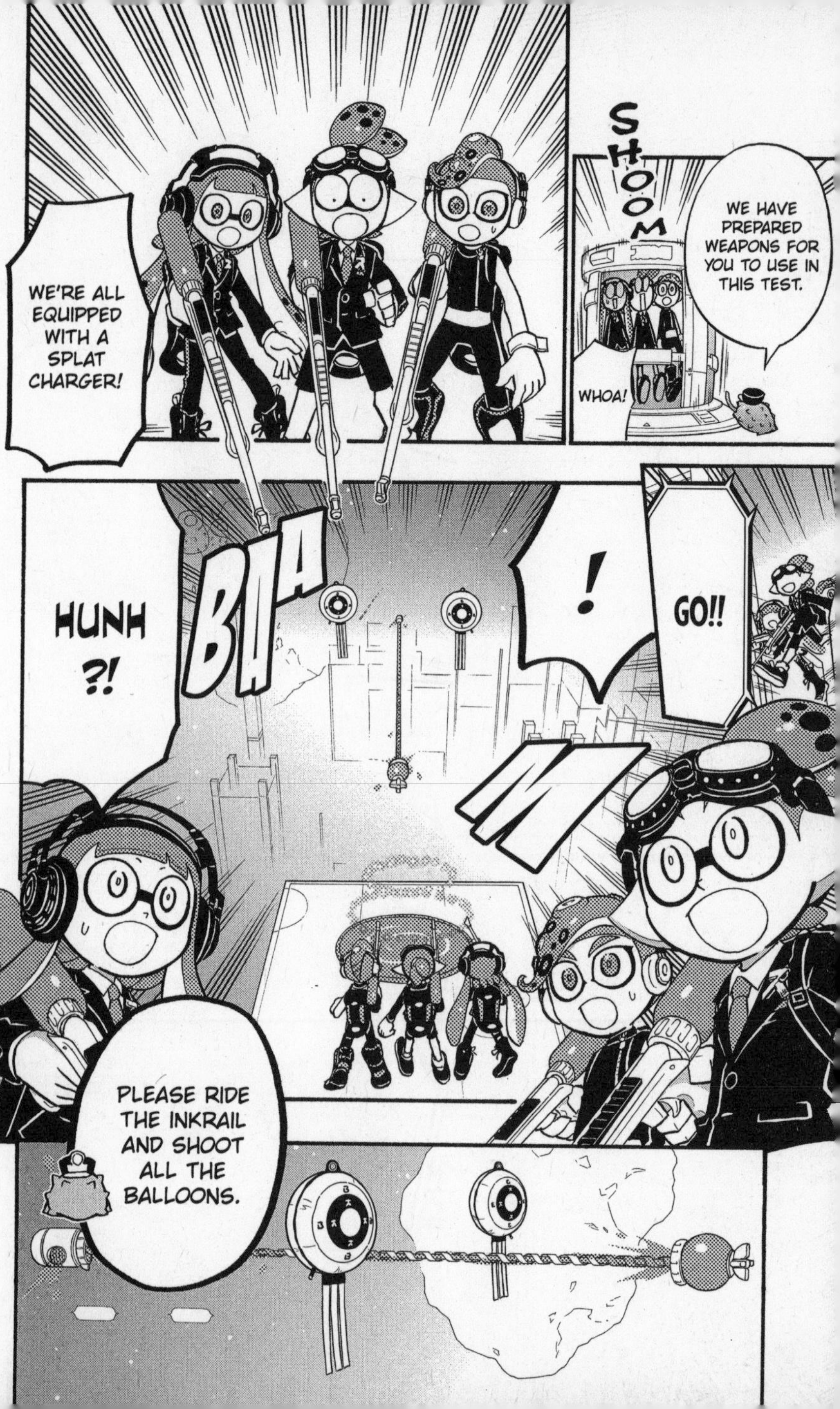
SHOOOM
WE HAVE PREPARED WEAPONS FOR YOU TO USE IN THIS TEST.
WHOA!
WE'RE ALL EQUIPPED WITH A SPLAT CHARGER!
GO!!
!
BAAM
HUNH ?!
PLEASE RIDE THE INKRAIL AND SHOOT ALL THE BALLOONS.

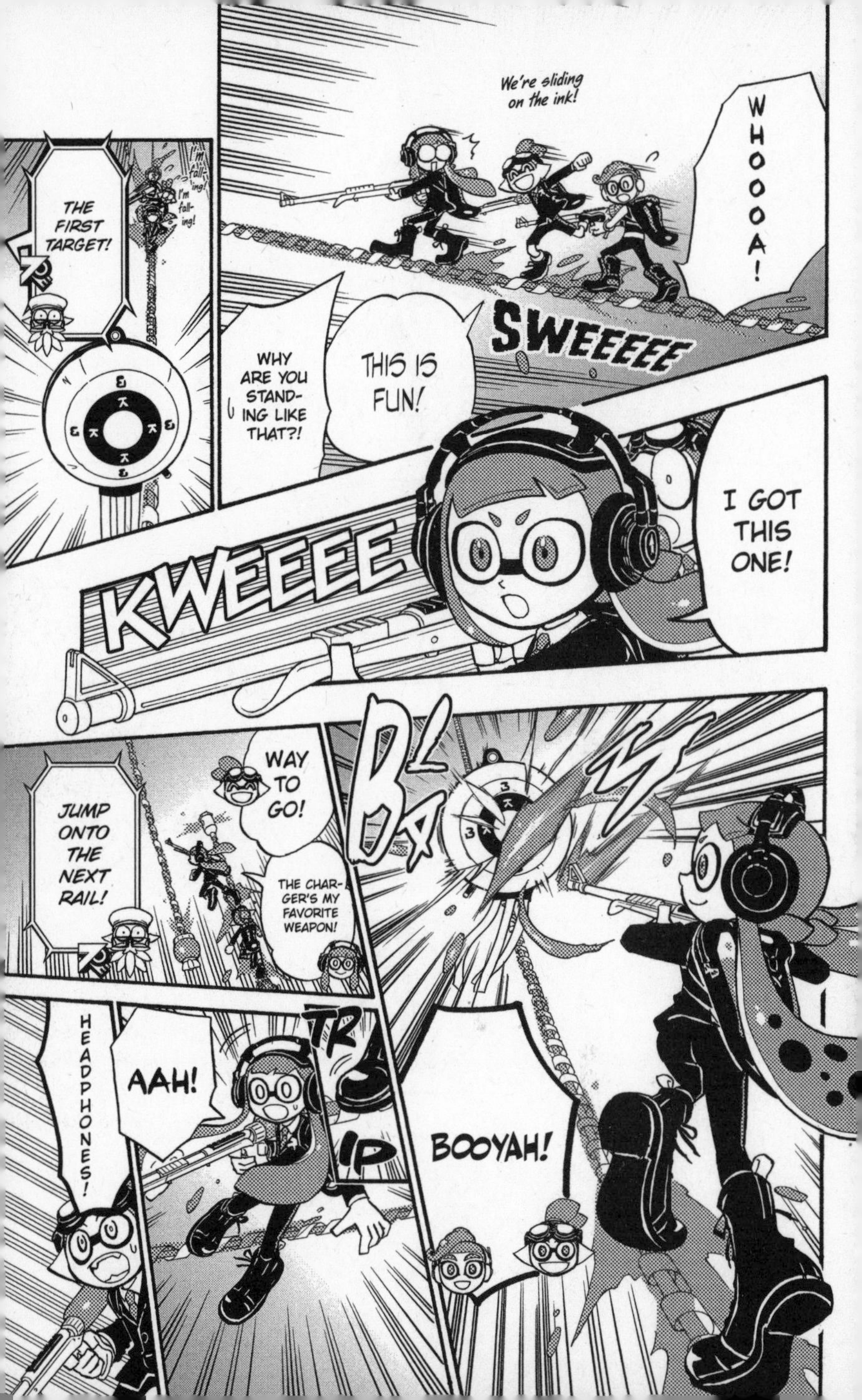
WHOOOA!
We're sliding on the ink!
SWEEEEEE
THIS IS FUN!
WHY ARE YOU STANDING LIKE THAT?!
THE FIRST TARGET!
I'm falling! I'm falling!
I GOT THIS ONE!
KWEEEEE
BLAM
WAY TO GO!
THE CHARGER'S MY FAVORITE WEAPON!
JUMP ONTO THE NEXT RAIL!
BOOYAH!
TRIP
AAH!
HEADPHONES!

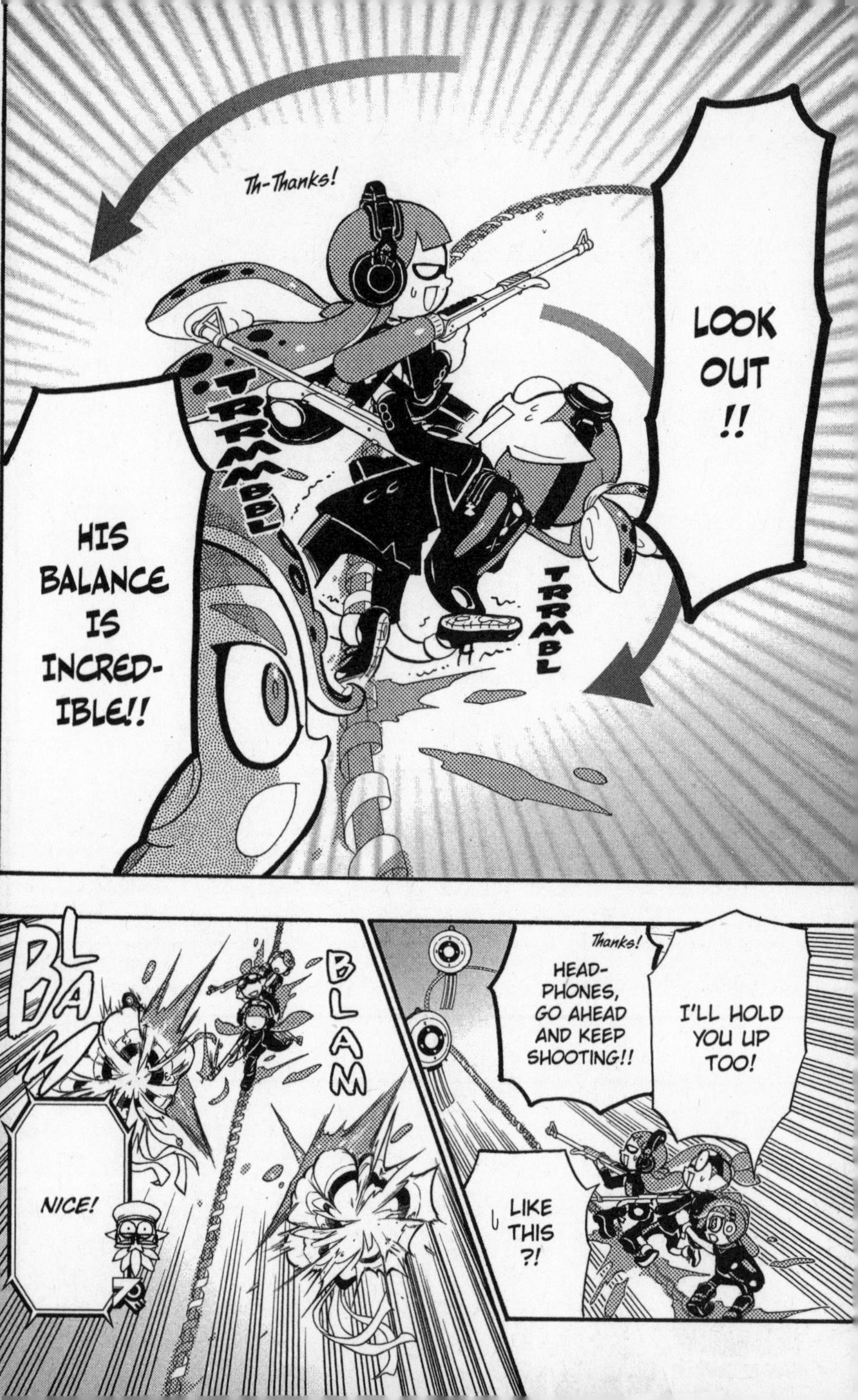
LOOK OUT!!
Th-Thanks!
TRRMMBBL
TRRMBL
HIS BALANCE IS INCREDIBLE!!
I'LL HOLD YOU UP TOO!
Thanks!
HEAD-PHONES, GO AHEAD AND KEEP SHOOTING!!
LIKE THIS?!
BLAM
BLAM
NICE!

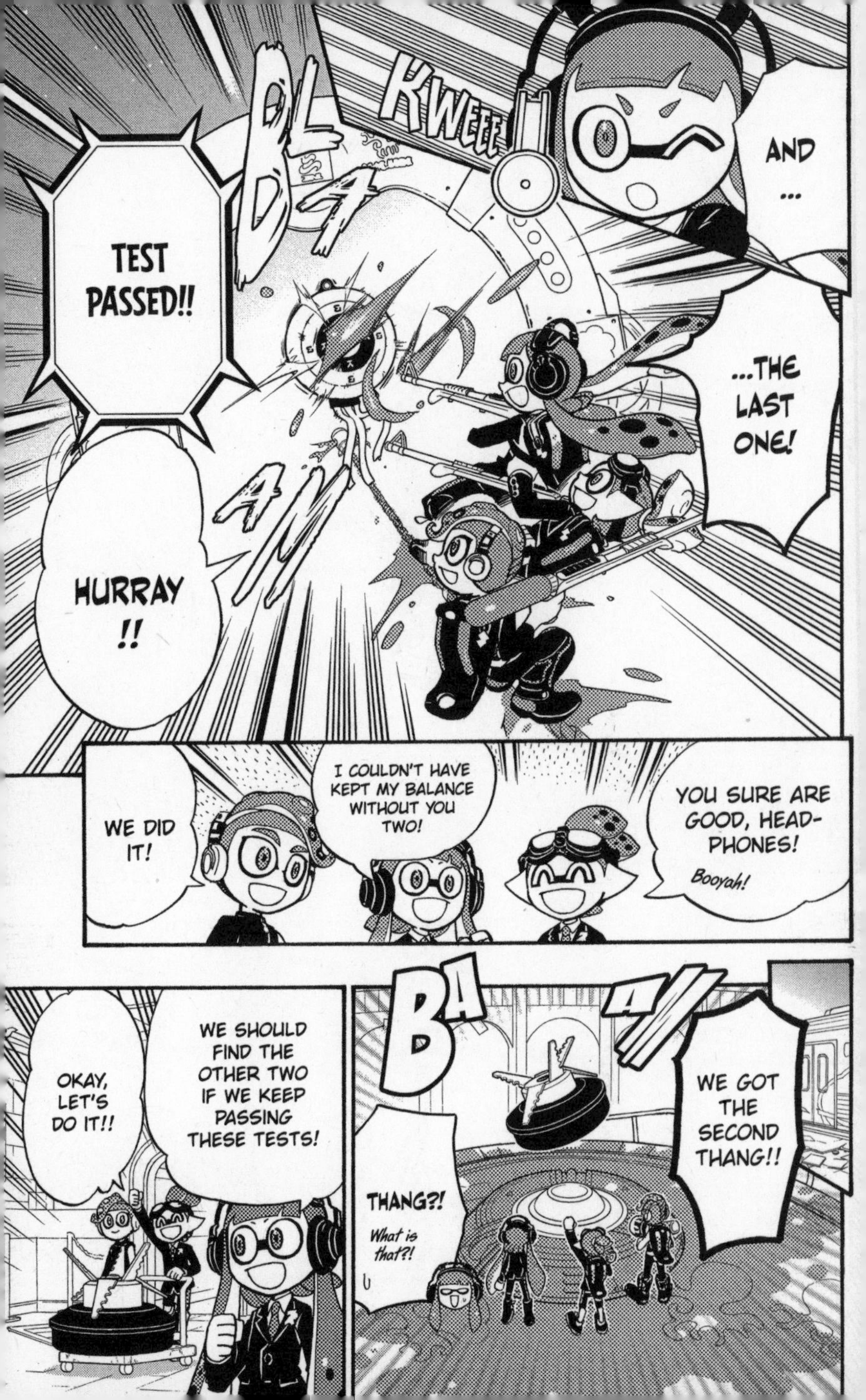
AND ...
KWEEE
...THE LAST ONE!
TEST PASSED!!
HURRAY !!
YOU SURE ARE GOOD, HEAD-PHONES!
Booyah!
I COULDN'T HAVE KEPT MY BALANCE WITHOUT YOU TWO!
WE DID IT!
WE GOT THE SECOND THANG!!
THANG?!
What is that?!
WE SHOULD FIND THE OTHER TWO IF WE KEEP PASSING THESE TESTS!
OKAY, LET'S DO IT!!

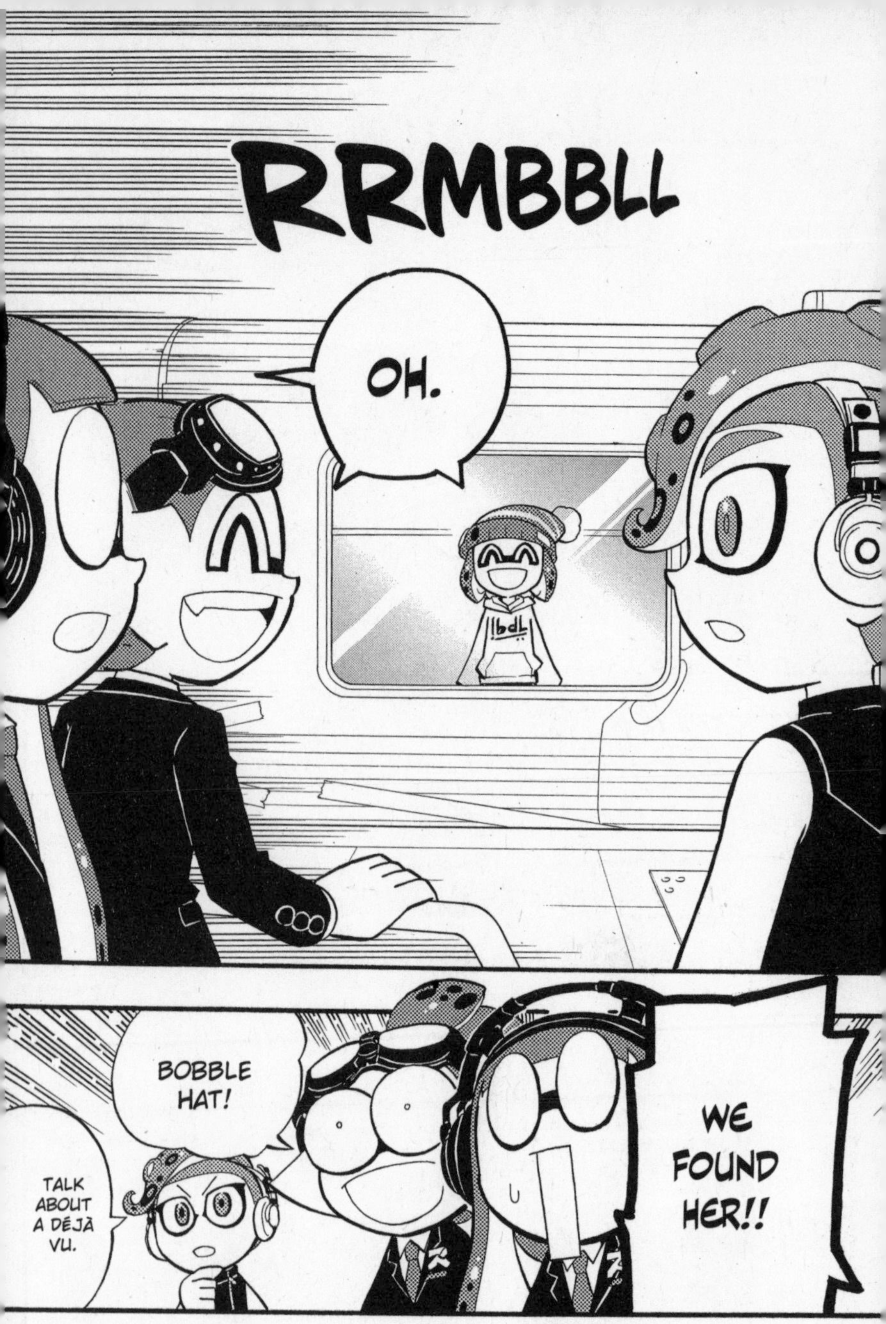
RRMBBLL
OH.
WE FOUND HER!!
BOBBLE HAT!
TALK ABOUT A DÉJÀ VU.

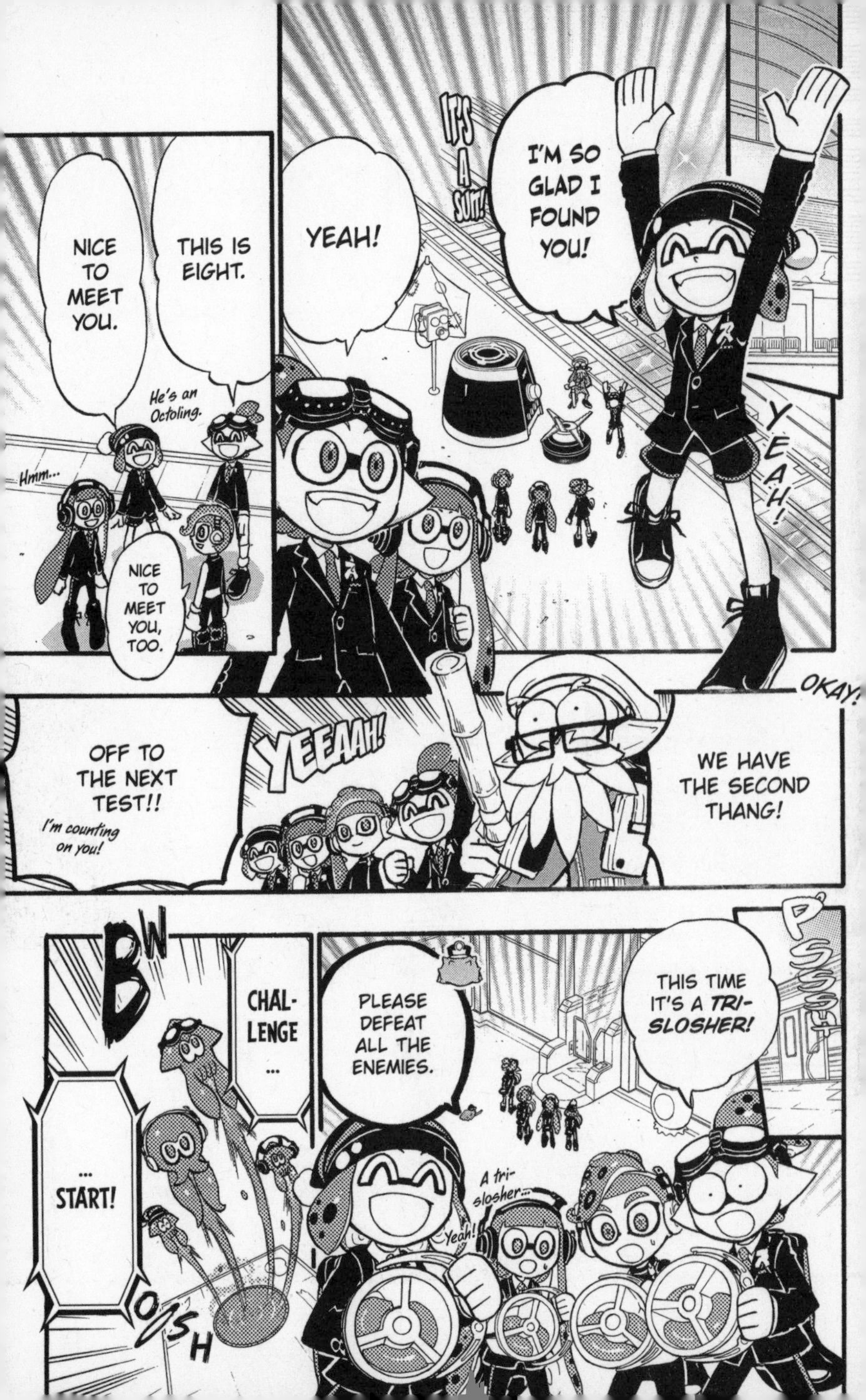
YEAH!
I'M SO GLAD I FOUND YOU!
IT'S A SUIT!
YEAH!
THIS IS EIGHT.
NICE TO MEET YOU.
He's an Octoling.
Hmm...
NICE TO MEET YOU, TOO.
OKAY!
WE HAVE THE SECOND THANG!
YEEAAH!
OFF TO THE NEXT TEST!!
I'm counting on you!
PSSSH
THIS TIME IT'S A TRI-SLOSHER!
PLEASE DEFEAT ALL THE ENEMIES.
A tri-slosher...
Yeah!
CHAL-LENGE ...
BWOOSH
... START!

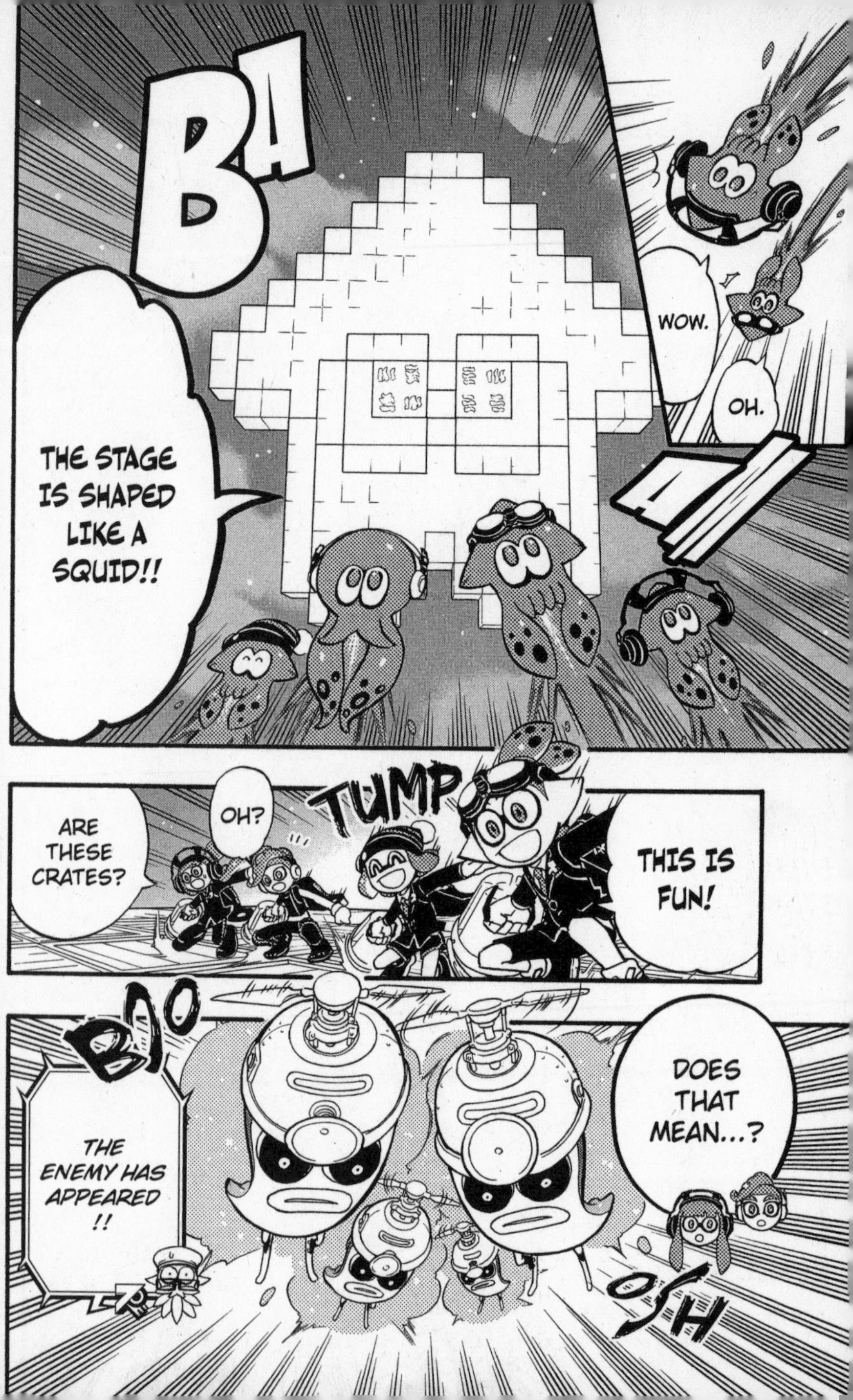
WOW.
OH.
BA
THE STAGE IS SHAPED LIKE A SQUID!!
THIS IS FUN!
TUMP
OH?
ARE THESE CRATES?
DOES THAT MEAN...?
OH
BOO
THE ENEMY HAS APPEARED!!

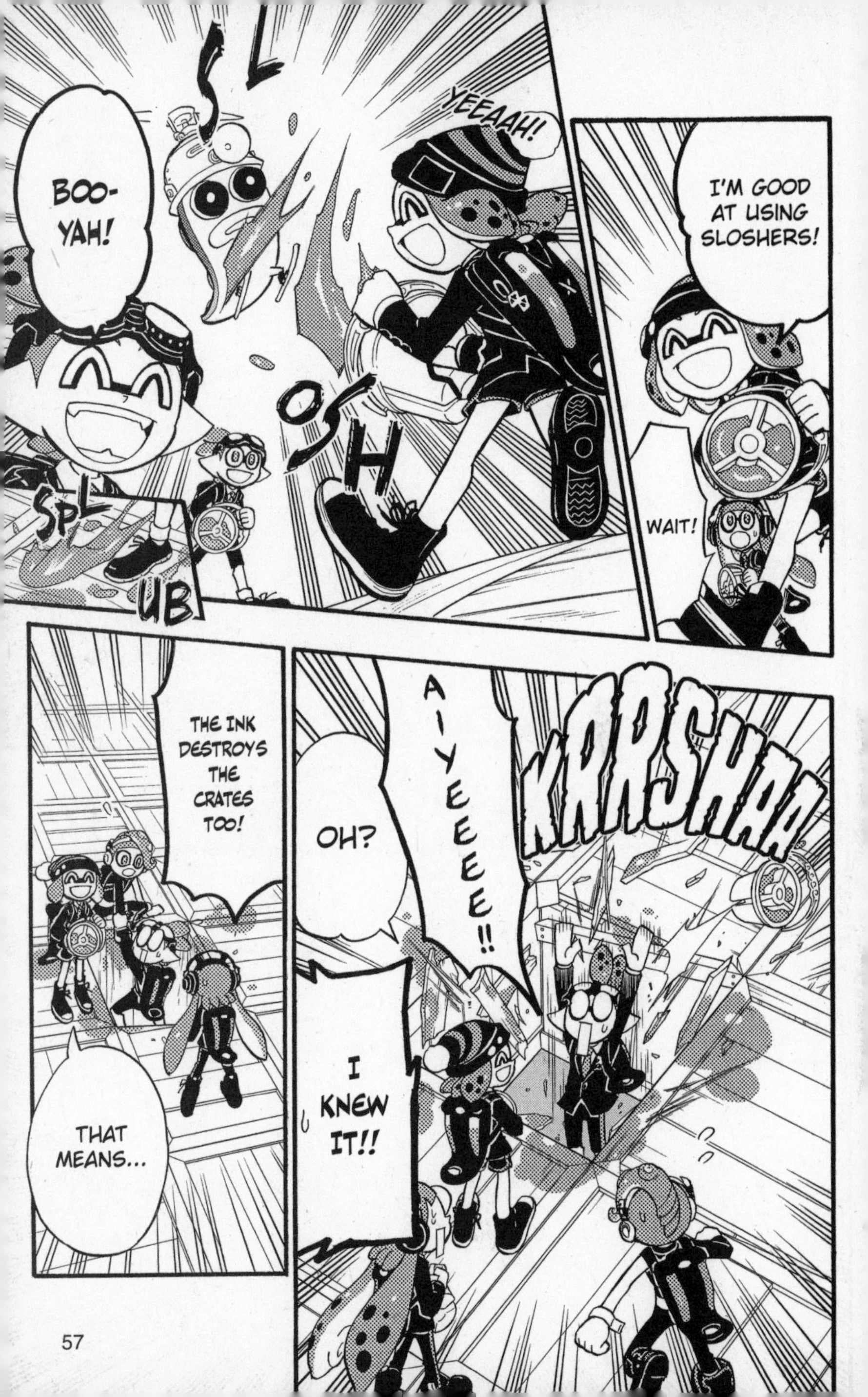
I'M GOOD AT USING SLOSHERS!
WAIT!
YEEAAH!
SL
OSH
BOO-YAH!
SPL
UB
KRRSHAA
AIYEEEEE!!
OH?
I KNEW IT!!
THE INK DESTROYS THE CRATES TOO!
THAT MEANS...

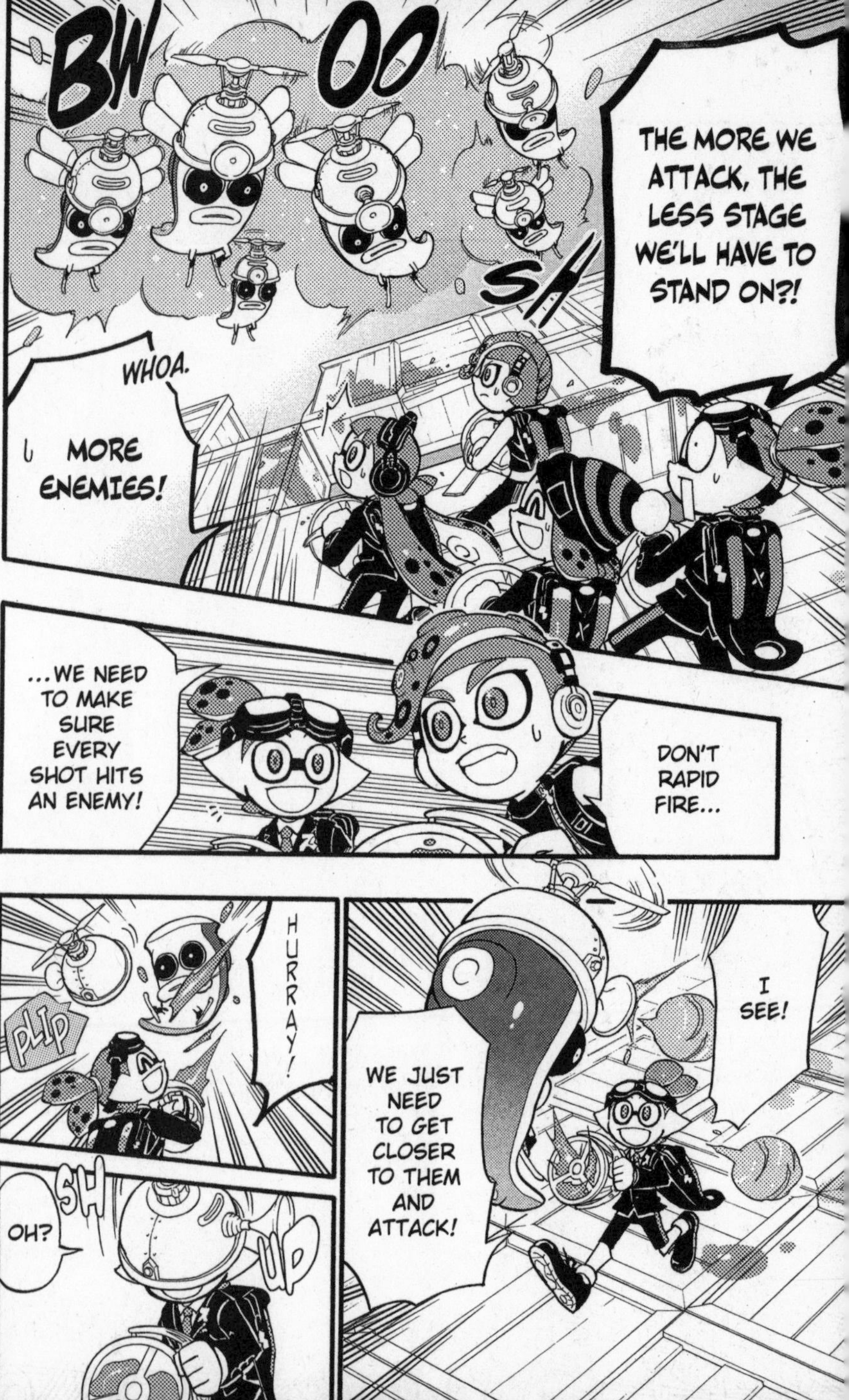
BWOO
THE MORE WE ATTACK, THE LESS STAGE WE'LL HAVE TO STAND ON?!
SH
WHOA.
MORE ENEMIES!
DON'T RAPID FIRE...
...WE NEED TO MAKE SURE EVERY SHOT HITS AN ENEMY!
I SEE!
WE JUST NEED TO GET CLOSER TO THEM AND ATTACK!
HURRAY!
PLIP
SH
UD
OH?

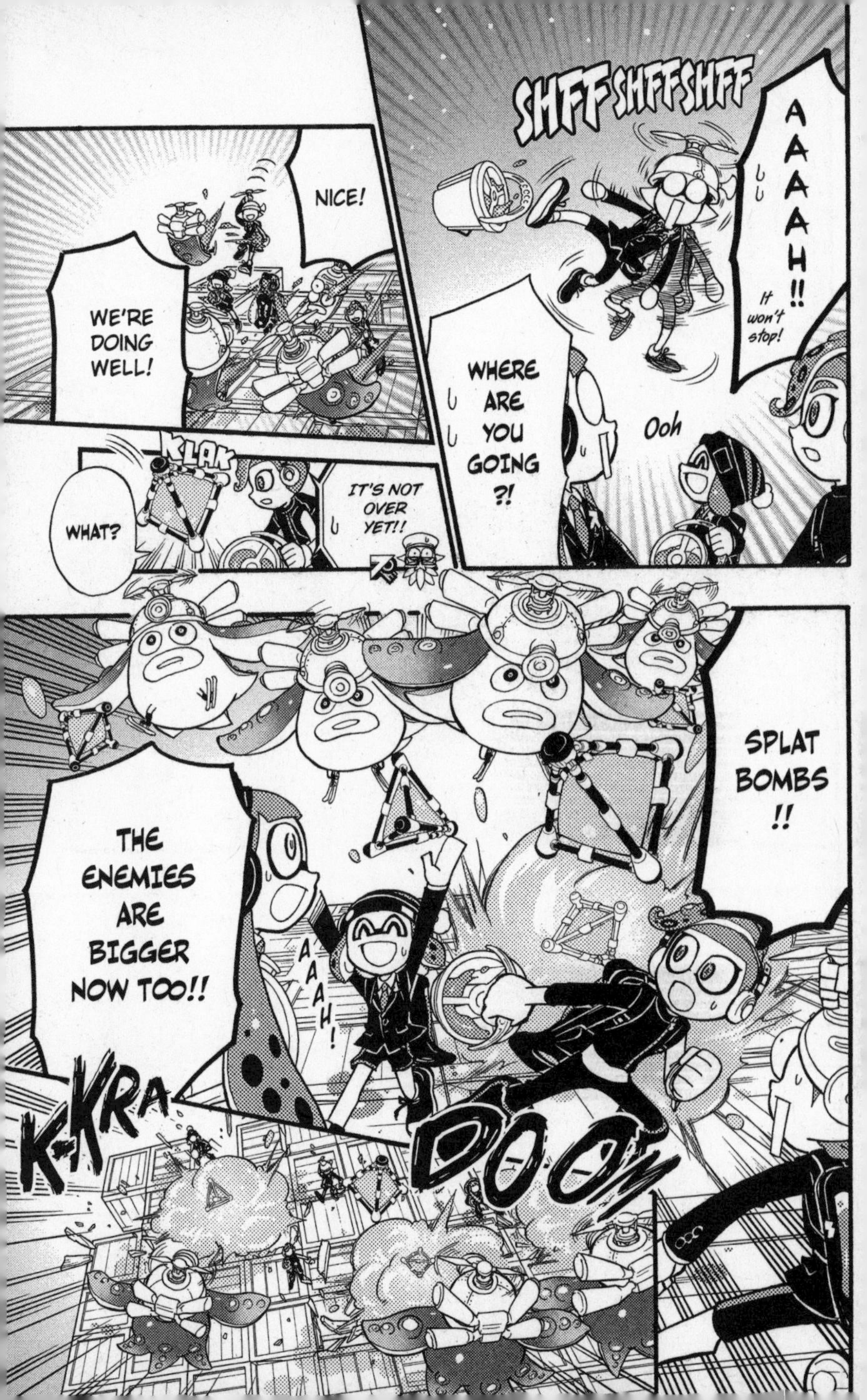
SHFF SHFFSHFF
AAAAH!!
It won't stop!
WHERE ARE YOU GOING?!
Ooh
NICE!
WE'RE DOING WELL!
IT'S NOT OVER YET!!
KLAK
WHAT?
SPLAT BOMBS!!
THE ENEMIES ARE BIGGER NOW TOO!!
AAAAH!
K-KRA
DOOM

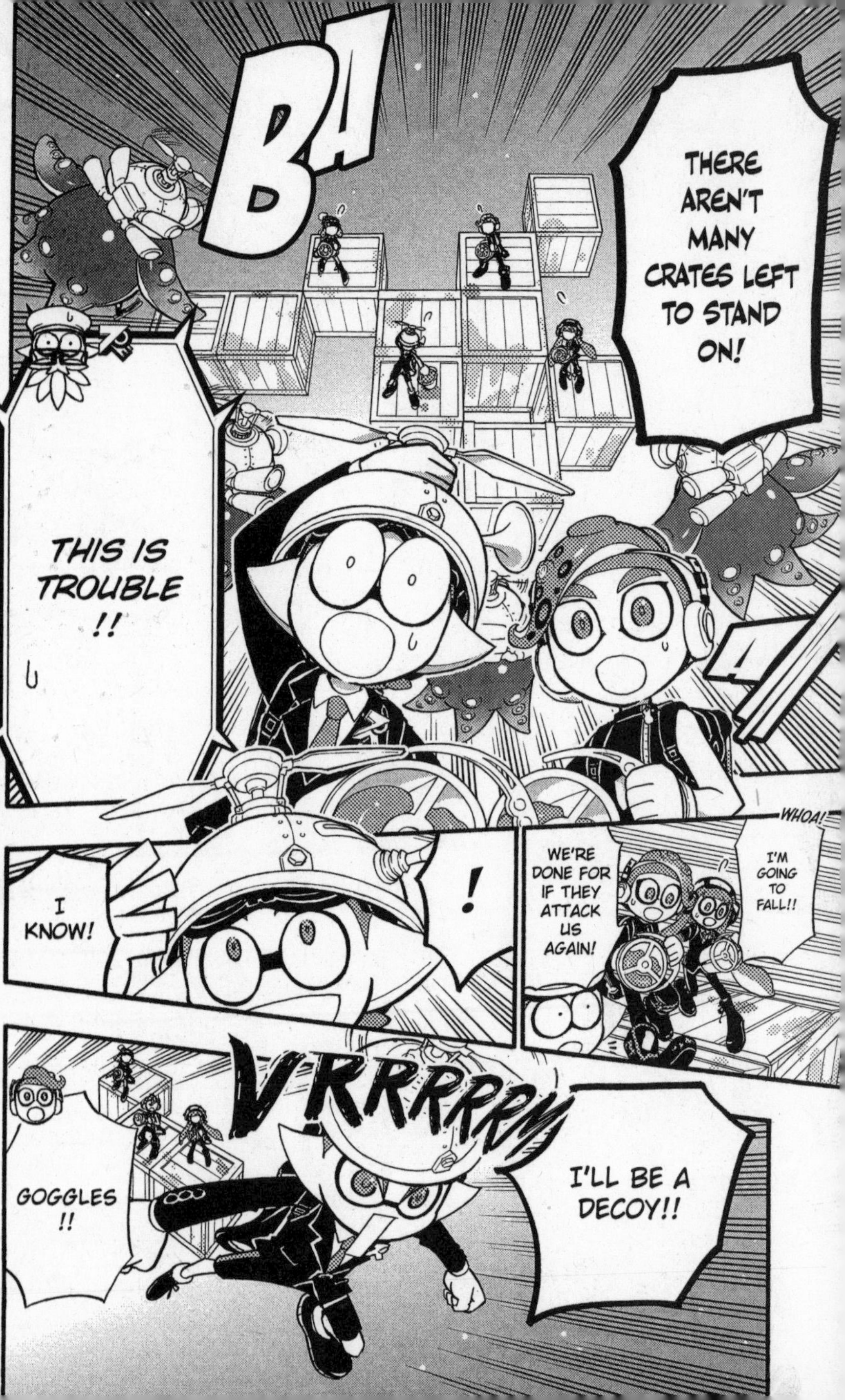
THERE AREN'T MANY CRATES LEFT TO STAND ON!
BA
THIS IS TROUBLE!!
WHOA!
I'M GOING TO FALL!!
WE'RE DONE FOR IF THEY ATTACK US AGAIN!
!
I KNOW!
VRRRRRM
I'LL BE A DECOY!!
GOGGLES!!

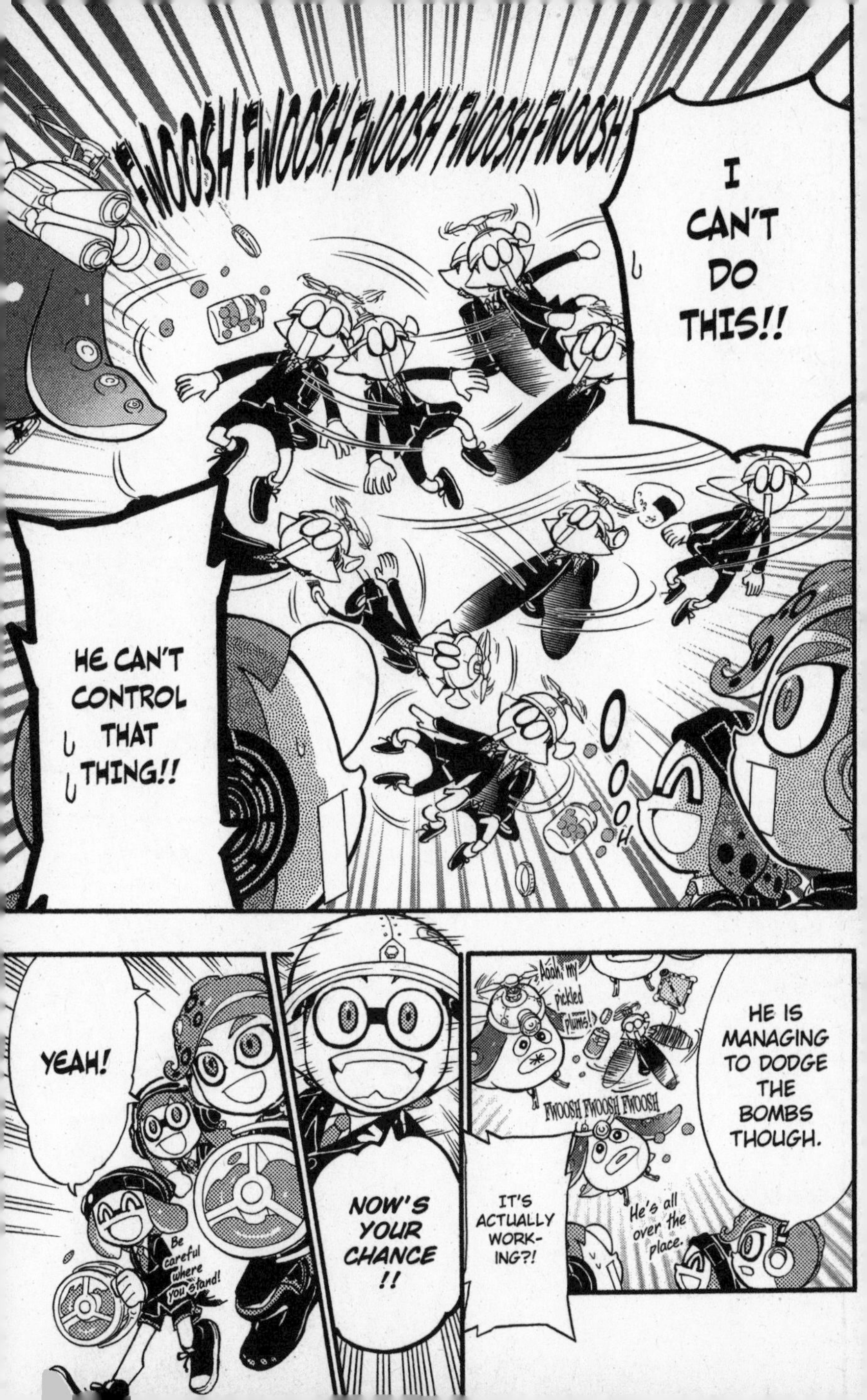
I CAN'T DO THIS!!
FWOOSH FWOOSH FWOOSH FWOOSH FWOOSH
OOOOH
HE CAN'T CONTROL THAT THING!!
HE IS MANAGING TO DODGE THE BOMBS THOUGH.
Aaah! my pickled plums!
FWOOSH FWOOSH FWOOSH
He's all over the place.
IT'S ACTUALLY WORK-ING?!
NOW'S YOUR CHANCE!!
YEAH!
Be careful where you stand!

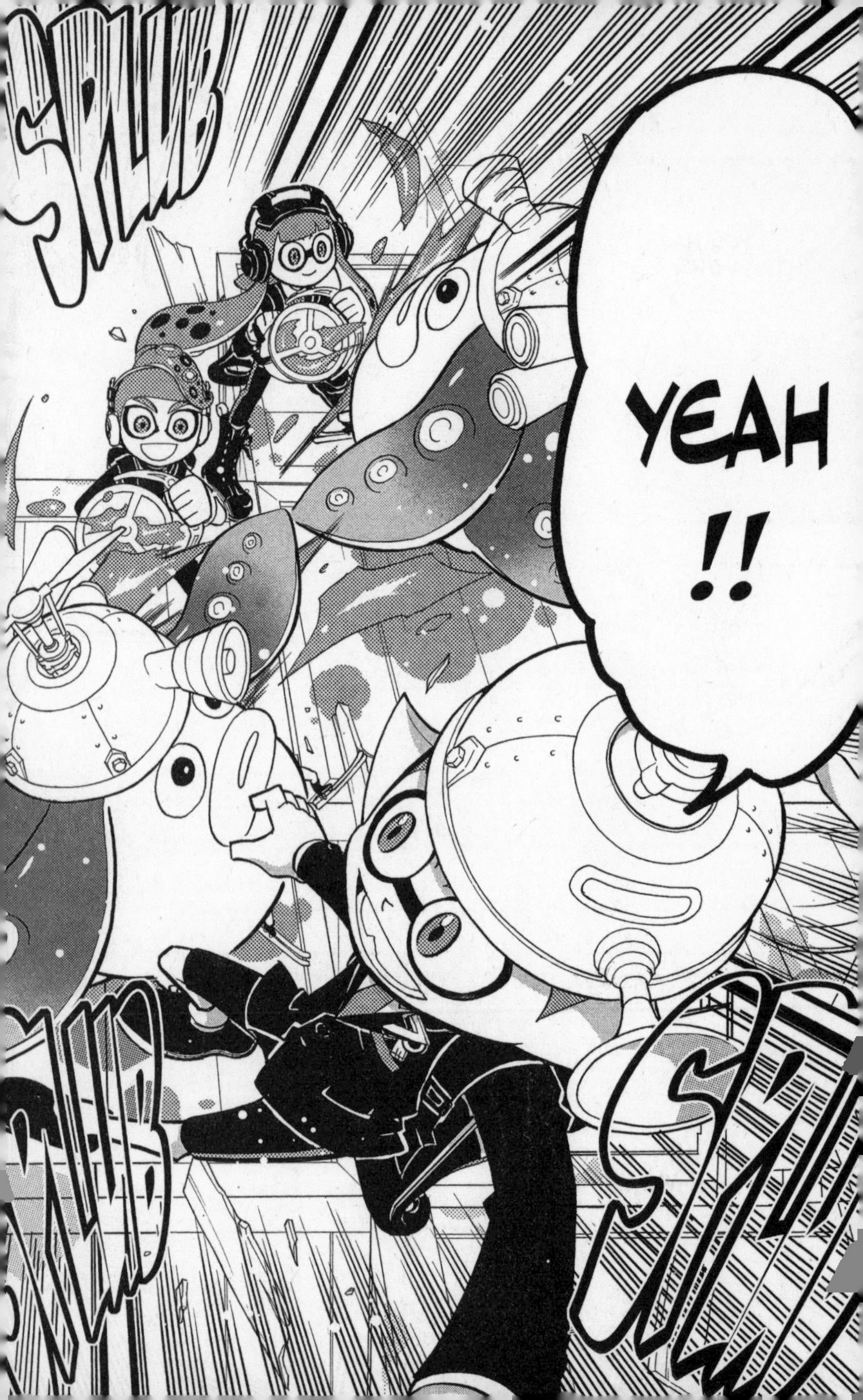
YEAH !!
SPLUB

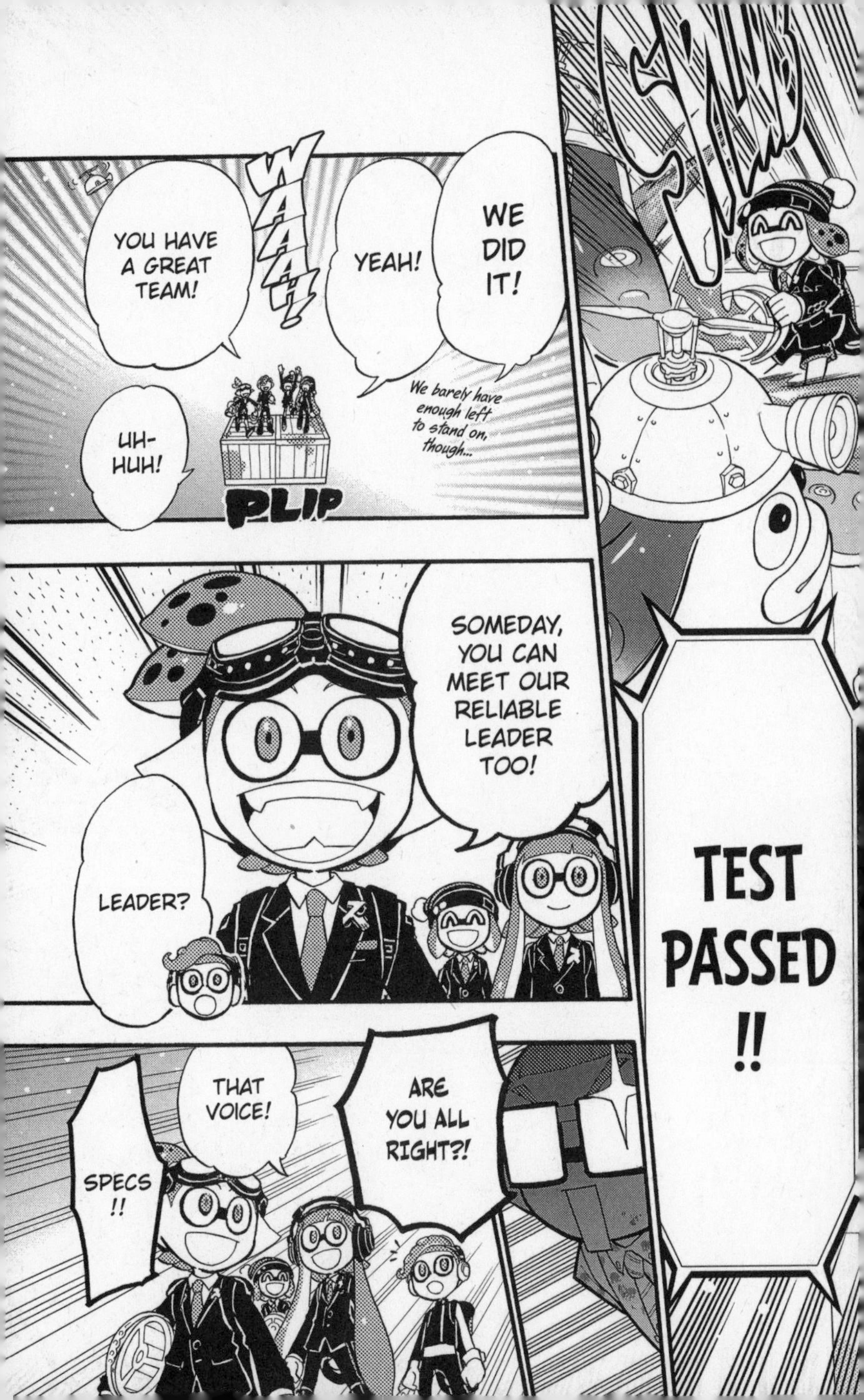
TEST PASSED !!
WE DID IT!
YEAH!
WAAAH!
YOU HAVE A GREAT TEAM!
We barely have enough left to stand on, though...
UH-HUH!
PLIP
SOMEDAY, YOU CAN MEET OUR RELIABLE LEADER TOO!
LEADER?
ARE YOU ALL RIGHT?!
THAT VOICE!
SPECS !!

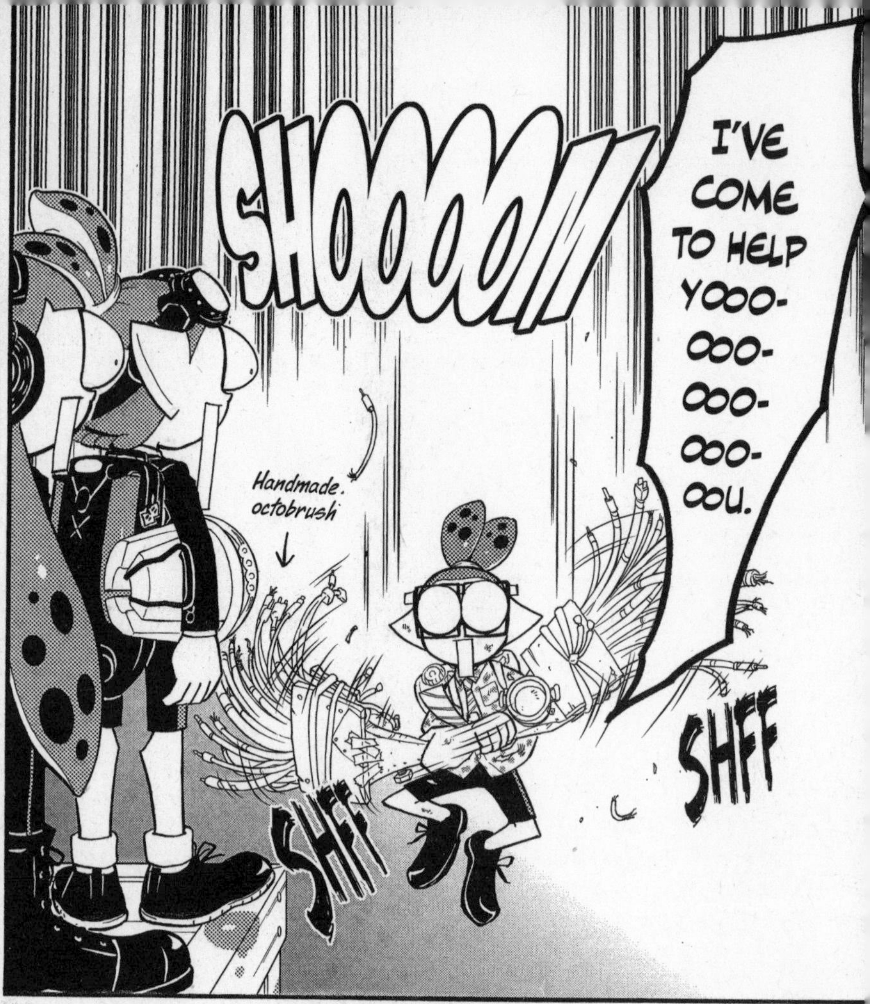
I'VE COME TO HELP YOOO-OOO-OOO-OOO-OOU.
SHOOOOOM
Handmade octobrush
SHFF
SHFF

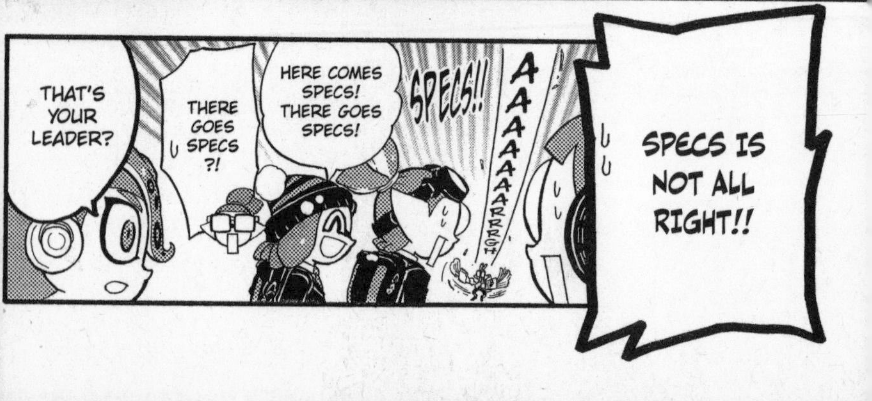
SPECS IS NOT ALL RIGHT!!
AAAAAAAAARRRGH
SPECS!!
HERE COMES SPECS! THERE GOES SPECS!
THERE GOES SPECS ?!
THAT'S YOUR LEADER?

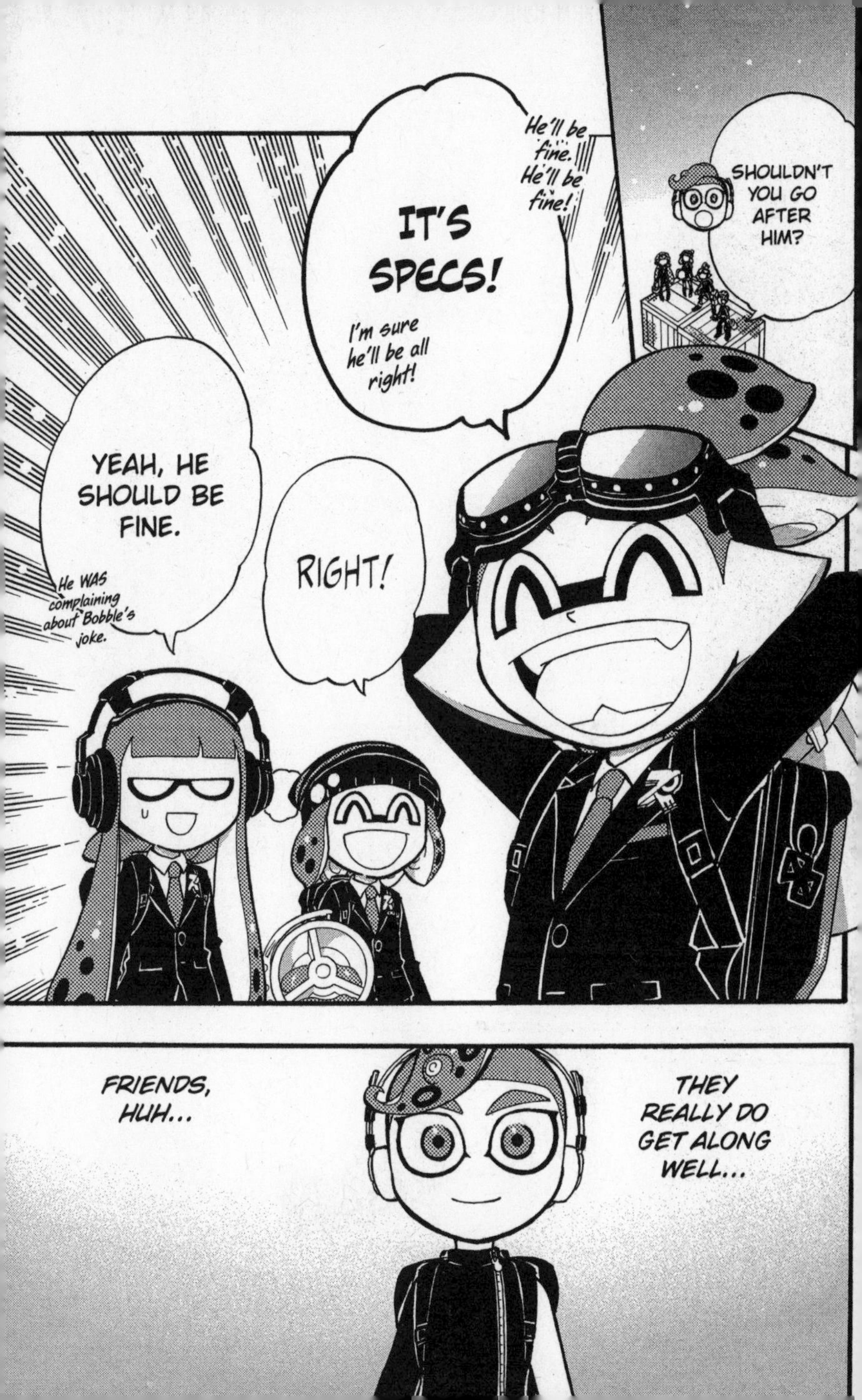
SHOULDN'T YOU GO AFTER HIM?
IT'S SPECS!
He'll be fine. He'll be fine!
I'm sure he'll be all right!
RIGHT!
YEAH, HE SHOULD BE FINE.
He WAS complaining about Bobble's joke.
THEY REALLY DO GET ALONG WELL...
FRIENDS, HUH...

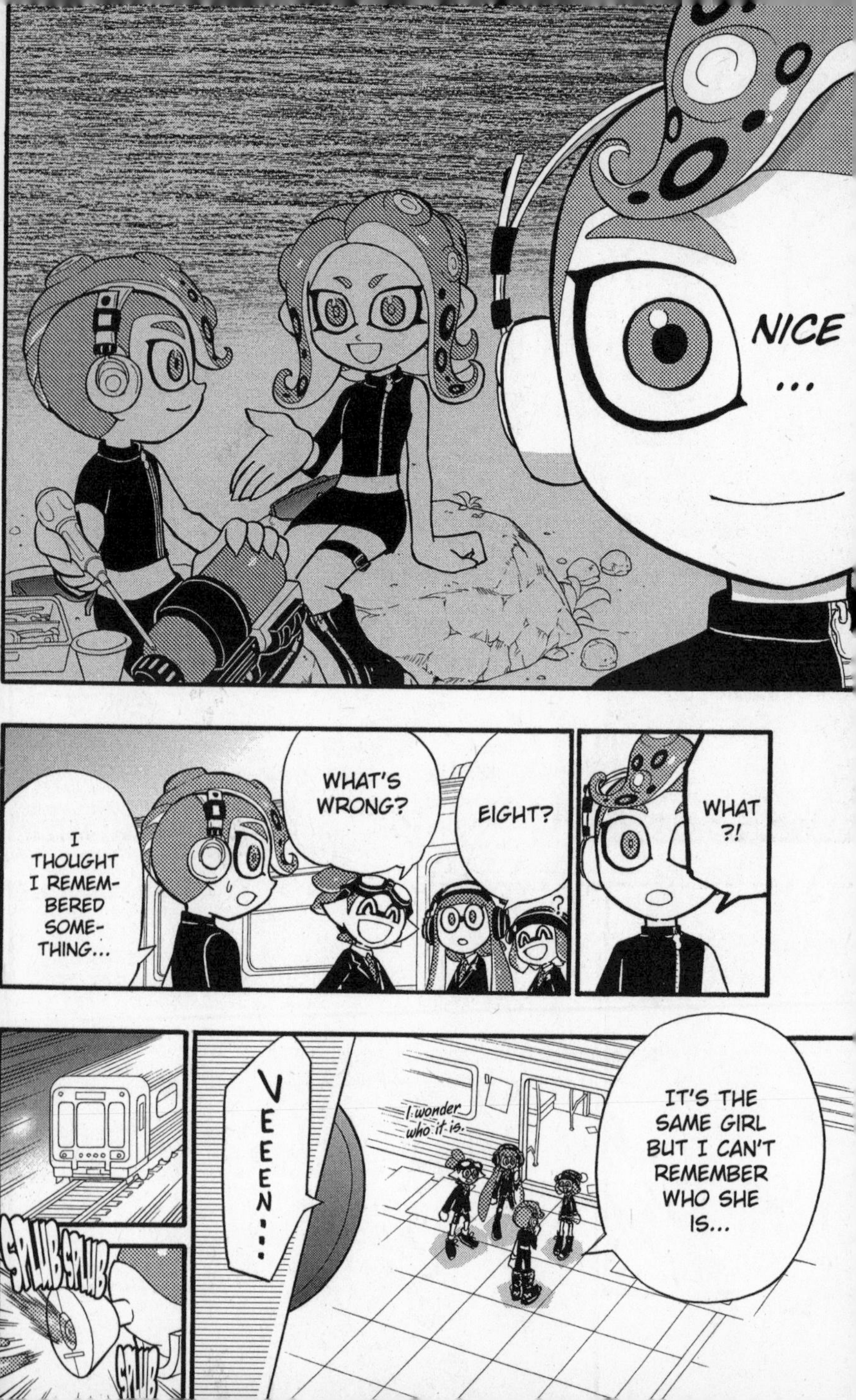
NICE ...
WHAT ?!
EIGHT?
WHAT'S WRONG?
I THOUGHT I REMEMBERED SOMETHING...
IT'S THE SAME GIRL BUT I CAN'T REMEMBER WHO SHE IS...
I wonder who it is.
VEEEEN...
SPLUB SPLUB
SPLUB

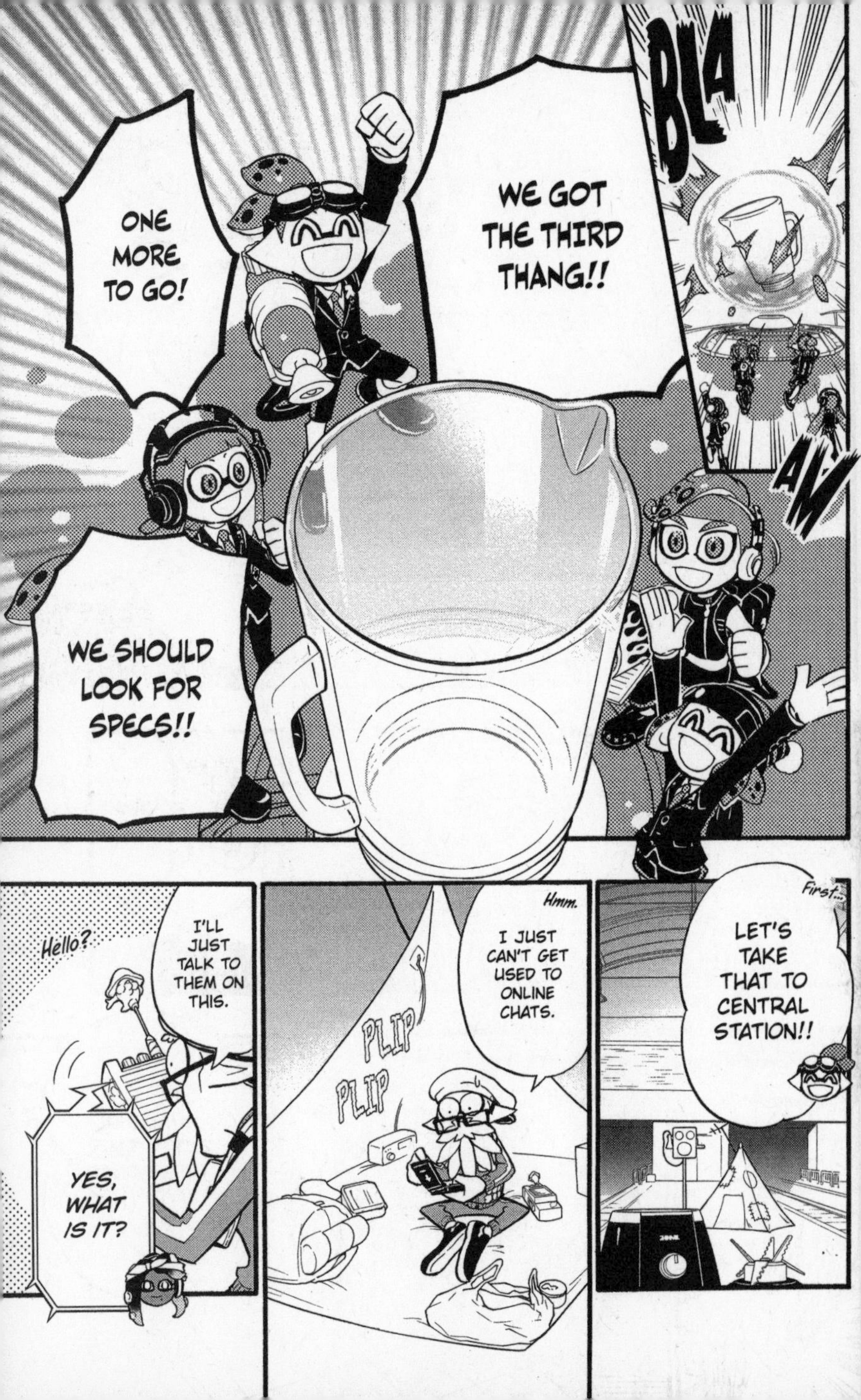
BLA
AM
WE GOT THE THIRD THANG!!
ONE MORE TO GO!
WE SHOULD LOOK FOR SPECS!!
First...
LET'S TAKE THAT TO CENTRAL STATION!!
Hmm.
I JUST CAN'T GET USED TO ONLINE CHATS.
PLIP
PLIP
I'LL JUST TALK TO THEM ON THIS.
Hello?
YES, WHAT IS IT?

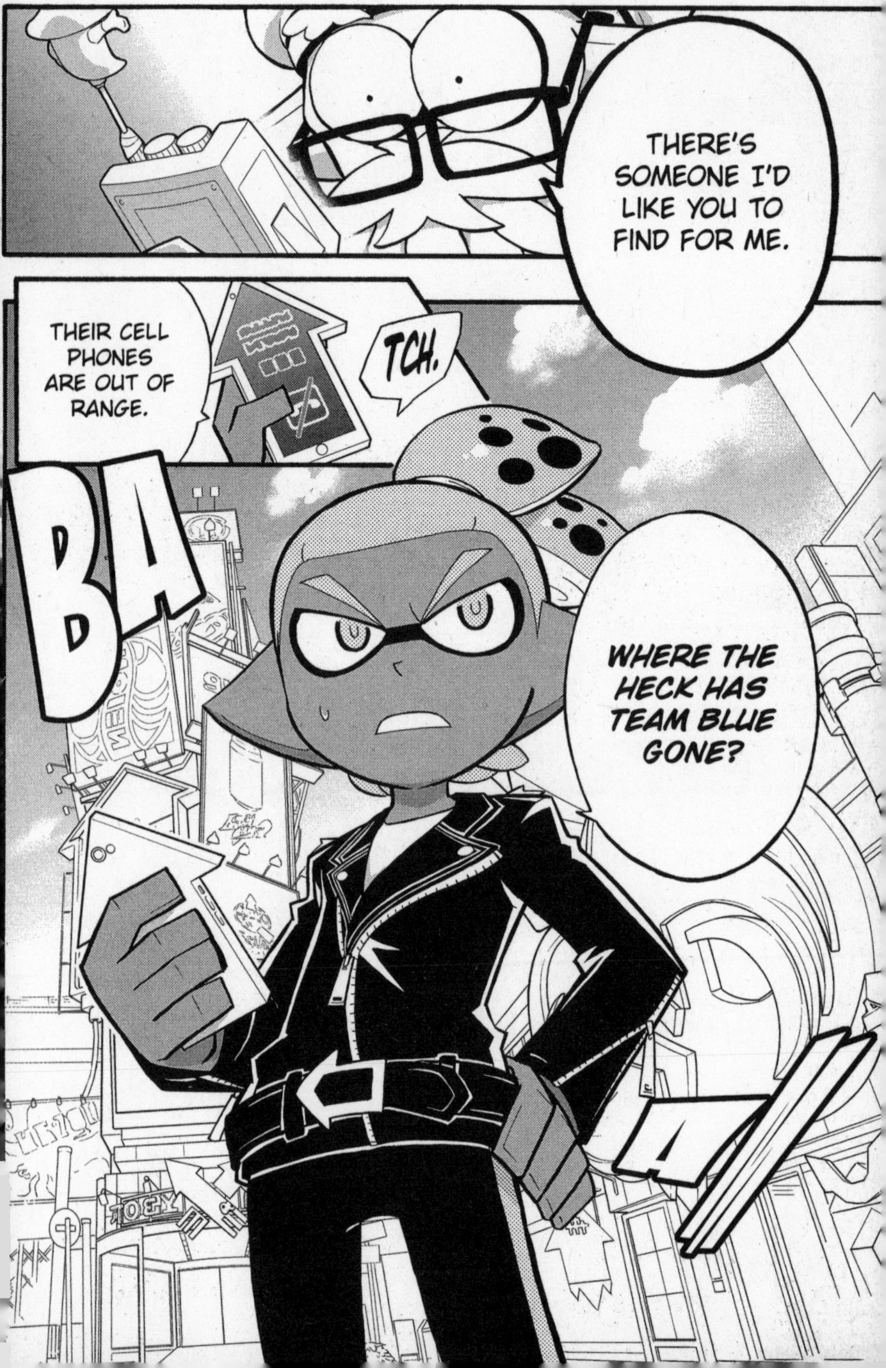
THERE'S SOMEONE I'D LIKE YOU TO FIND FOR ME.
TCH.
THEIR CELL PHONES ARE OUT OF RANGE.
WHERE THE HECK HAS TEAM BLUE GONE?
BA
A

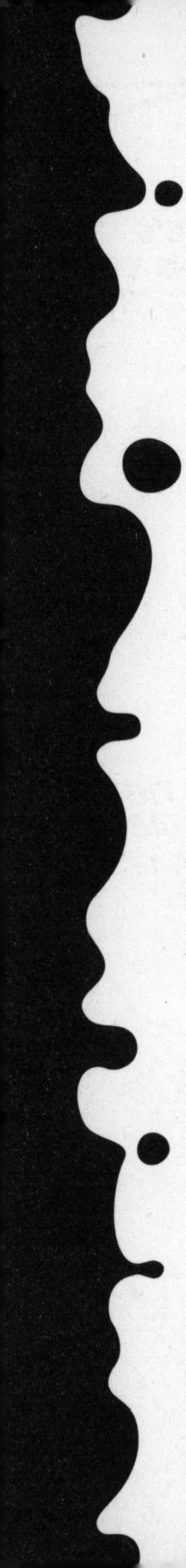

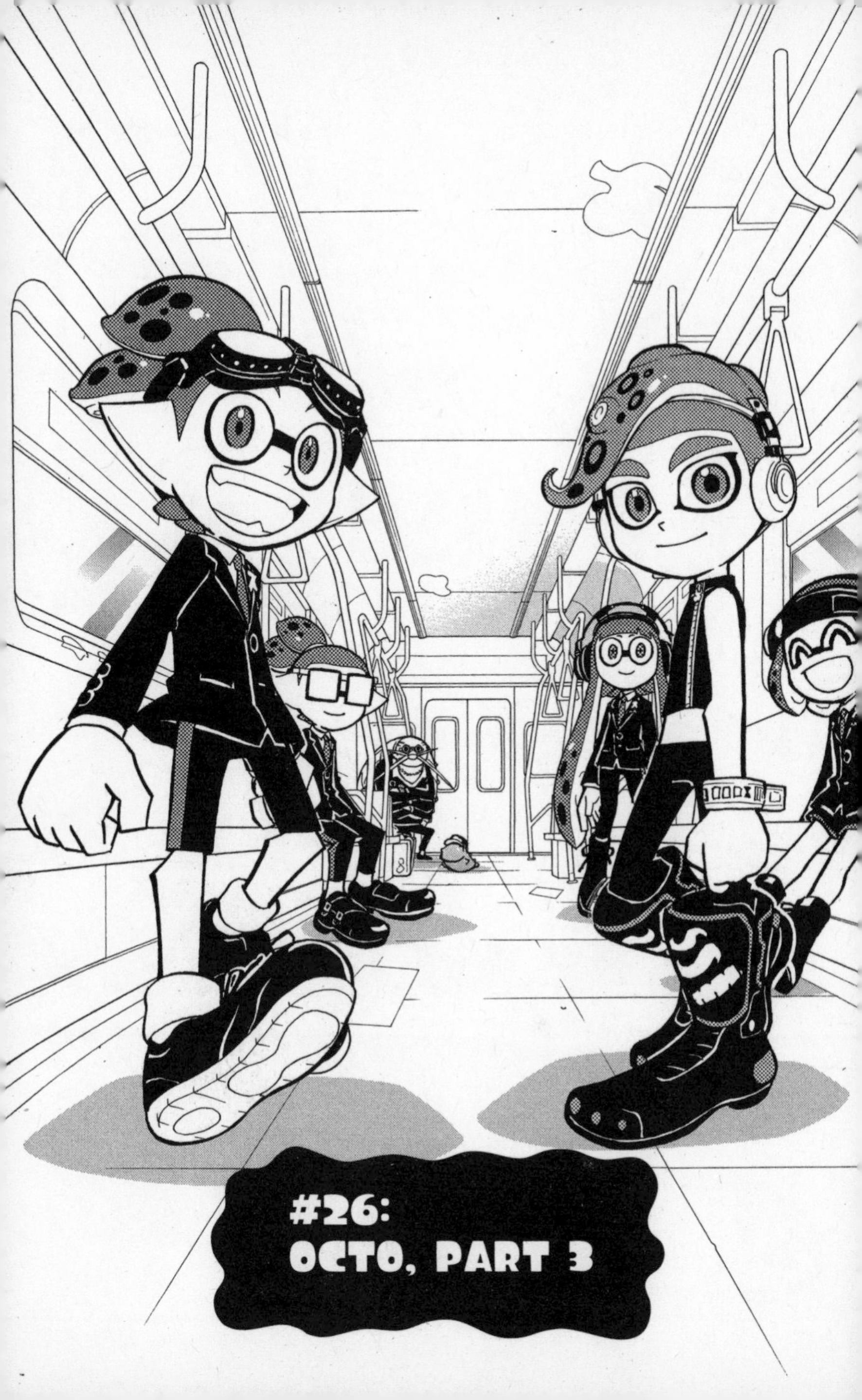
#26:
OCTO, PART 3

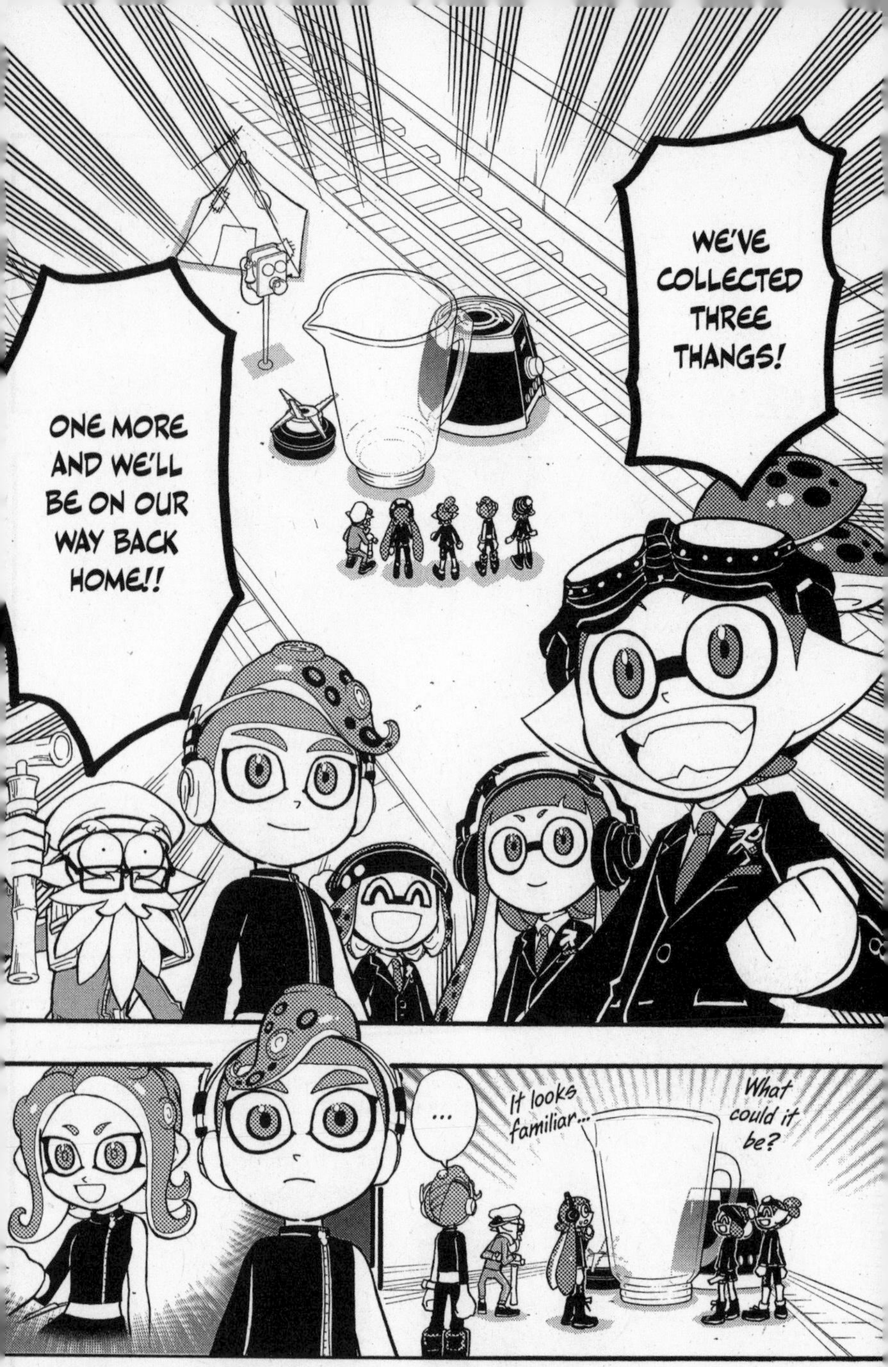
WE'VE COLLECTED THREE THANGS!
ONE MORE AND WE'LL BE ON OUR WAY BACK HOME!!
What could it be?
It looks familiar...
...

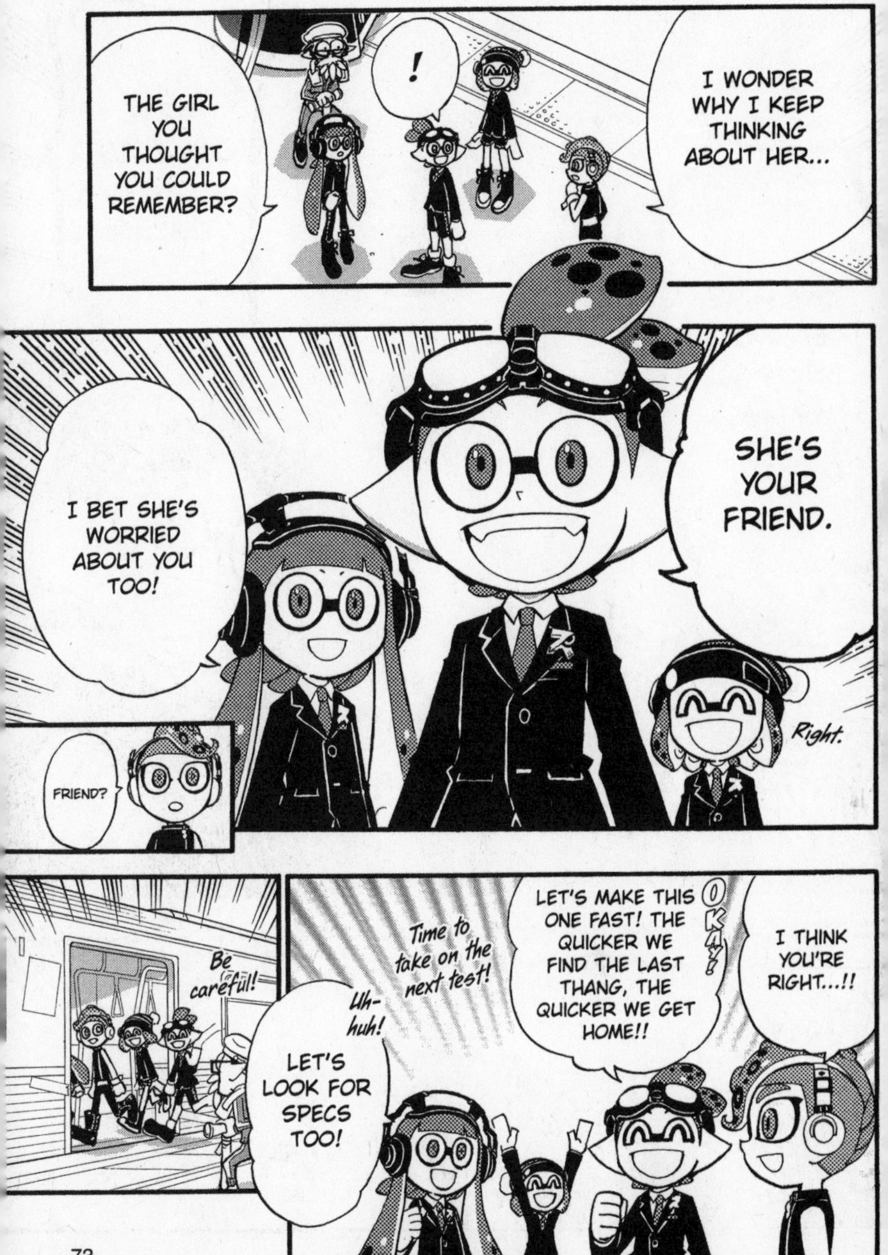

I WONDER WHY I KEEP THINKING ABOUT HER...
!
THE GIRL YOU THOUGHT YOU COULD REMEMBER?
SHE'S YOUR FRIEND.
Right.
I BET SHE'S WORRIED ABOUT YOU TOO!
FRIEND?
I THINK YOU'RE RIGHT...!!
OKAY!
LET'S MAKE THIS ONE FAST! THE QUICKER WE FIND THE LAST THANG, THE QUICKER WE GET HOME!!
Time to take on the next test!
Uh-huh!
LET'S LOOK FOR SPECS TOO!
Be careful!

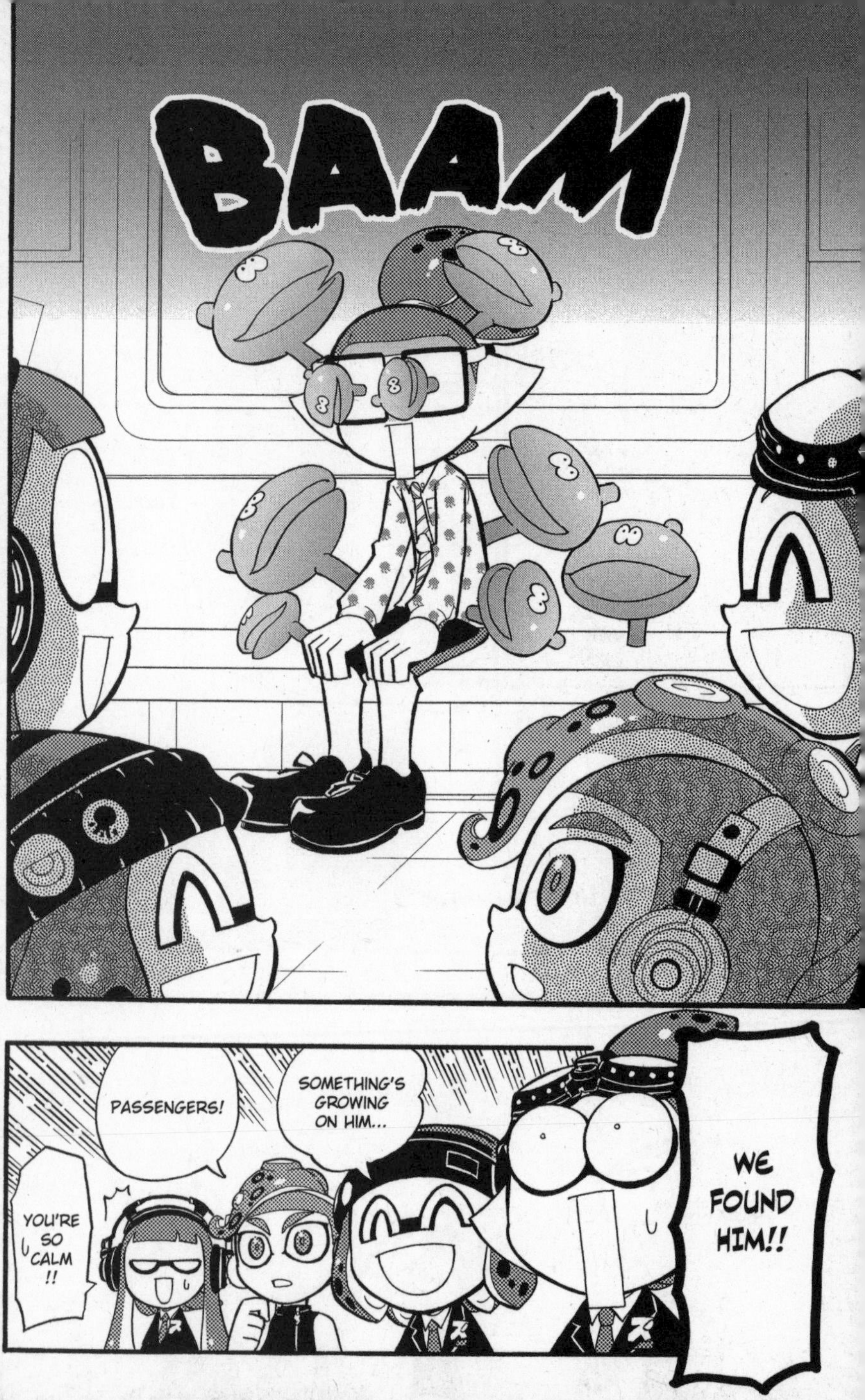
BAAM
WE FOUND HIM!!
SOMETHING'S GROWING ON HIM...
PASSENGERS!
YOU'RE SO CALM!!

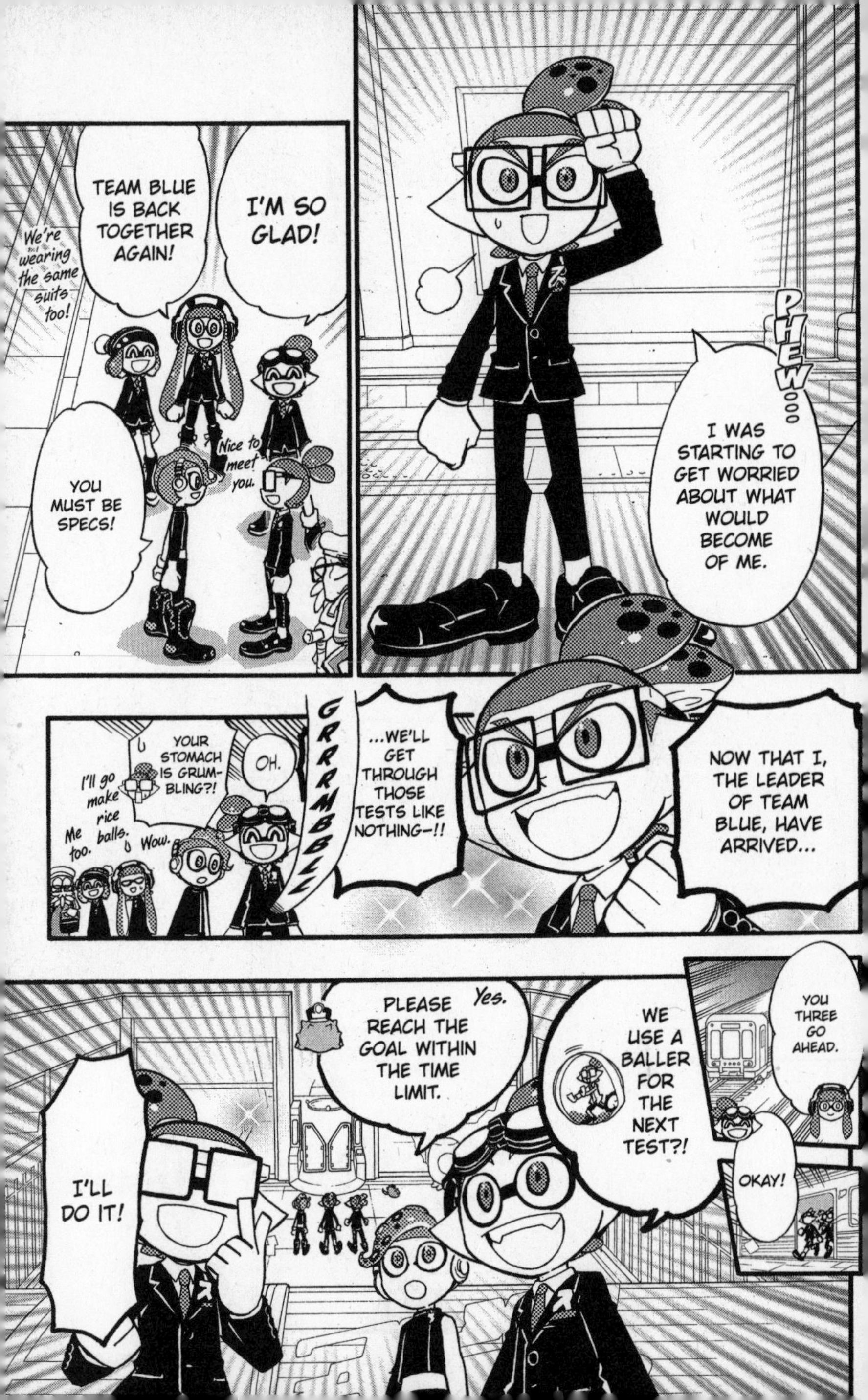
PHEWOOO
I WAS STARTING TO GET WORRIED ABOUT WHAT WOULD BECOME OF ME.
I'M SO GLAD!
TEAM BLUE IS BACK TOGETHER AGAIN!
We're wearing the same suits too!
Nice to meet you.
YOU MUST BE SPECS!
NOW THAT I, THE LEADER OF TEAM BLUE, HAVE ARRIVED...
...WE'LL GET THROUGH THOSE TESTS LIKE NOTHING--!!
GRRRMBBLLL
OH.
YOUR STOMACH IS GRUMBLING?!
I'll go make rice balls.
Wow.
Me too.
YOU THREE GO AHEAD.
OKAY!
WE USE A BALLER FOR THE NEXT TEST?!
Yes.
PLEASE REACH THE GOAL WITHIN THE TIME LIMIT.
I'LL DO IT!

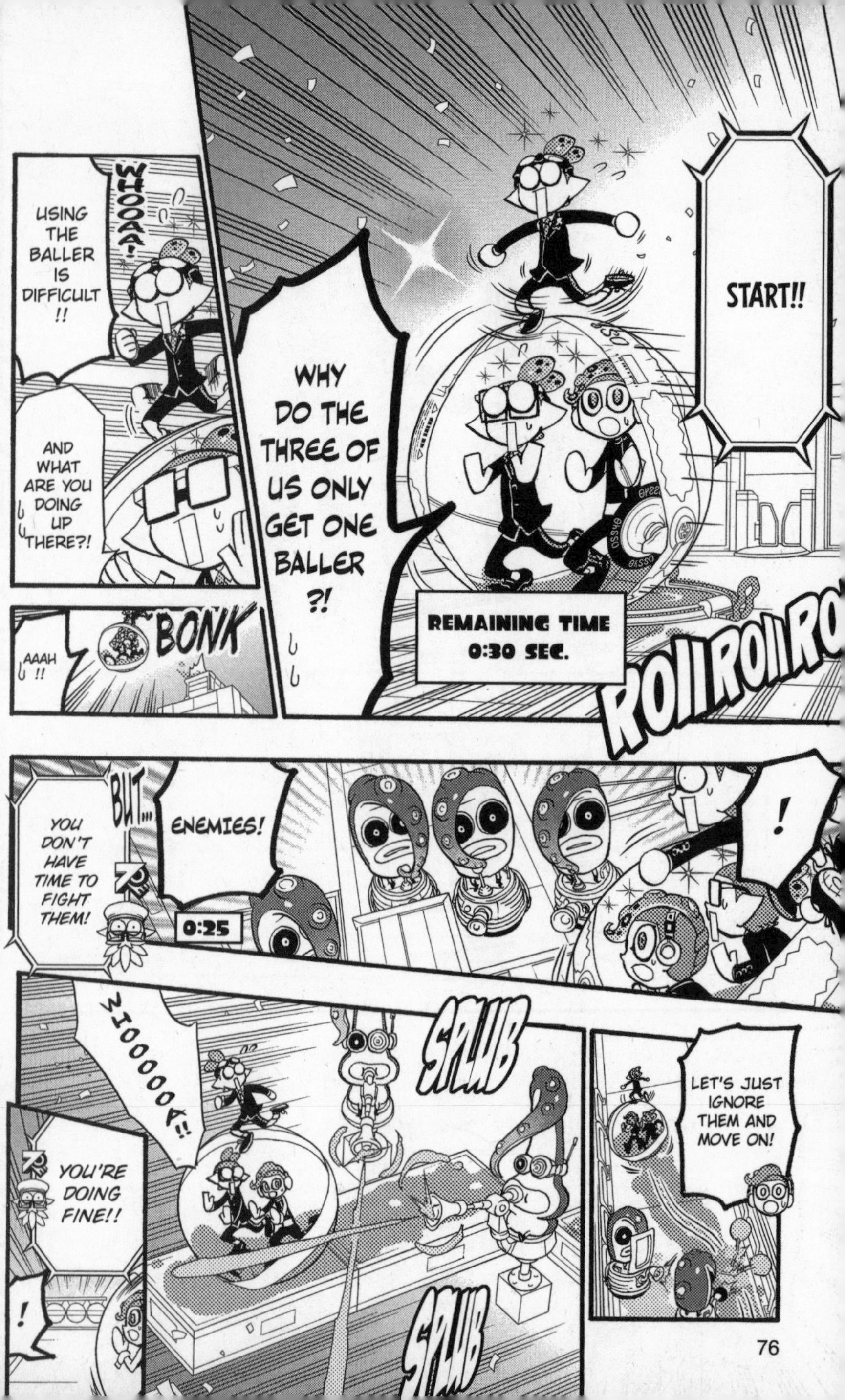
START!!
ROLL ROLL RO
WHY DO THE THREE OF US ONLY GET ONE BALLER?!
REMAINING TIME 0:30 SEC.
WHOOAAA!
USING THE BALLER IS DIFFICULT!!
AND WHAT ARE YOU DOING UP THERE?!
BONK
AAAH!!
!
ENEMIES!
0:25
BUT...
YOU DON'T HAVE TIME TO FIGHT THEM!
LET'S JUST IGNORE THEM AND MOVE ON!
SPLUB
WHOOOOOA!!
YOU'RE DOING FINE!!
!
SPLUB

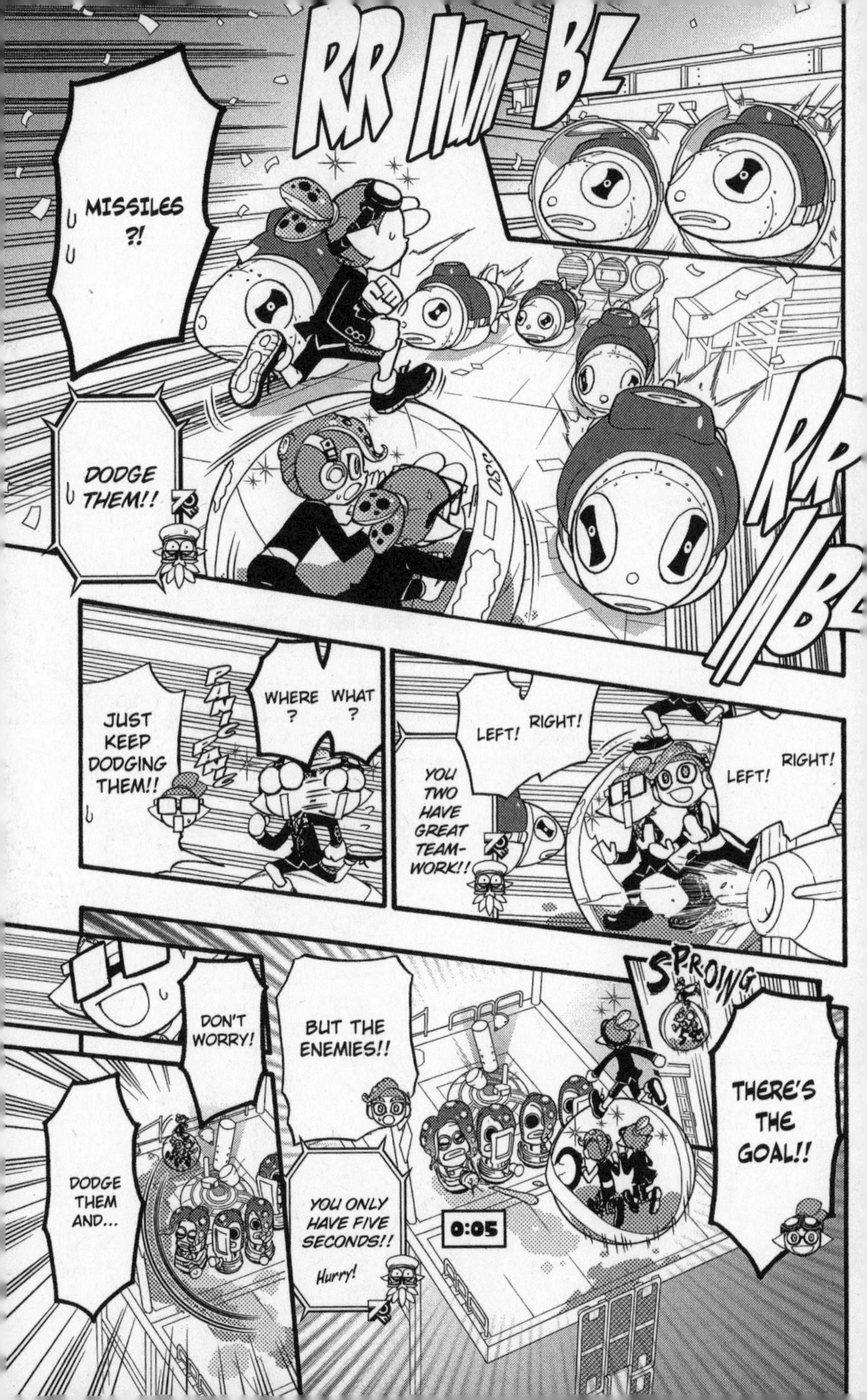
RRMMBL
MISSILES ?!
DODGE THEM!!
LEFT! RIGHT!
LEFT! RIGHT!
YOU TWO HAVE GREAT TEAMWORK!!
WHERE? WHAT?
JUST KEEP DODGING THEM!!
S-P-R-O-ING
THERE'S THE GOAL!!
0:05
BUT THE ENEMIES!!
YOU ONLY HAVE FIVE SECONDS!!
Hurry!
DON'T WORRY!
DODGE THEM AND...

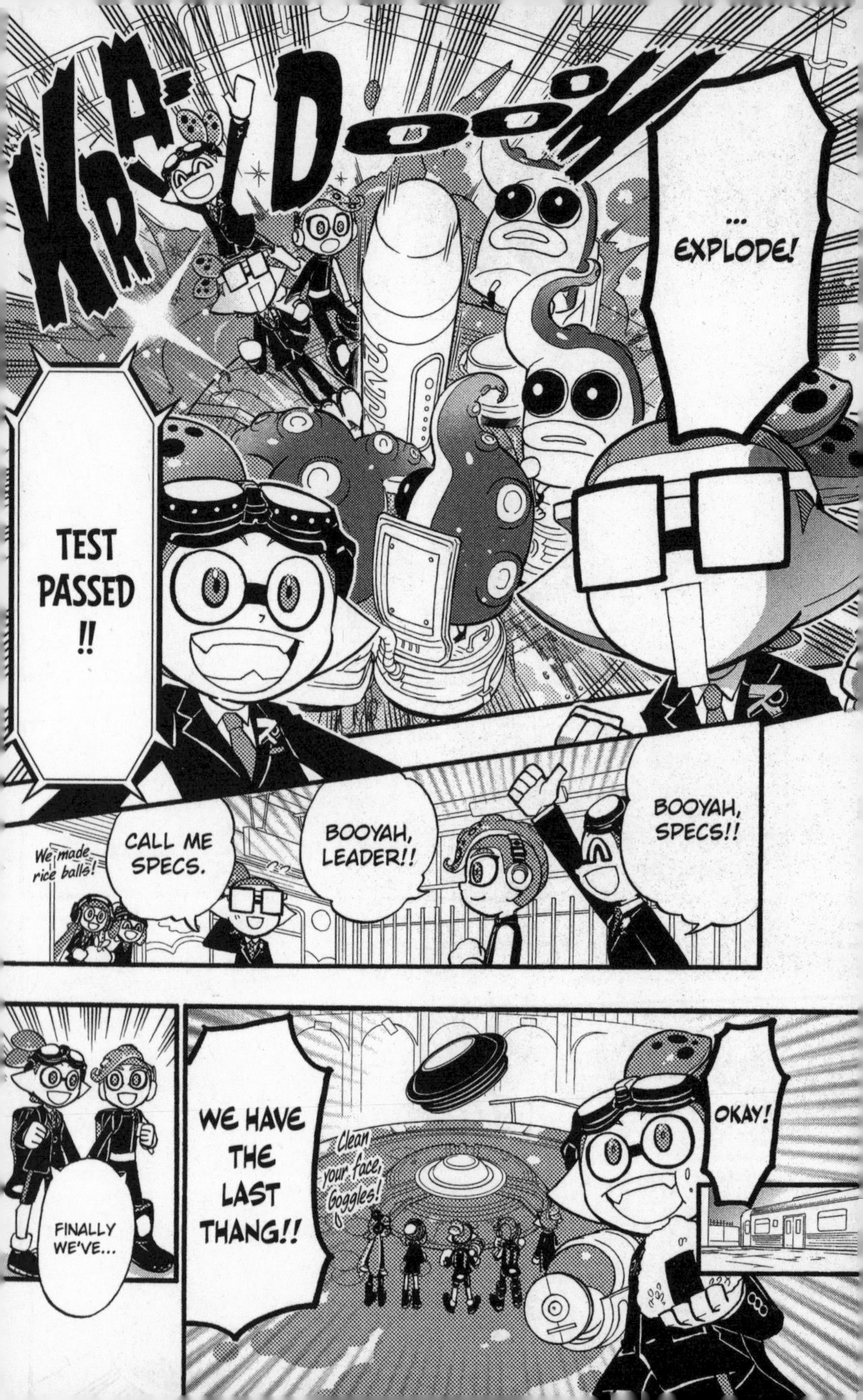
KRA-DOOOOM
...EXPLODE!
TEST PASSED!!
BOOYAH, SPECS!!
BOOYAH, LEADER!!
CALL ME SPECS.
We made rice balls!
OKAY!
WE HAVE THE LAST THANG!!
Clean your face, Goggles!
FINALLY WE'VE...

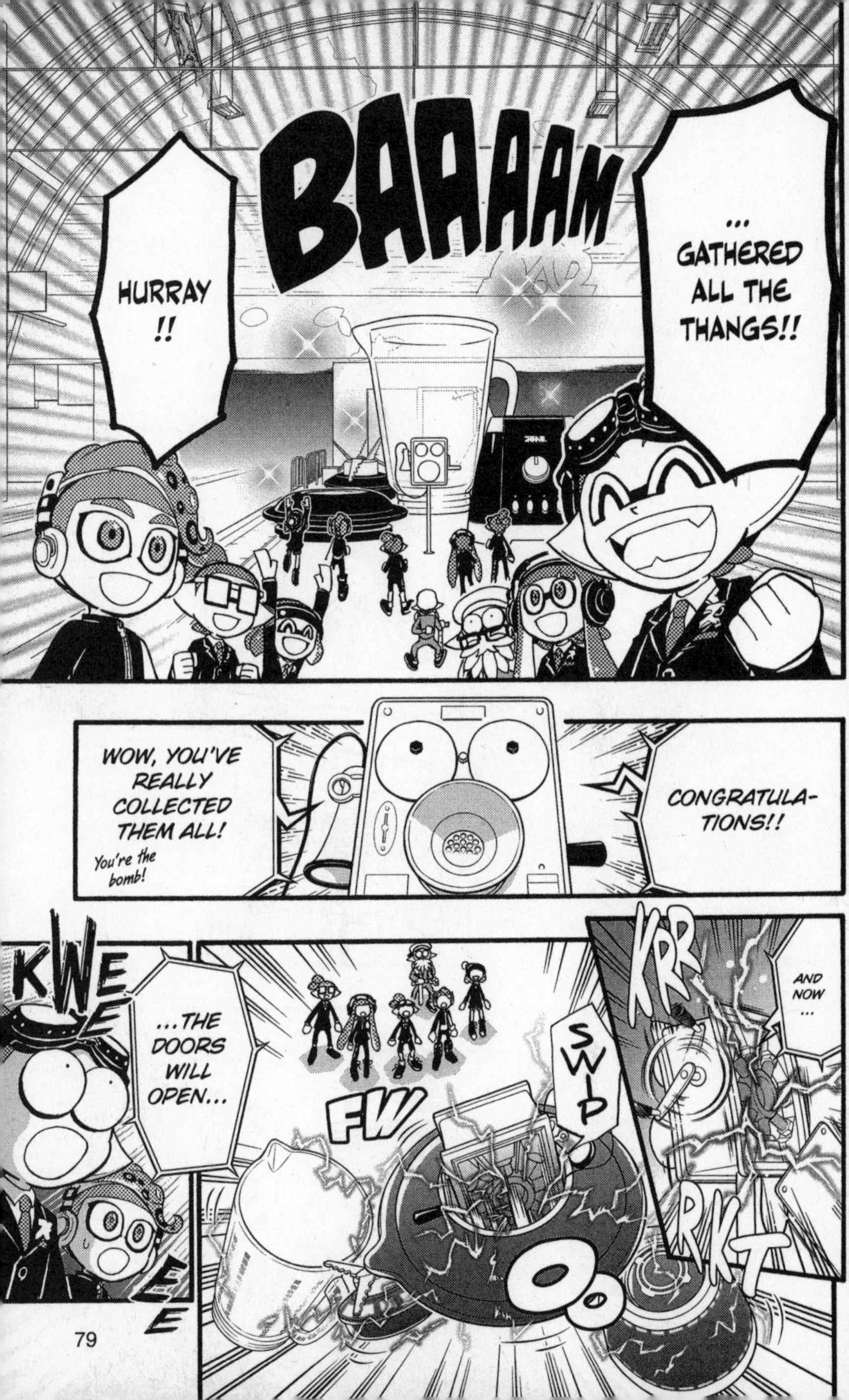
...GATHERED ALL THE THANGS!!
BAAAAM
HURRAY!!
CONGRATULA-TIONS!!
WOW, YOU'VE REALLY COLLECTED THEM ALL!
You're the bomb!
KRR
AND NOW...
SWIP
RKT
FW
...THE DOORS WILL OPEN...
KWEEEE

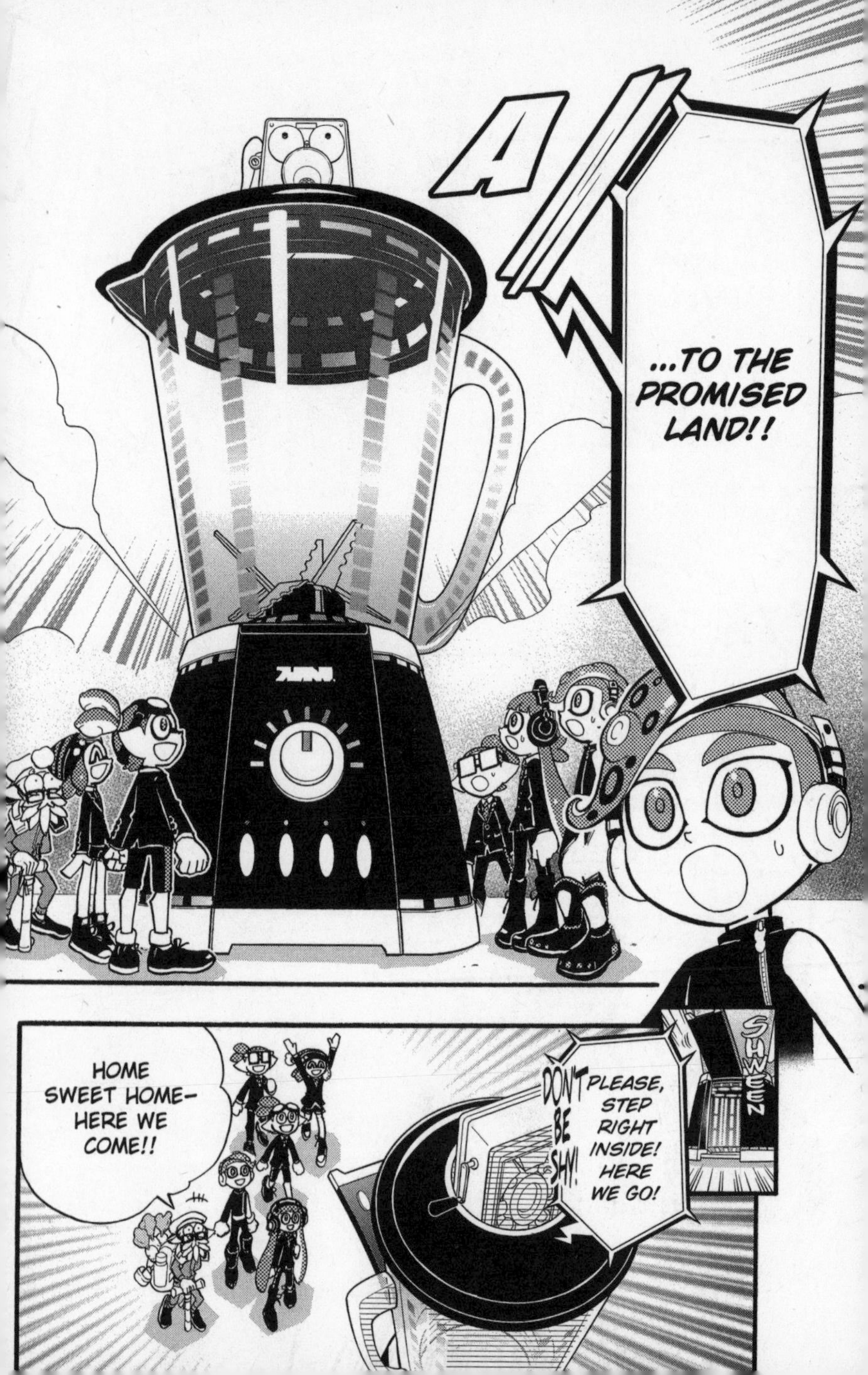
A
...TO THE PROMISED LAND!!
PLEASE, STEP RIGHT INSIDE! HERE WE GO!
DON'T BE SHY!
HOME SWEET HOME—HERE WE COME!!

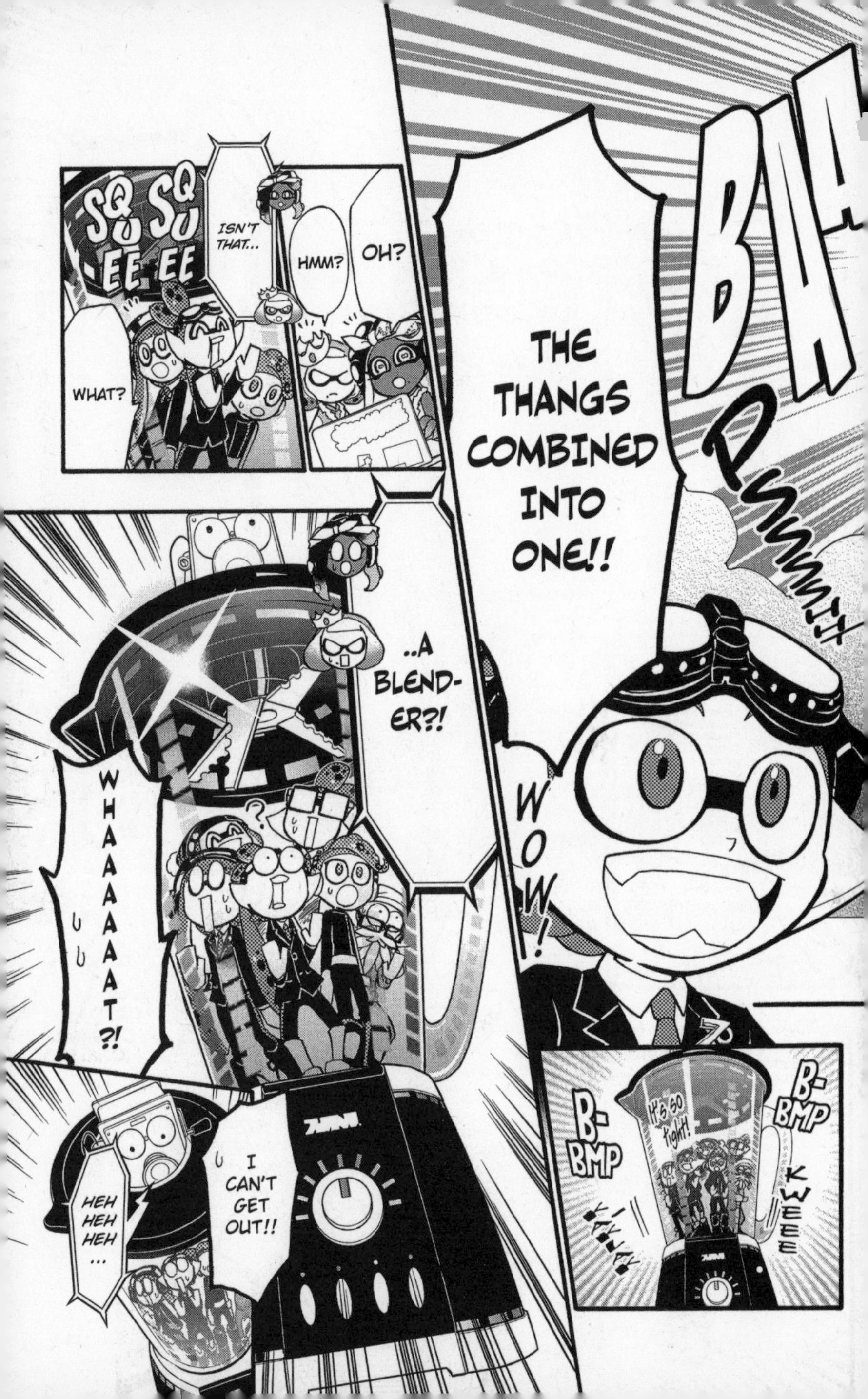
BA
D!!
THE THANGS COMBINED INTO ONE!!
WOW!
OH?
HMM?
ISN'T THAT...
SQUEE SQUEE
WHAT?
..A BLENDER?!
WHAAAAAAAT?!
B-BMP
KWEEE
It's so tight!
B-BMP
I CAN'T GET OUT!!
HEH HEH HEH...

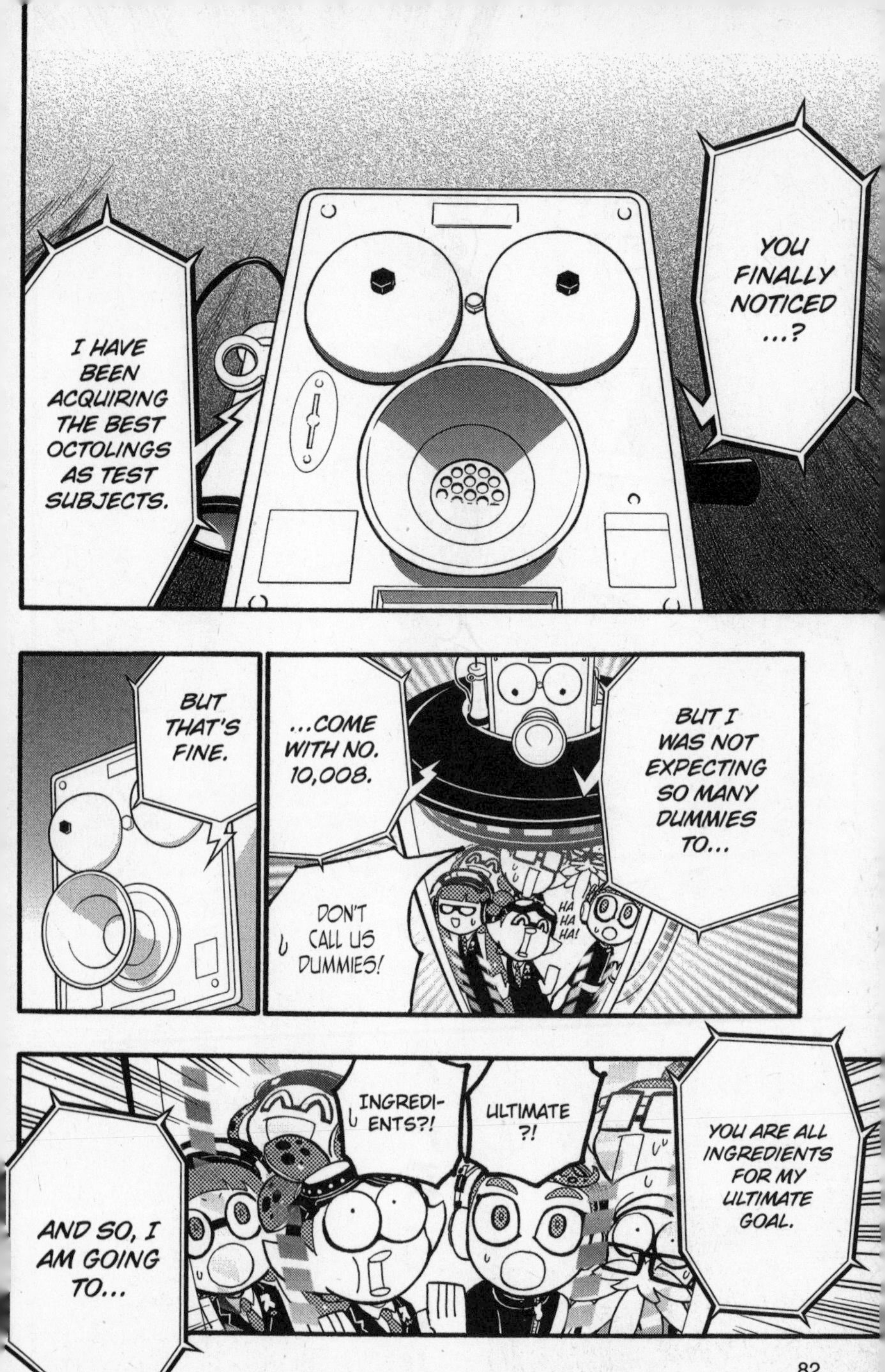

YOU FINALLY NOTICED ...?
I HAVE BEEN ACQUIRING THE BEST OCTOLINGS AS TEST SUBJECTS.
BUT I WAS NOT EXPECTING SO MANY DUMMIES TO...
...COME WITH NO. 10,008.
HA HA HA!
DON'T CALL US DUMMIES!
BUT THAT'S FINE.
YOU ARE ALL INGREDIENTS FOR MY ULTIMATE GOAL.
ULTIMATE ?!
INGREDI-ENTS?!
AND SO, I AM GOING TO...

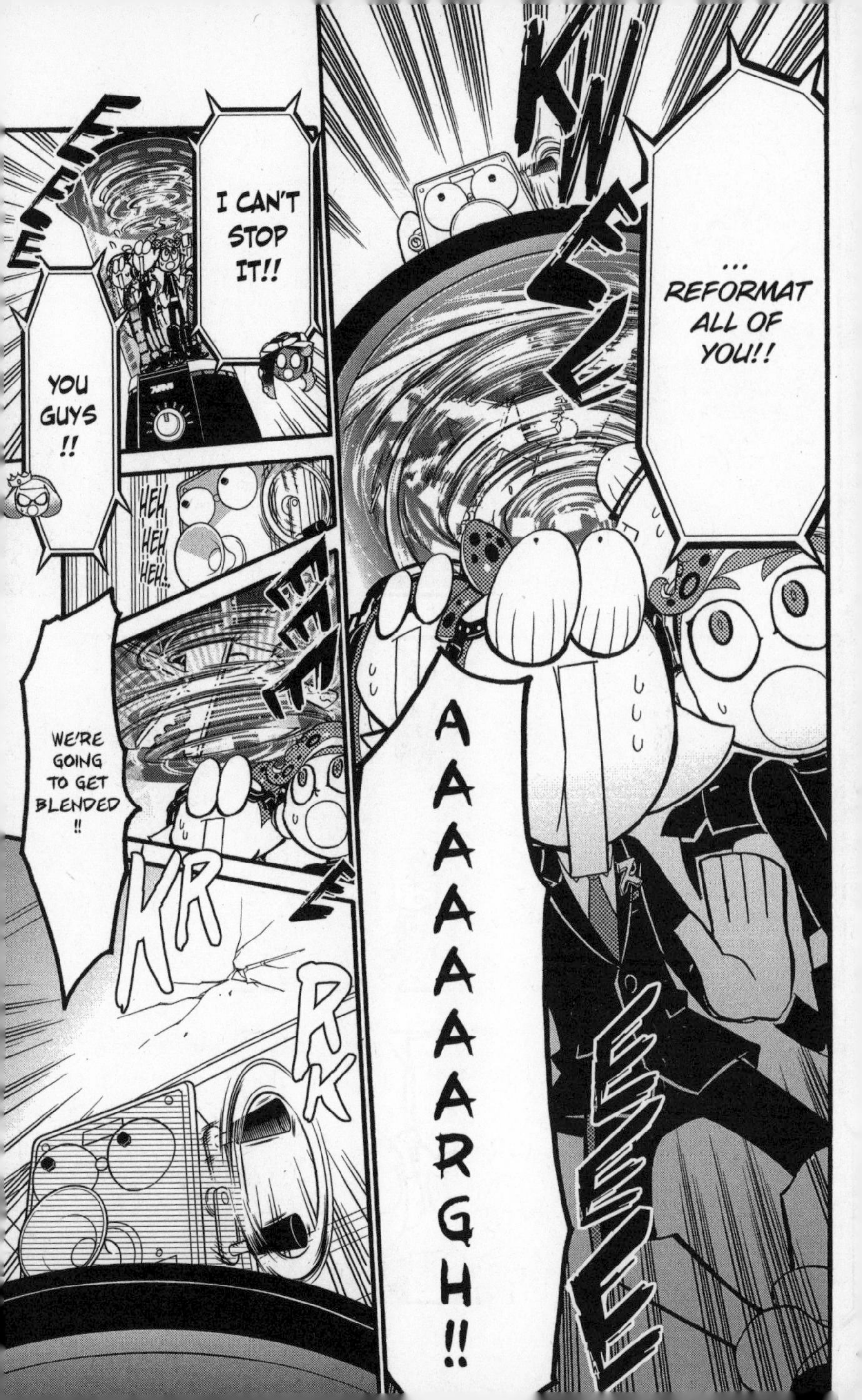
...REFORMAT ALL OF YOU!!
AAAAAAAARGH!!
I CAN'T STOP IT!!
YOU GUYS!!
HEH HEH HEH!!
WE'RE GOING TO GET BLENDED!!

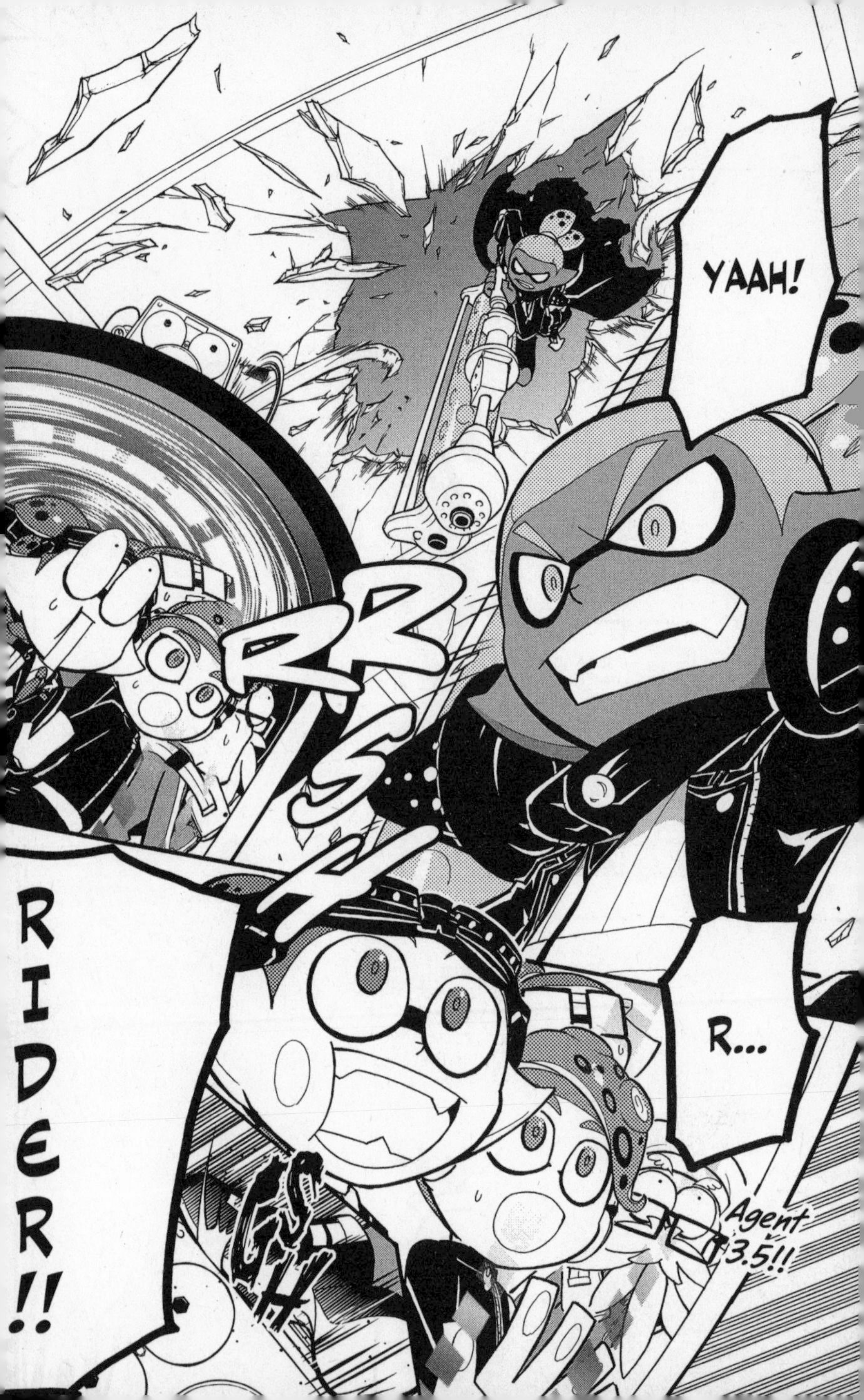
YAAH!
R...
RIDER!!
Agent 3.5!!

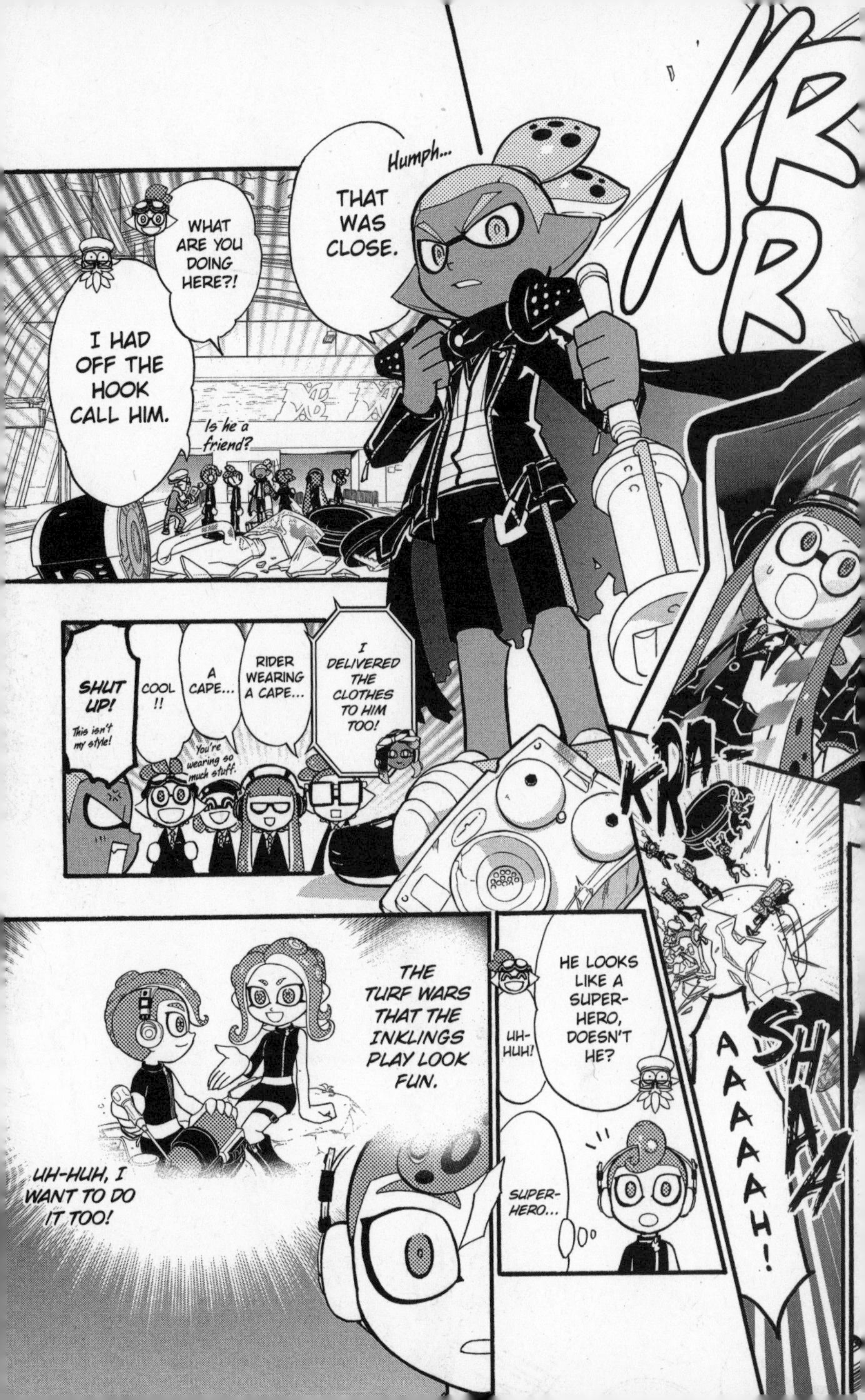
Humph...
THAT WAS CLOSE.
WHAT ARE YOU DOING HERE?!
I HAD OFF THE HOOK CALL HIM.
Is he a friend?
I DELIVERED THE CLOTHES TO HIM TOO!
RIDER WEARING A CAPE...
A CAPE...
COOL !!
You're wearing so much stuff.
SHUT UP!
This isn't my style!
KRA-
AAAAAH!
HE LOOKS LIKE A SUPER-HERO, DOESN'T HE?
UH-HUH!
SUPER-HERO...
THE TURF WARS THAT THE INKLINGS PLAY LOOK FUN.
UH-HUH, I WANT TO DO IT TOO!

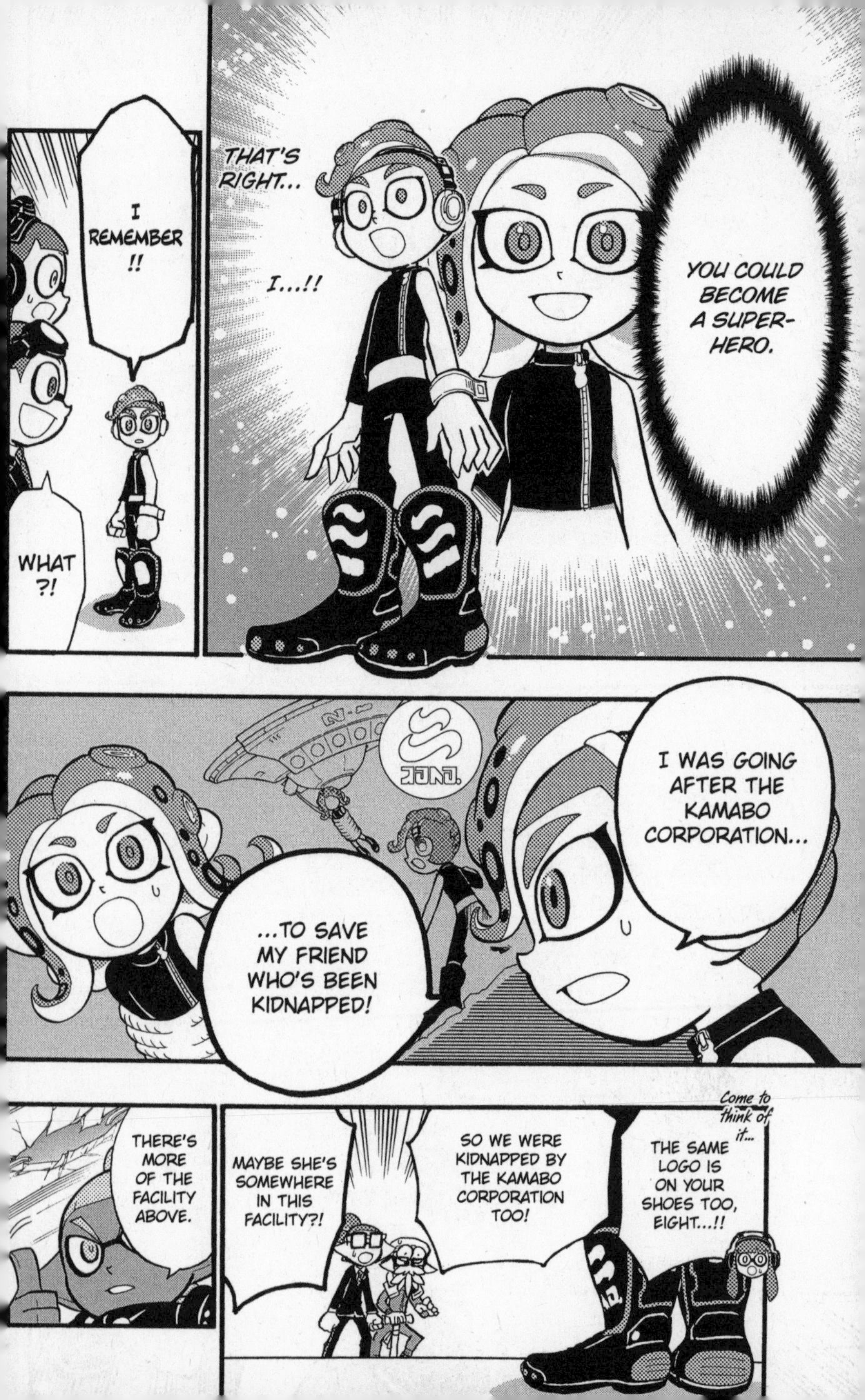
YOU COULD BECOME A SUPER-HERO.
THAT'S RIGHT...
I...!!
I REMEMBER !!
WHAT ?!
I WAS GOING AFTER THE KAMABO CORPORATION...
...TO SAVE MY FRIEND WHO'S BEEN KIDNAPPED!
Come to think of it...
THE SAME LOGO IS ON YOUR SHOES TOO, EIGHT...!!
SO WE WERE KIDNAPPED BY THE KAMABO CORPORATION TOO!
MAYBE SHE'S SOMEWHERE IN THIS FACILITY?!
THERE'S MORE OF THE FACILITY ABOVE.

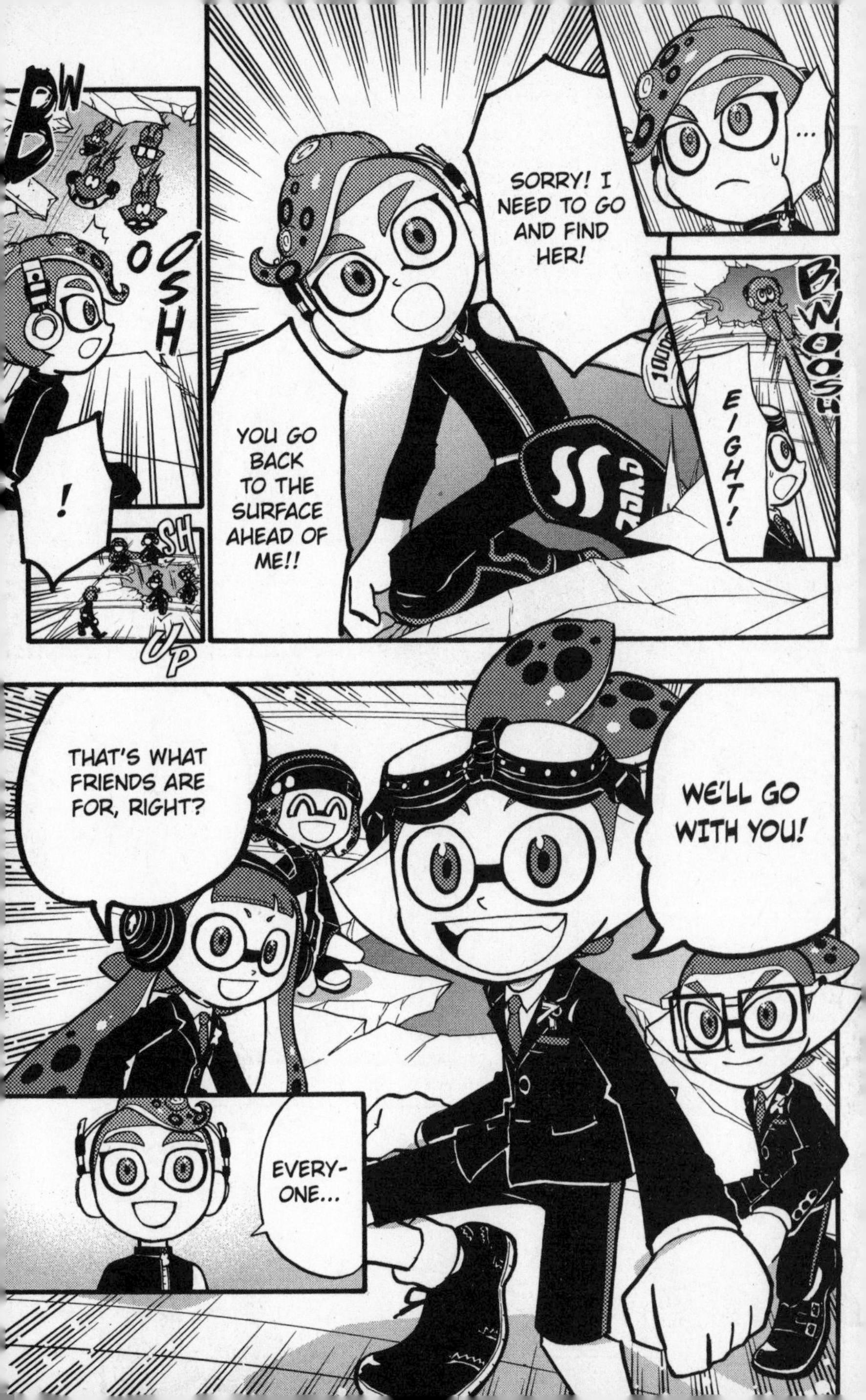
...
BWOOSH
EIGHT!
SORRY! I NEED TO GO AND FIND HER!
YOU GO BACK TO THE SURFACE AHEAD OF ME!!
BWOOSH
!
SHUP
WE'LL GO WITH YOU!
THAT'S WHAT FRIENDS ARE FOR, RIGHT?
EVERY-ONE...

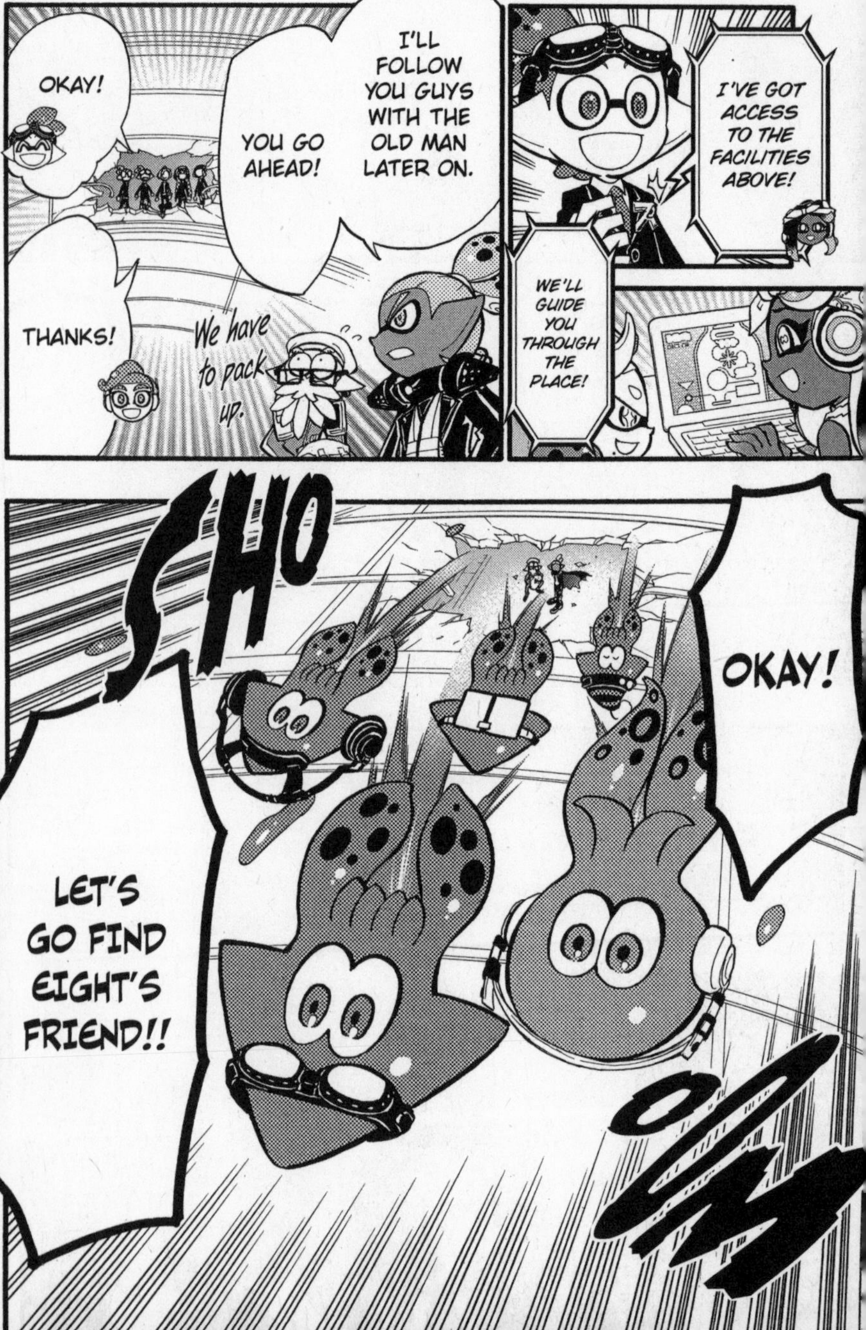

I'VE GOT ACCESS TO THE FACILITIES ABOVE!
WE'LL GUIDE YOU THROUGH THE PLACE!
I'LL FOLLOW YOU GUYS WITH THE OLD MAN LATER ON.
YOU GO AHEAD!
We have to pack up.
OKAY!
THANKS!
OKAY!
SHO
LET'S GO FIND EIGHT'S FRIEND!!

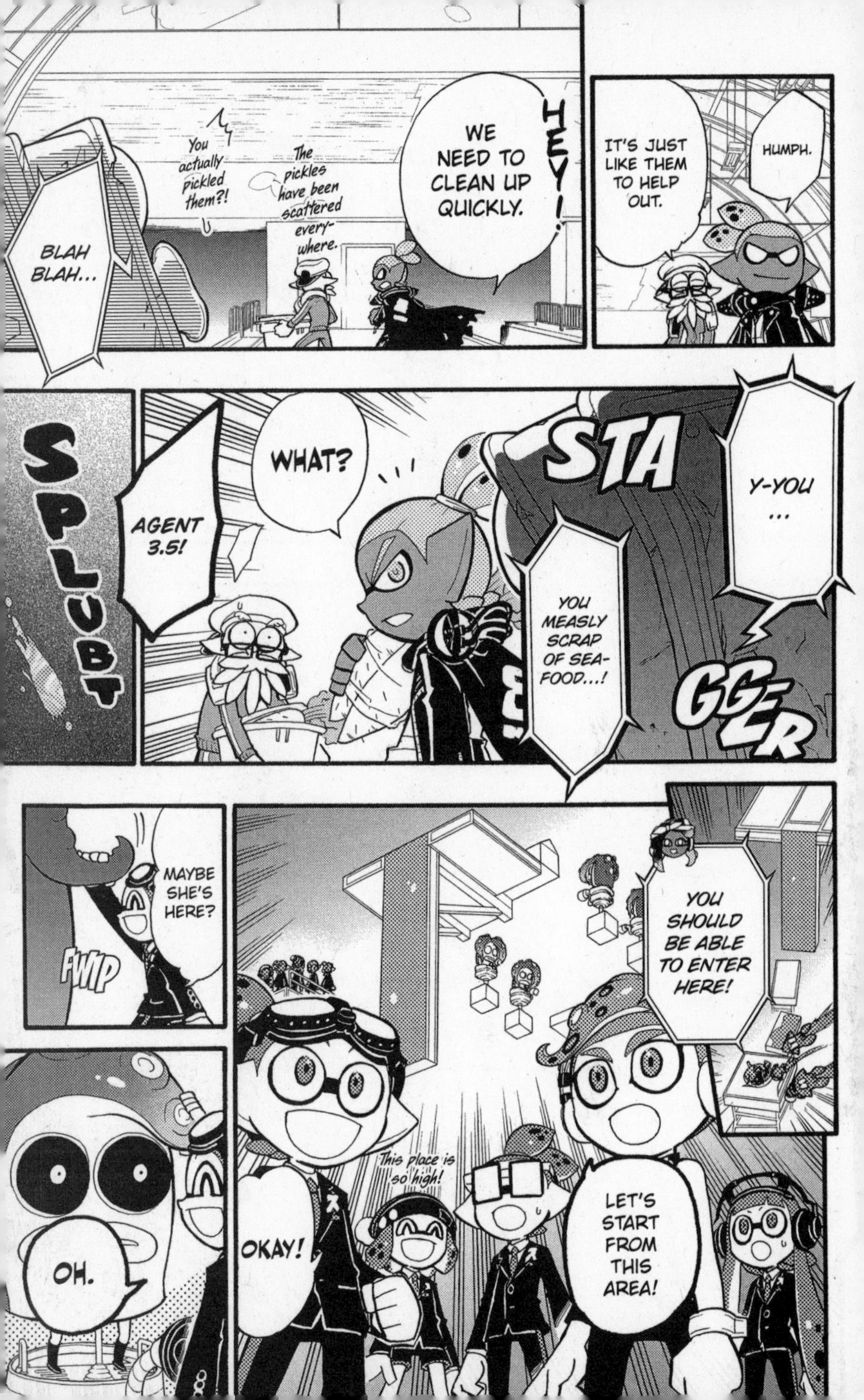
HUMPH.
IT'S JUST LIKE THEM TO HELP OUT.
HEY!
WE NEED TO CLEAN UP QUICKLY.
The pickles have been scattered every-where.
You actually pickled them?!
BLAH BLAH...
Y-YOU ...
STA
GGER
YOU MEASLY SCRAP OF SEA-FOOD...!
WHAT?
AGENT 3.5!
SPLUBT
YOU SHOULD BE ABLE TO ENTER HERE!
LET'S START FROM THIS AREA!
This place is so high!
OKAY!
MAYBE SHE'S HERE?
FWIP
OH.

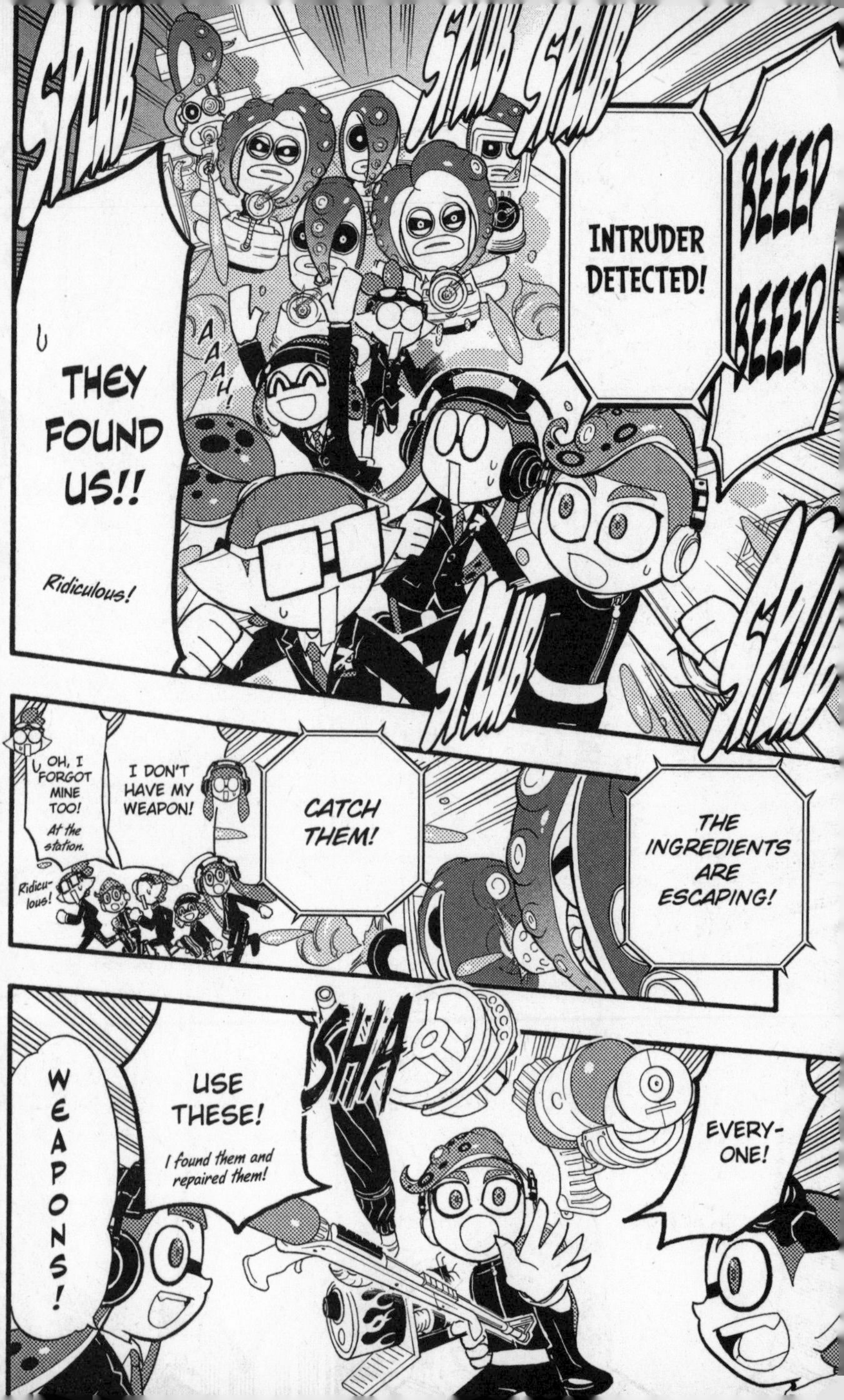
BEEEP BEEEP
INTRUDER DETECTED!
AAAH!
THEY FOUND US!!
Ridiculous!
THE INGREDIENTS ARE ESCAPING!
CATCH THEM!
I DON'T HAVE MY WEAPON!
OH, I FORGOT MINE TOO!
At the station.
Ridicu-lous!
EVERY-ONE!
SHA
USE THESE!
I found them and repaired them!
WEAPONS!

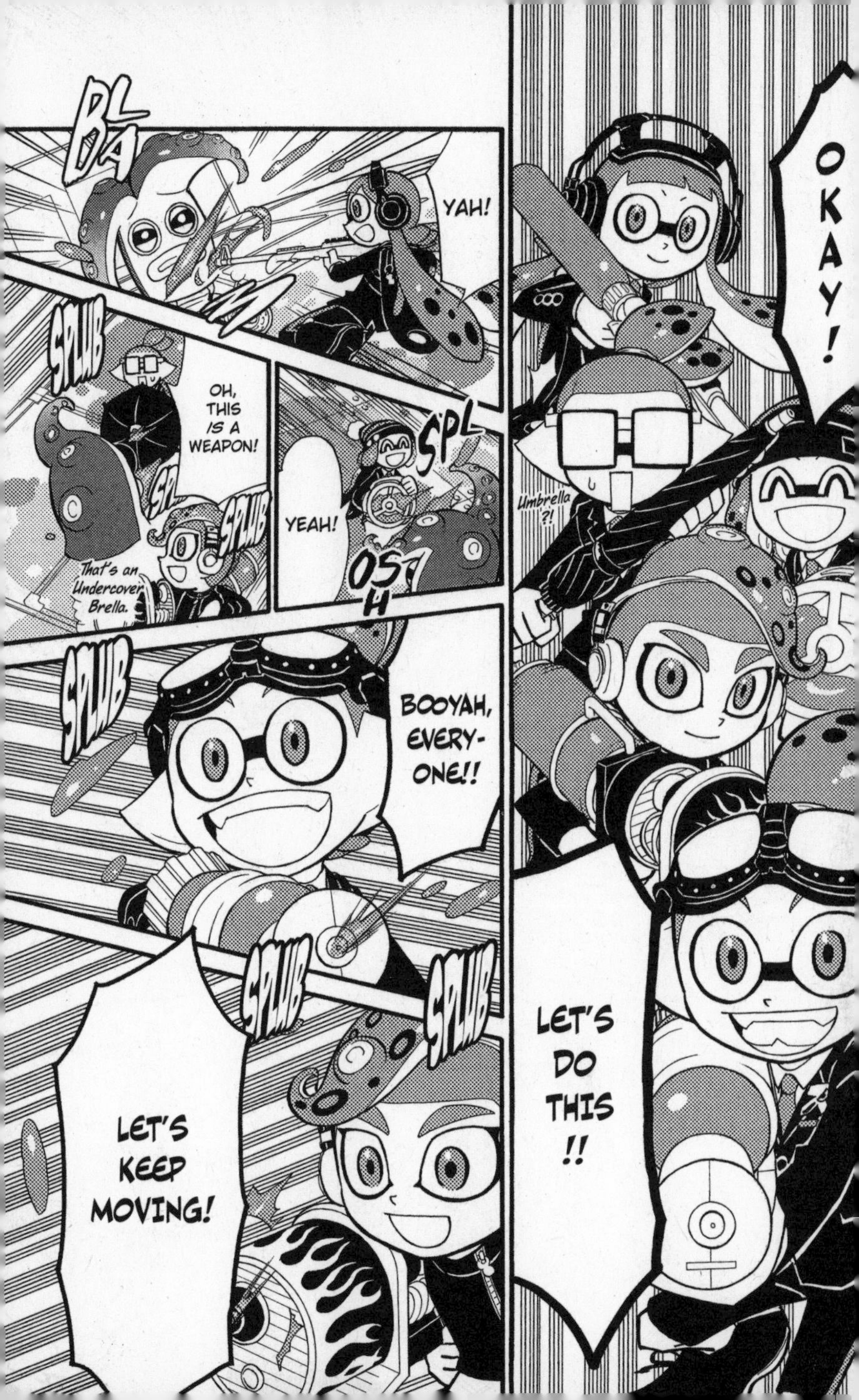
OKAY!
Umbrella?!
LET'S DO THIS!!
BLA
YAH!
SPL
YEAH!
OSH
SPLUB
OH, THIS IS A WEAPON!
SPL
SPLUB
That's an Undercover Brella.
SPLUB
BOOYAH, EVERYONE!!
SPLUB
SPLUB
LET'S KEEP MOVING!

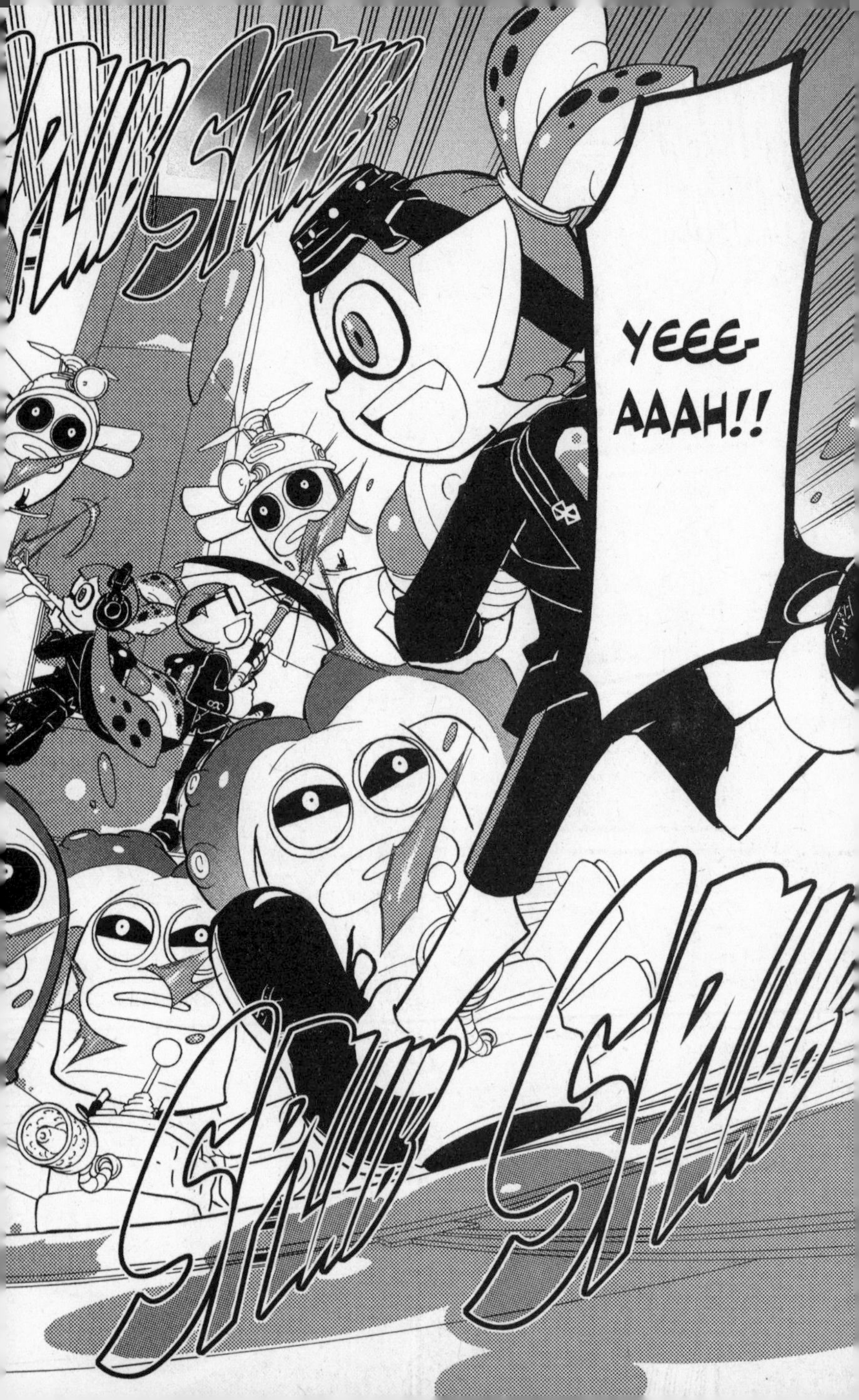
YEEE-AAAH!!

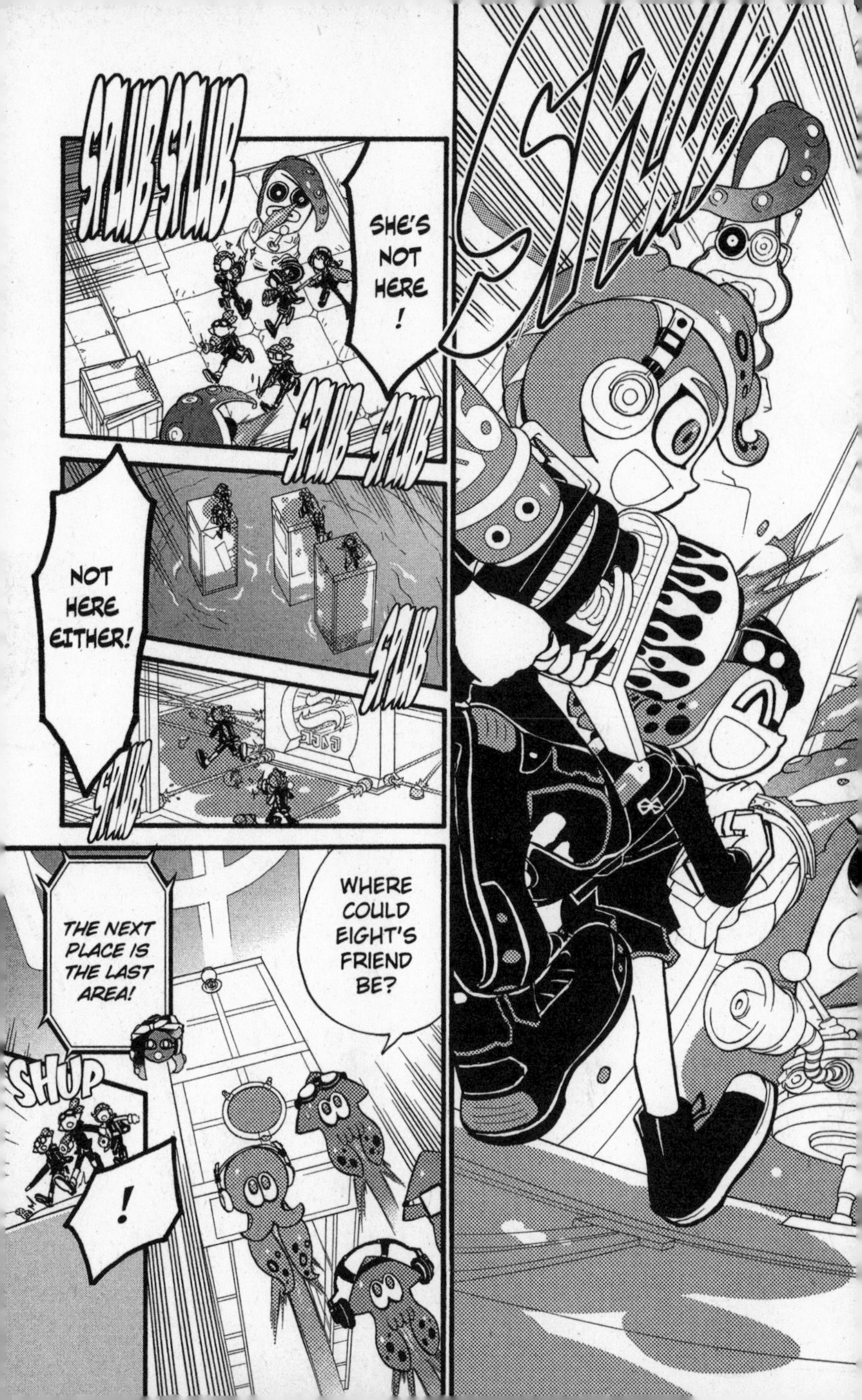
SPLUB SPLUB
SHE'S NOT HERE!
SPLUB SPLUB
NOT HERE EITHER!
SPLUB
SPLUB
WHERE COULD EIGHT'S FRIEND BE?
THE NEXT PLACE IS THE LAST AREA!
SHUP
!

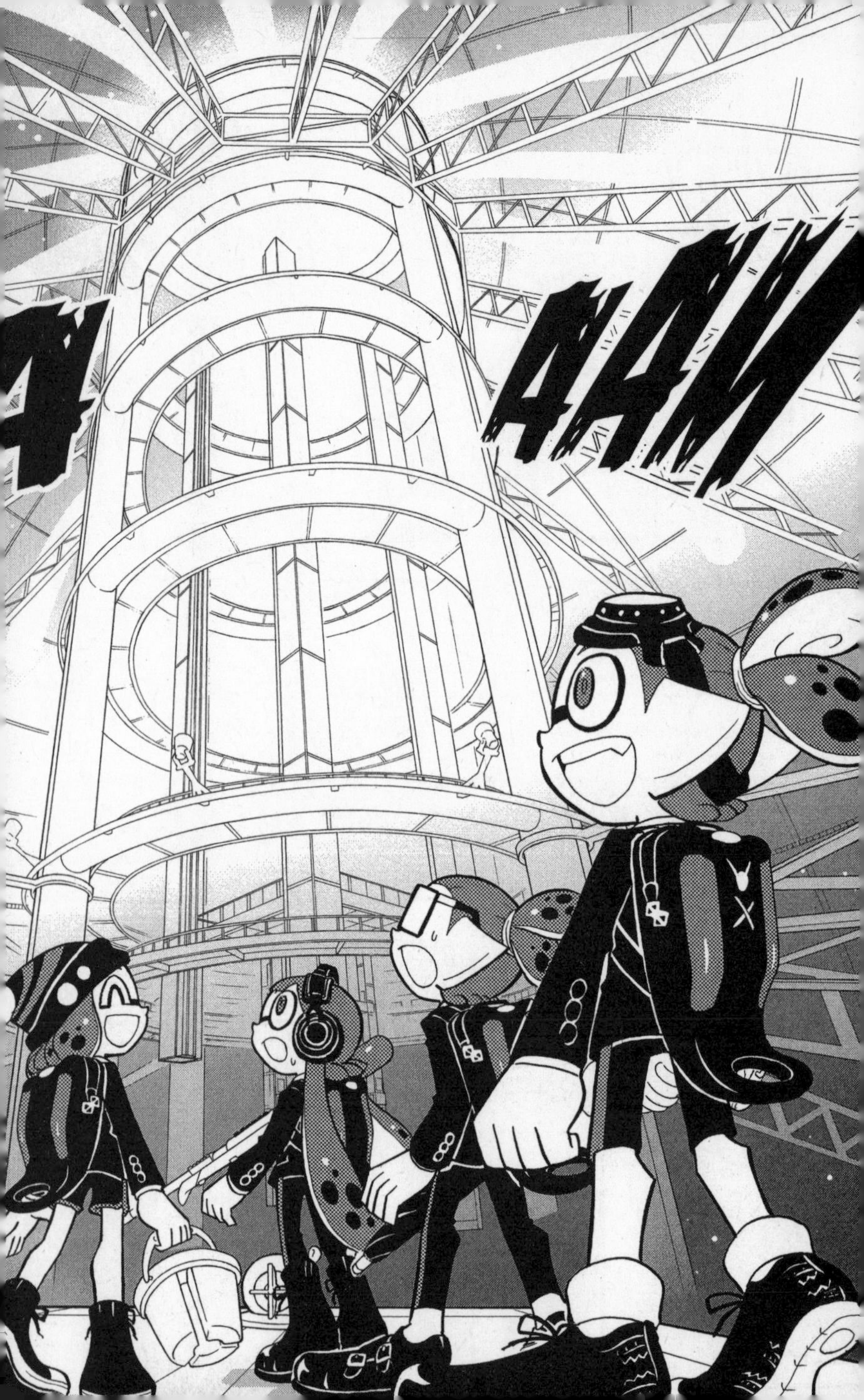
AAA

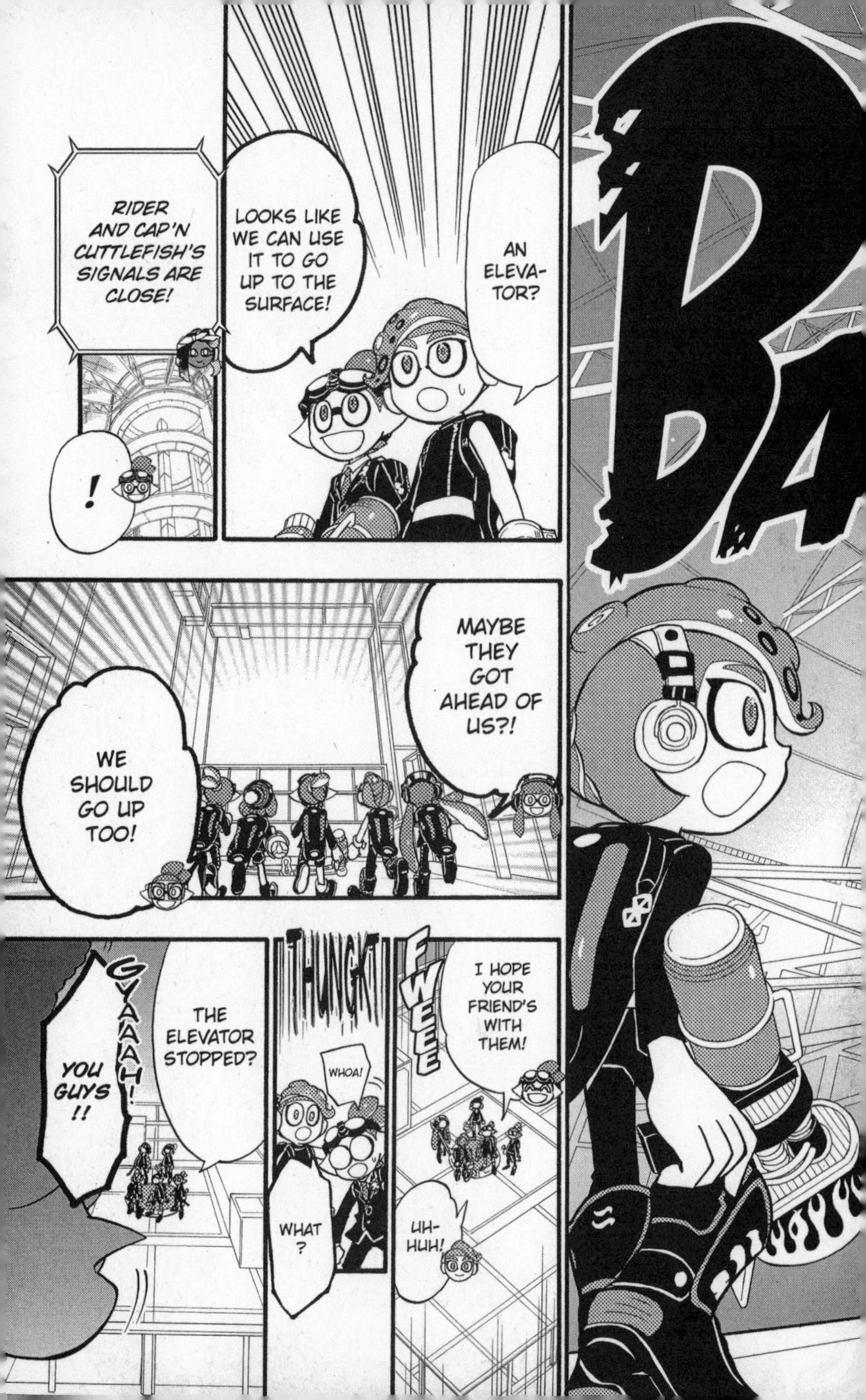
BA
AN ELEVATOR?
LOOKS LIKE WE CAN USE IT TO GO UP TO THE SURFACE!
RIDER AND CAP'N CUTTLEFISH'S SIGNALS ARE CLOSE!
!
MAYBE THEY GOT AHEAD OF US?!
WE SHOULD GO UP TOO!
I HOPE YOUR FRIEND'S WITH THEM!
UH-HUH!
FWEEE
THUNK!
WHOA!
WHAT?
THE ELEVATOR STOPPED?
GYAAAAH!
YOU GUYS!!

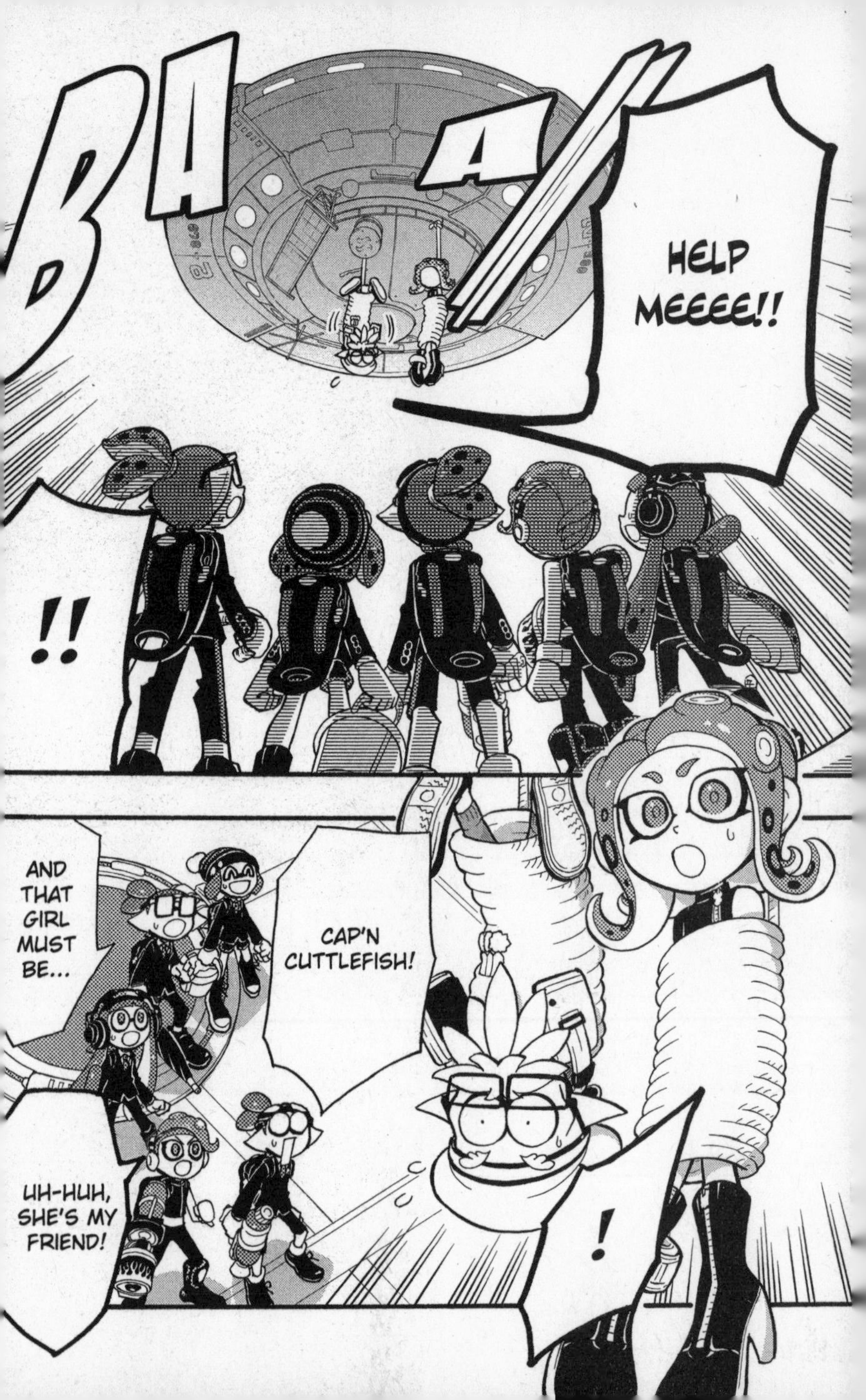
BAA
HELP MEEEE!!
!!
CAP'N CUTTLEFISH!
!
AND THAT GIRL MUST BE...
UH-HUH, SHE'S MY FRIEND!

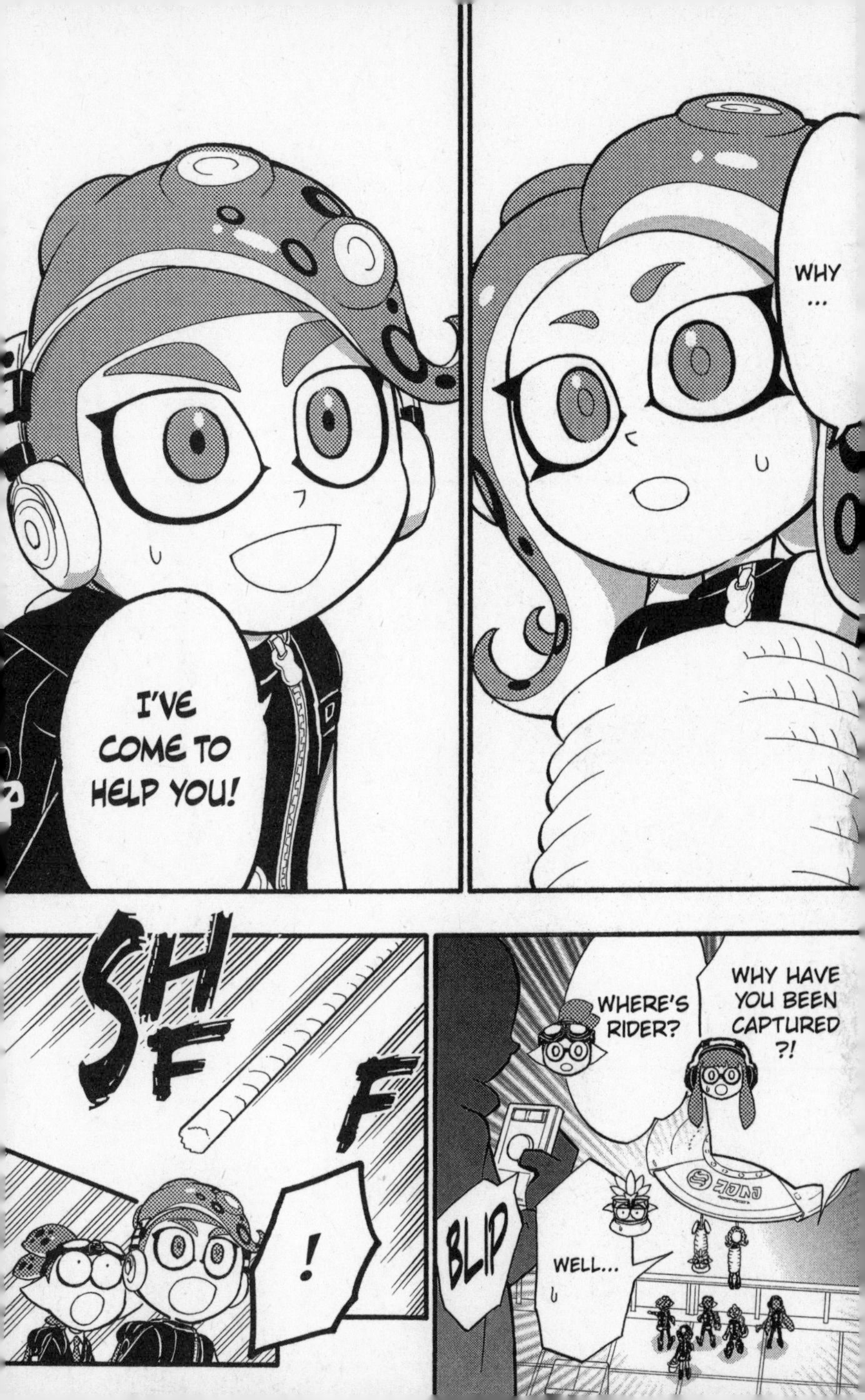
WHY ...
I'VE COME TO HELP YOU!
WHY HAVE YOU BEEN CAPTURED ?!
WHERE'S RIDER?
WELL...
BLIP
SHFF
!

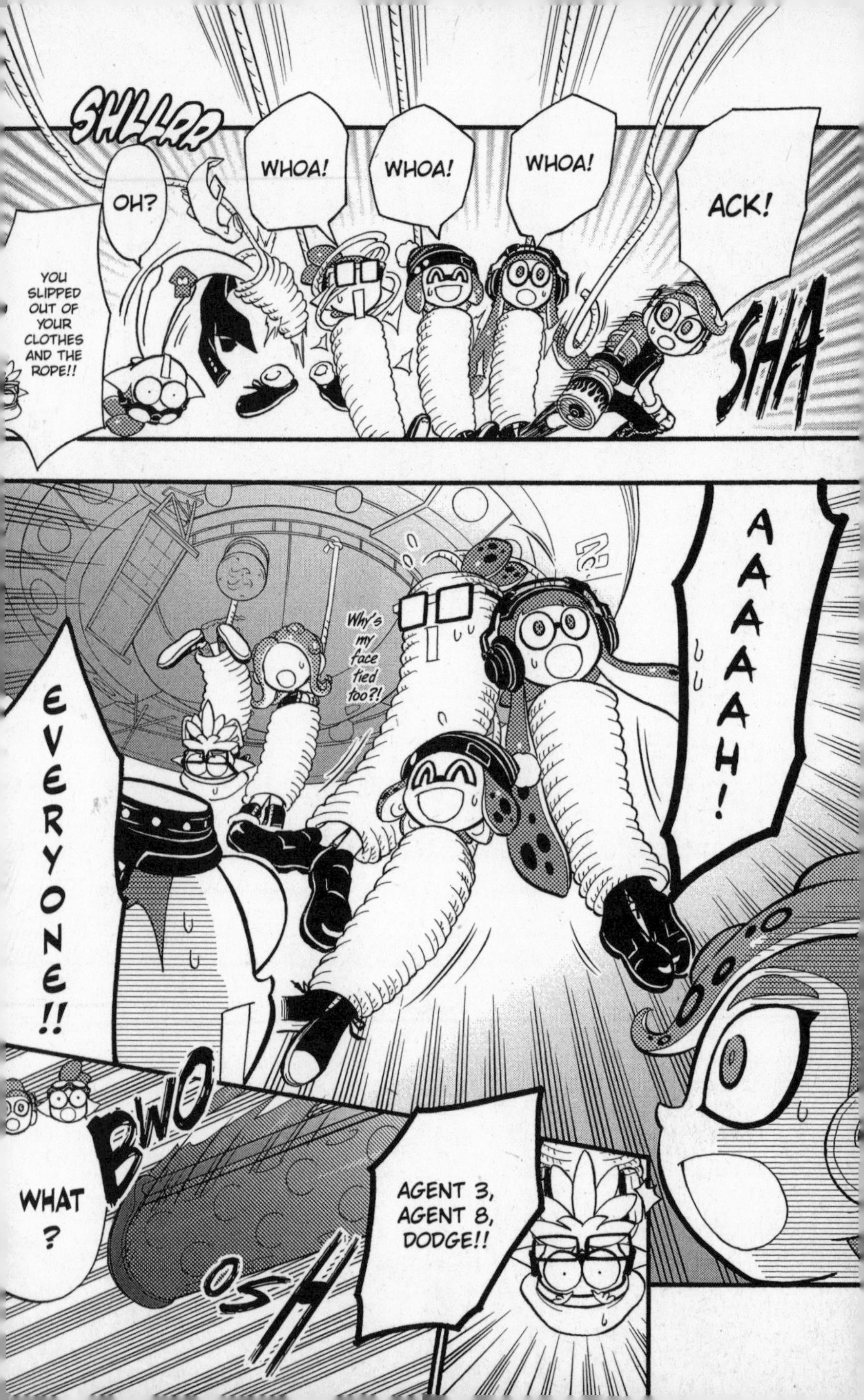
SHA
ACK!
WHOA!
WHOA!
WHOA!
OH?
SHLLRR
YOU SLIPPED OUT OF YOUR CLOTHES AND THE ROPE!!
AAAAAH!
?!
Why's my face tied too?!
EVERYONE!!
AGENT 3, AGENT 8, DODGE!!
BWO
WHAT?
OSH

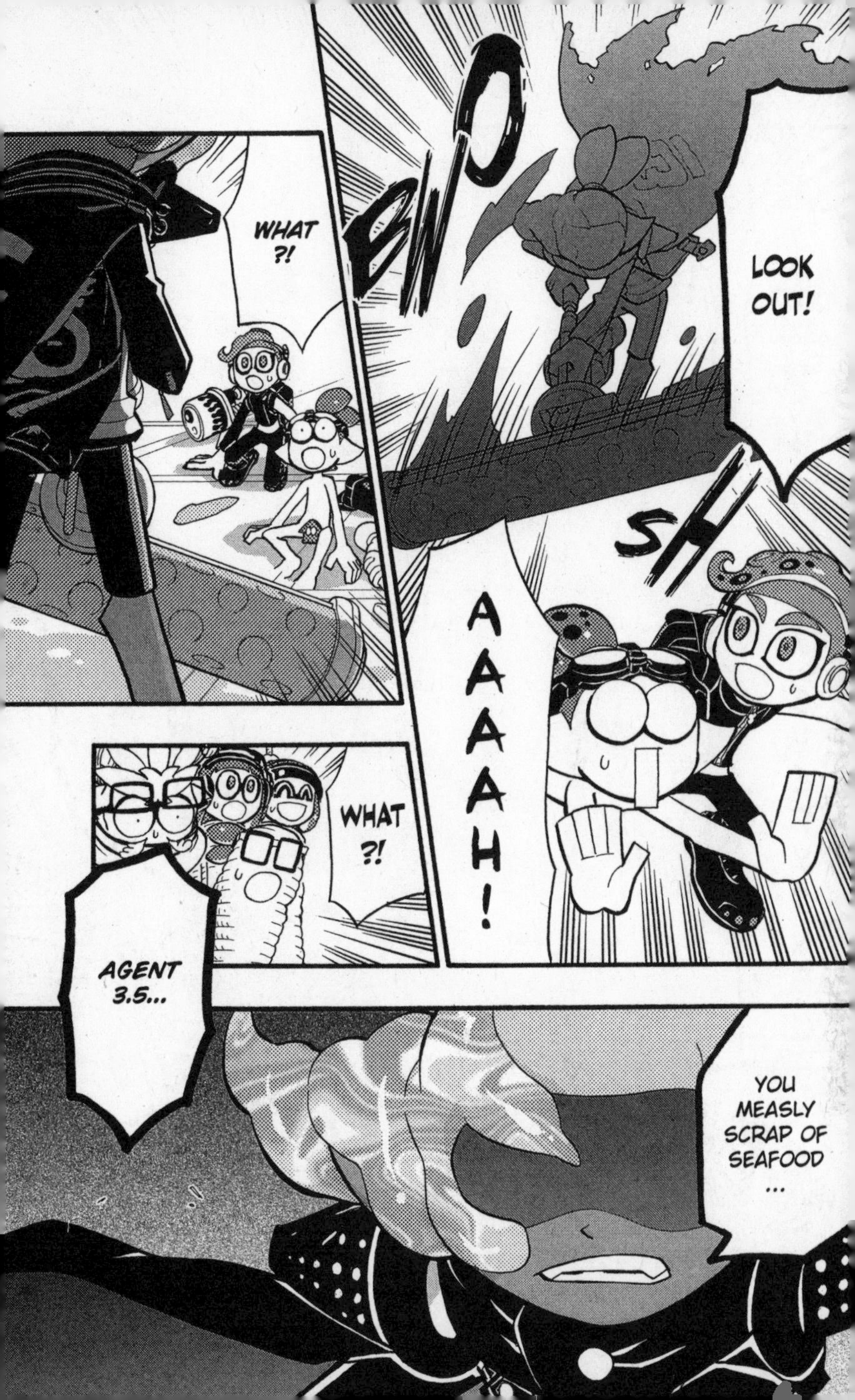
LOOK OUT!
SH
AAAAH!
WHAT ?!
WHAT ?!
YOU MEASLY SCRAP OF SEAFOOD ...
AGENT 3.5...

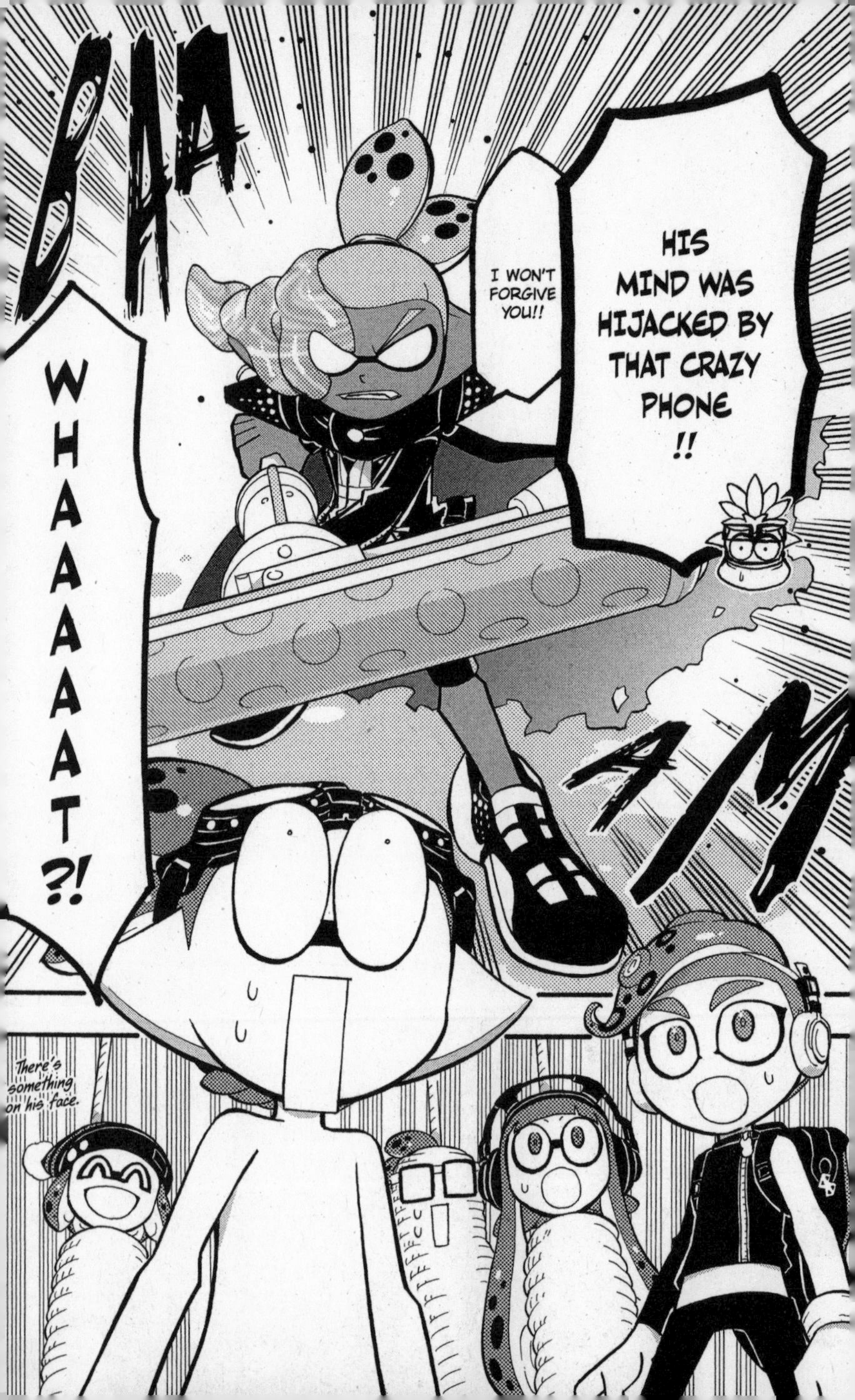
HIS MIND WAS HIJACKED BY THAT CRAZY PHONE!!
I WON'T FORGIVE YOU!!
BA
AM
WHAAAAAAT?!
There's something on his face.

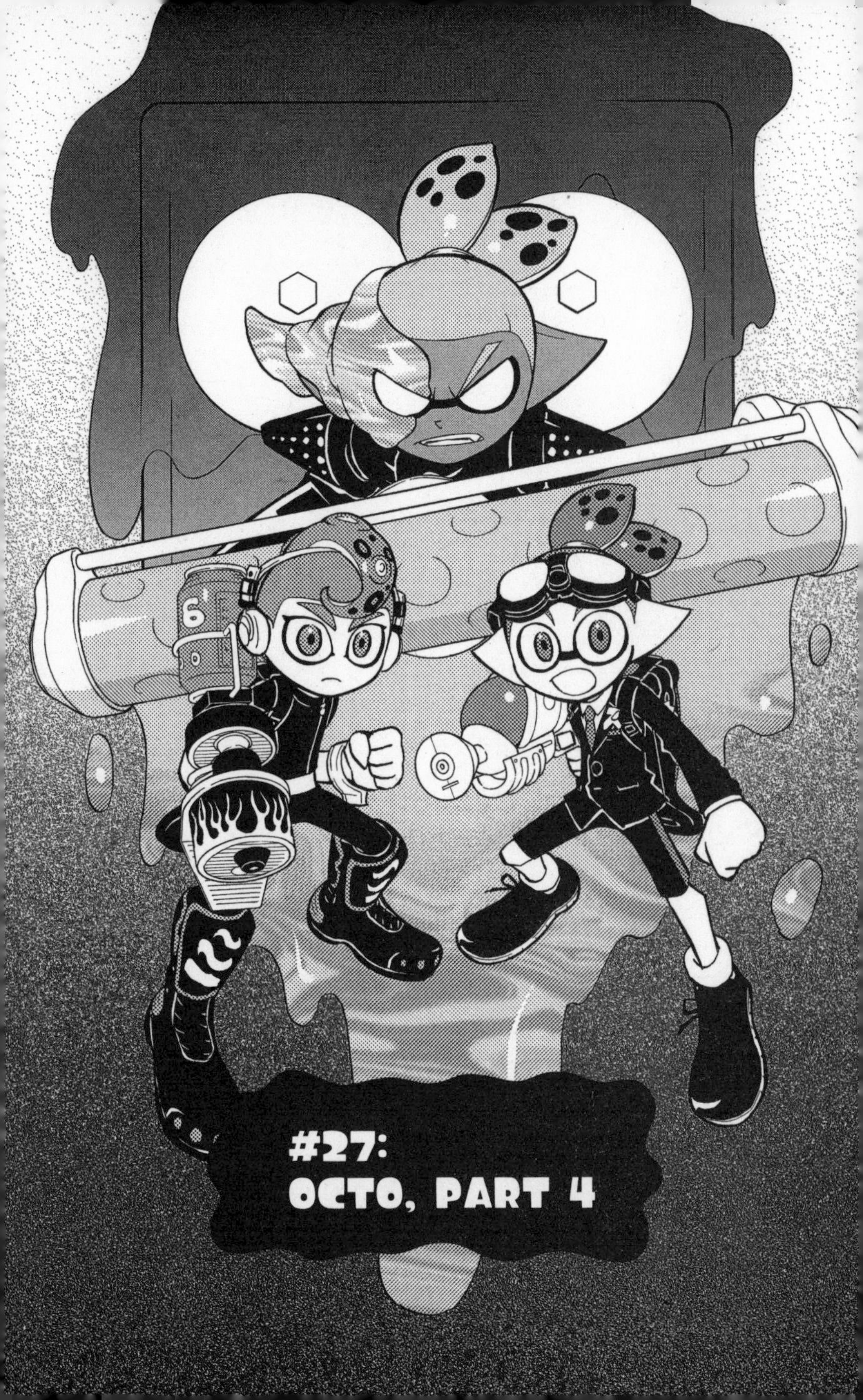
#27:
OCTO, PART 4

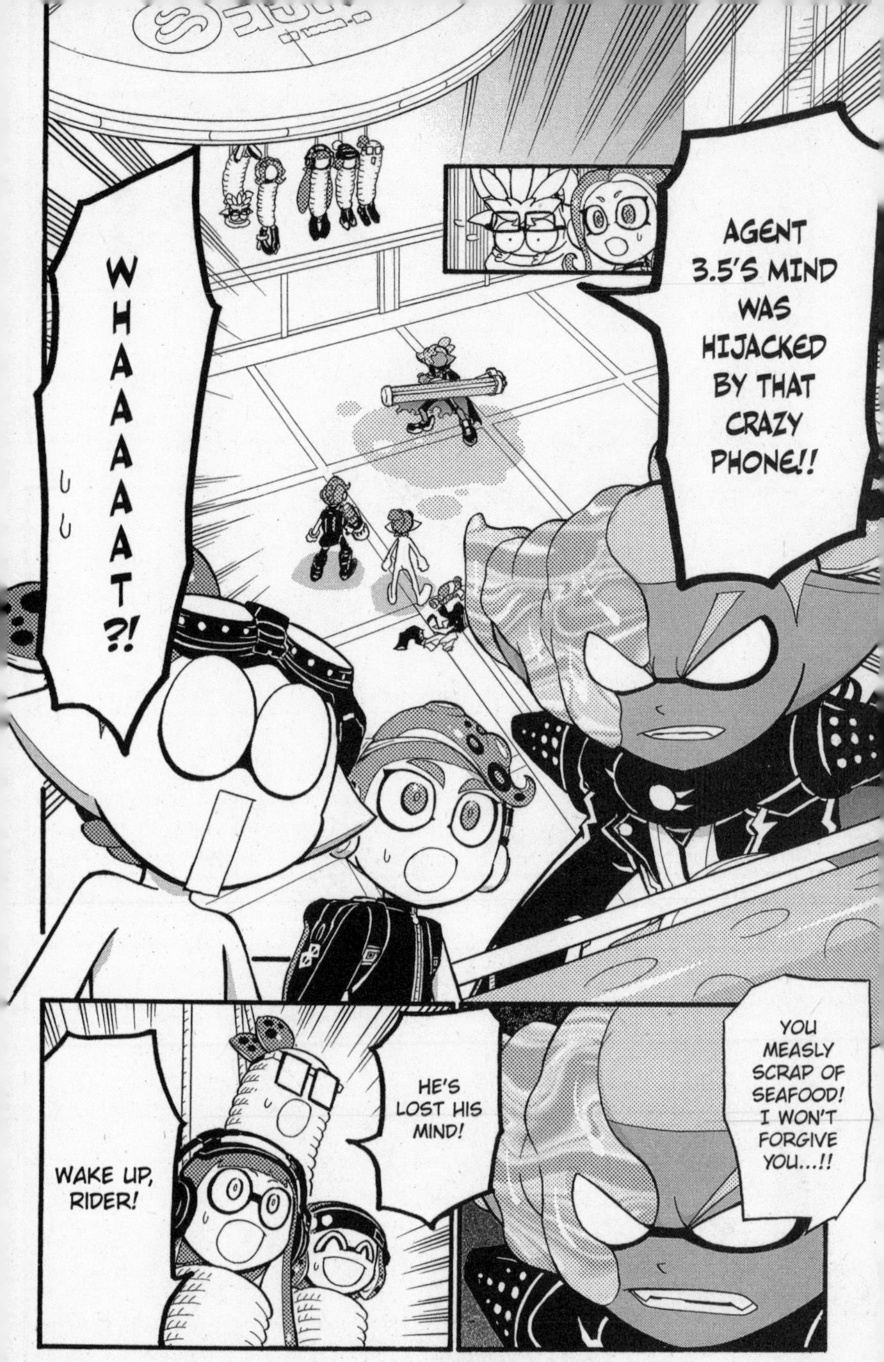
AGENT 3.5'S MIND WAS HIJACKED BY THAT CRAZY PHONE!!
WHAAAAAT?!
YOU MEASLY SCRAP OF SEAFOOD! I WON'T FORGIVE YOU...!!
HE'S LOST HIS MIND!
WAKE UP, RIDER!

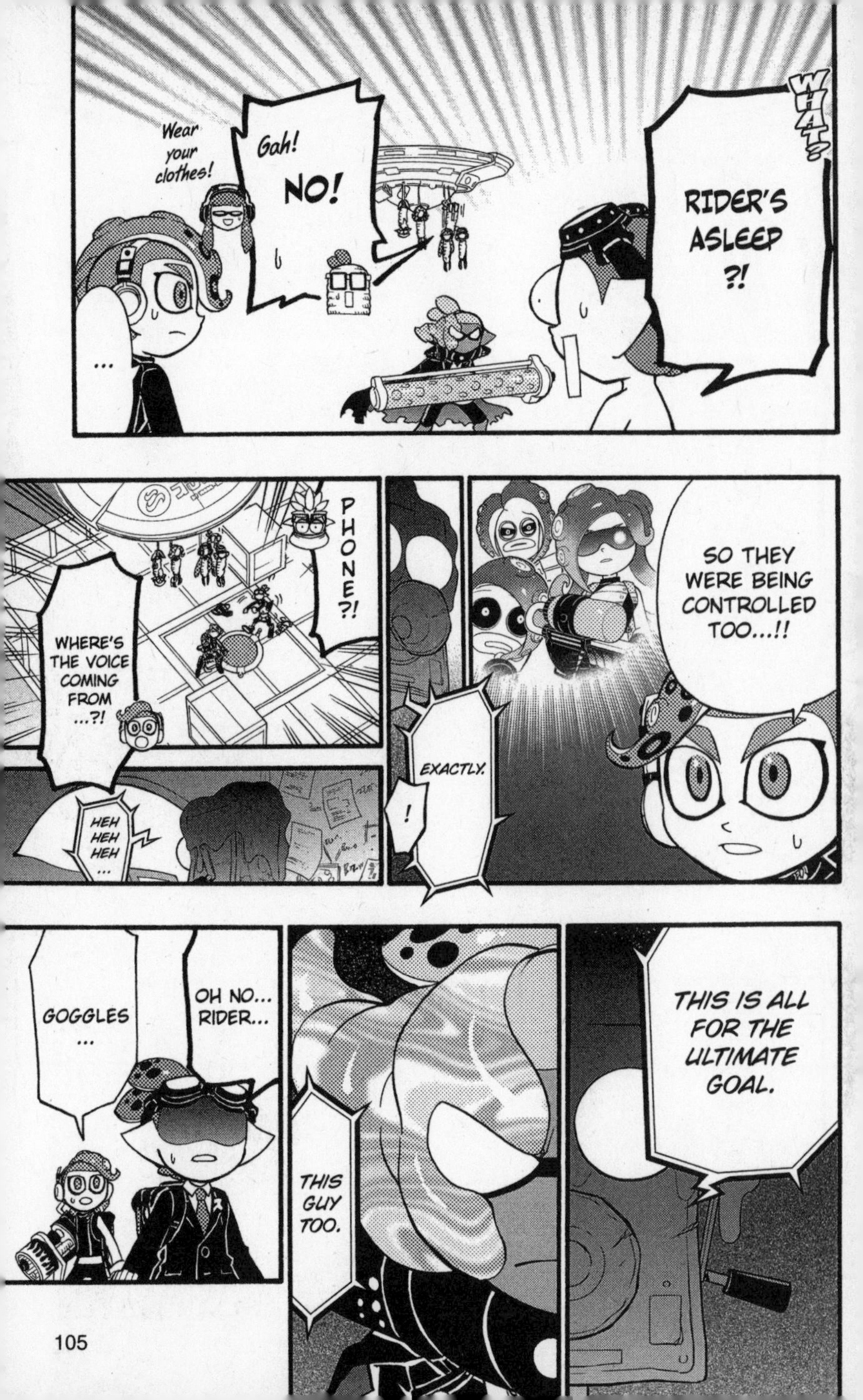
WHAT?!
RIDER'S ASLEEP ?!
Gah! NO!
Wear your clothes!
...
SO THEY WERE BEING CONTROLLED TOO...!!
!
EXACTLY.
PHONE?!
WHERE'S THE VOICE COMING FROM ...?!
HEH HEH HEH ...
THIS IS ALL FOR THE ULTIMATE GOAL.
THIS GUY TOO.
OH NO... RIDER...
GOGGLES ...

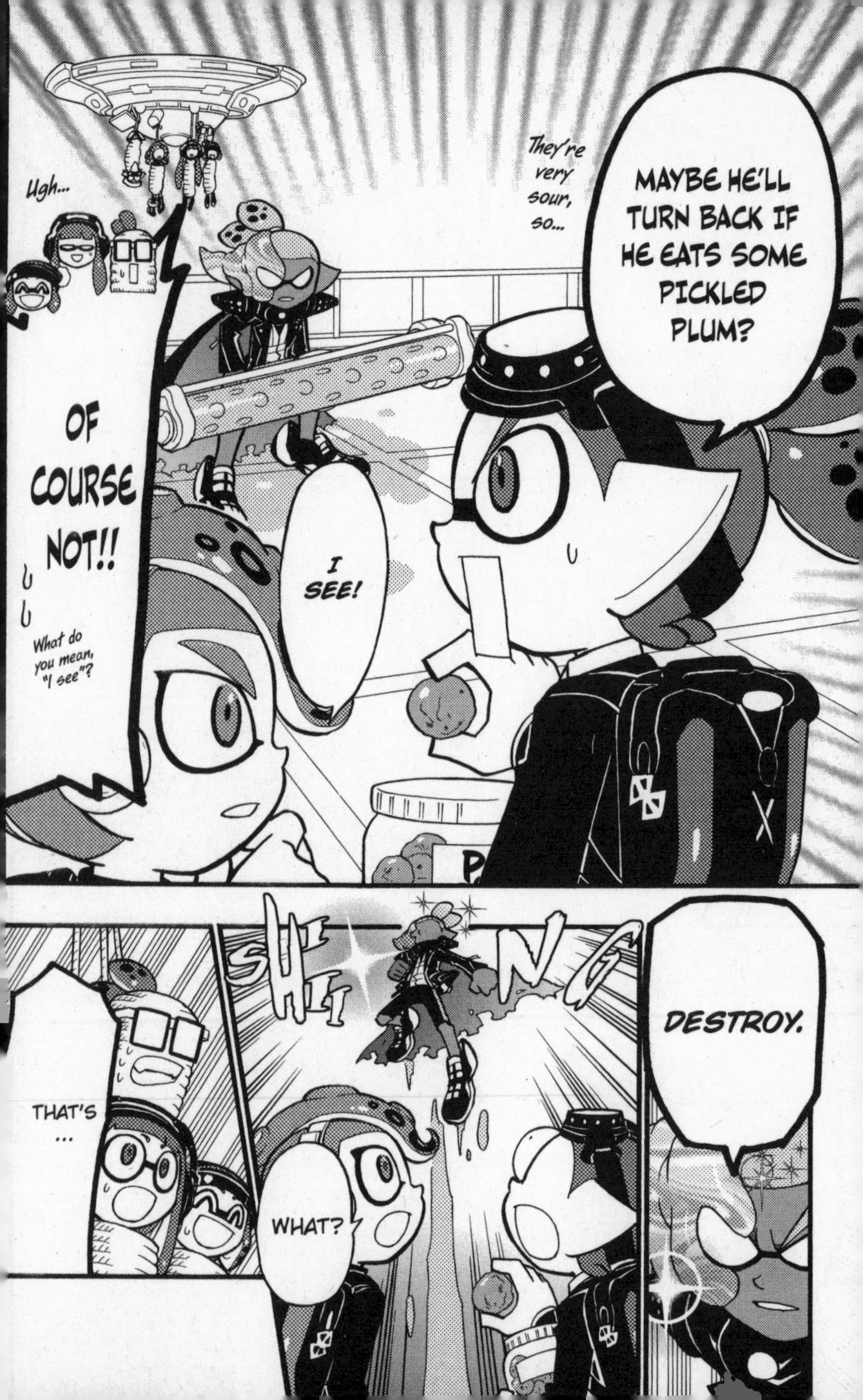

MAYBE HE'LL TURN BACK IF HE EATS SOME PICKLED PLUM?
They're very sour, so...
I SEE!
Ugh...
OF COURSE NOT!!
What do you mean, "I see"?
DESTROY.
SHIIING
WHAT?
THAT'S ...

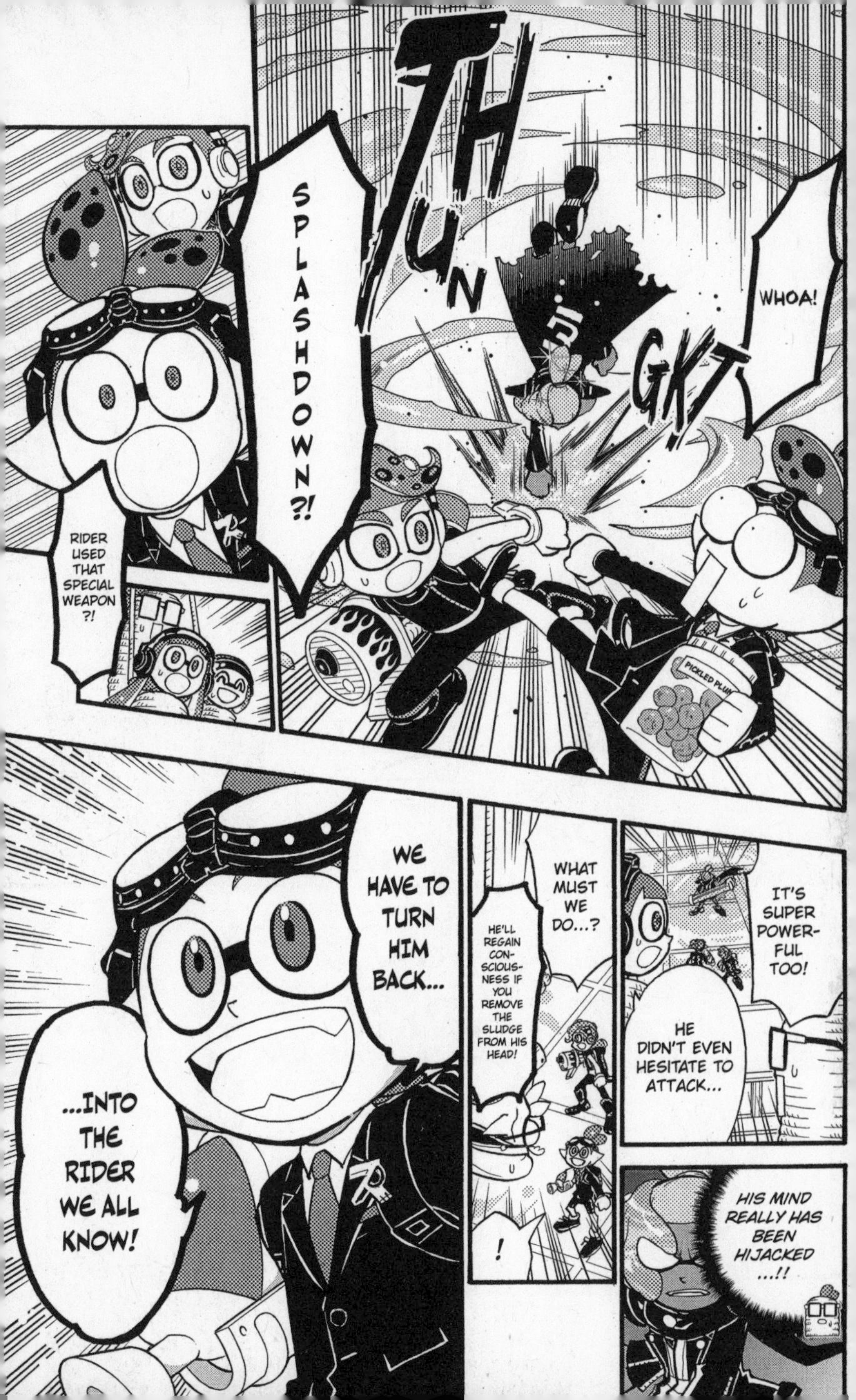
THUNK
WHOA!
GKT
PICKLED PLUM
SPLASHDOWN?!
RIDER USED THAT SPECIAL WEAPON?!
IT'S SUPER POWERFUL TOO!
HE DIDN'T EVEN HESITATE TO ATTACK...
HIS MIND REALLY HAS BEEN HIJACKED...!!
WHAT MUST WE DO...?
HE'LL REGAIN CONSCIOUSNESS IF YOU REMOVE THE SLUDGE FROM HIS HEAD!
!
WE HAVE TO TURN HIM BACK...
...INTO THE RIDER WE ALL KNOW!

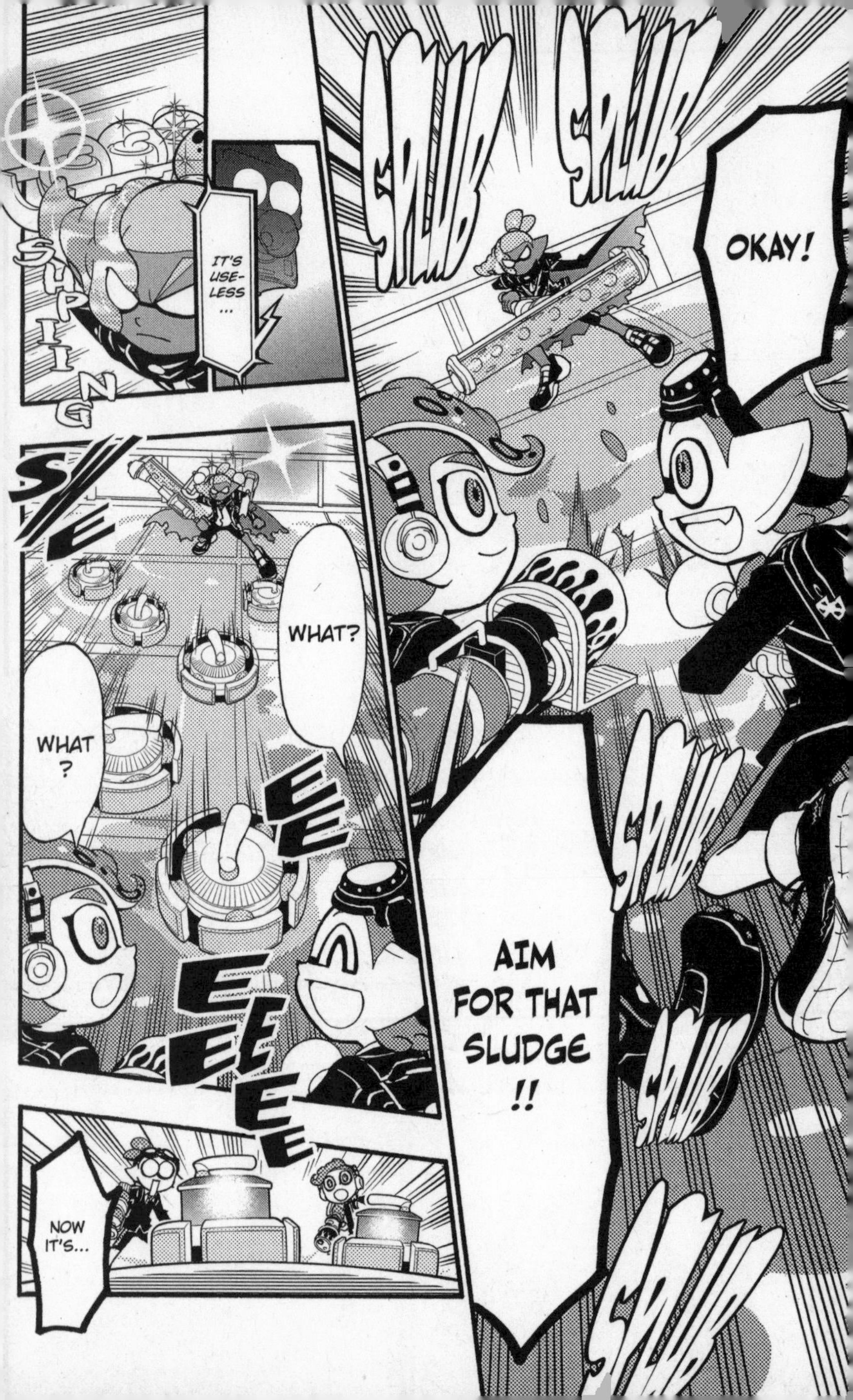
SPLUB
SPLUB
OKAY!
AIM FOR THAT SLUDGE!!
IT'S USELESS...
SHPIIING
WHAT?
WHAT?
NOW IT'S...

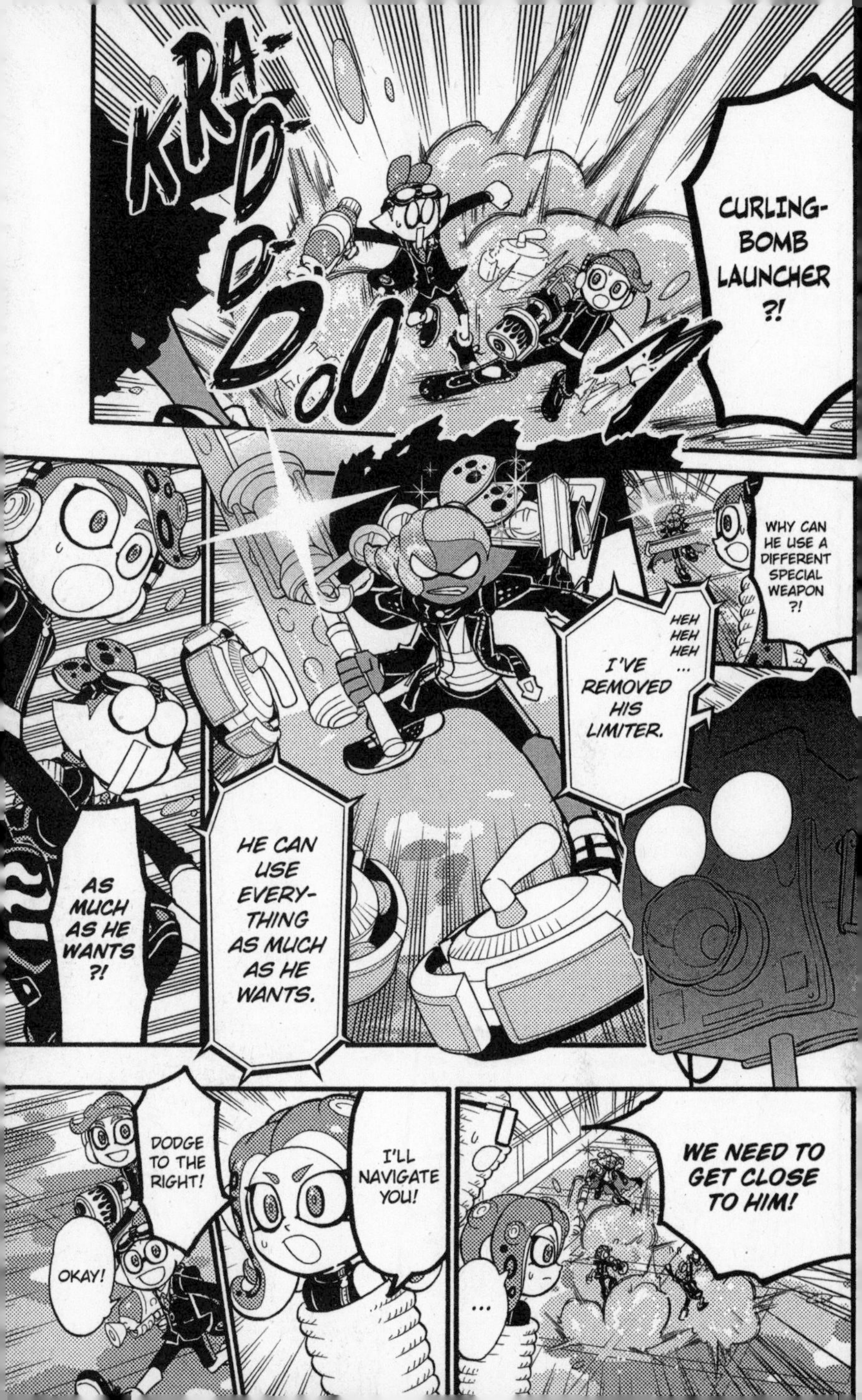
CURLING-BOMB LAUNCHER ?!
KRA-D-D-DOOM
WHY CAN HE USE A DIFFERENT SPECIAL WEAPON ?!
HEH HEH HEH ...
I'VE REMOVED HIS LIMITER.
HE CAN USE EVERYTHING AS MUCH AS HE WANTS.
AS MUCH AS HE WANTS ?!
WE NEED TO GET CLOSE TO HIM!
...
I'LL NAVIGATE YOU!
DODGE TO THE RIGHT!
OKAY!

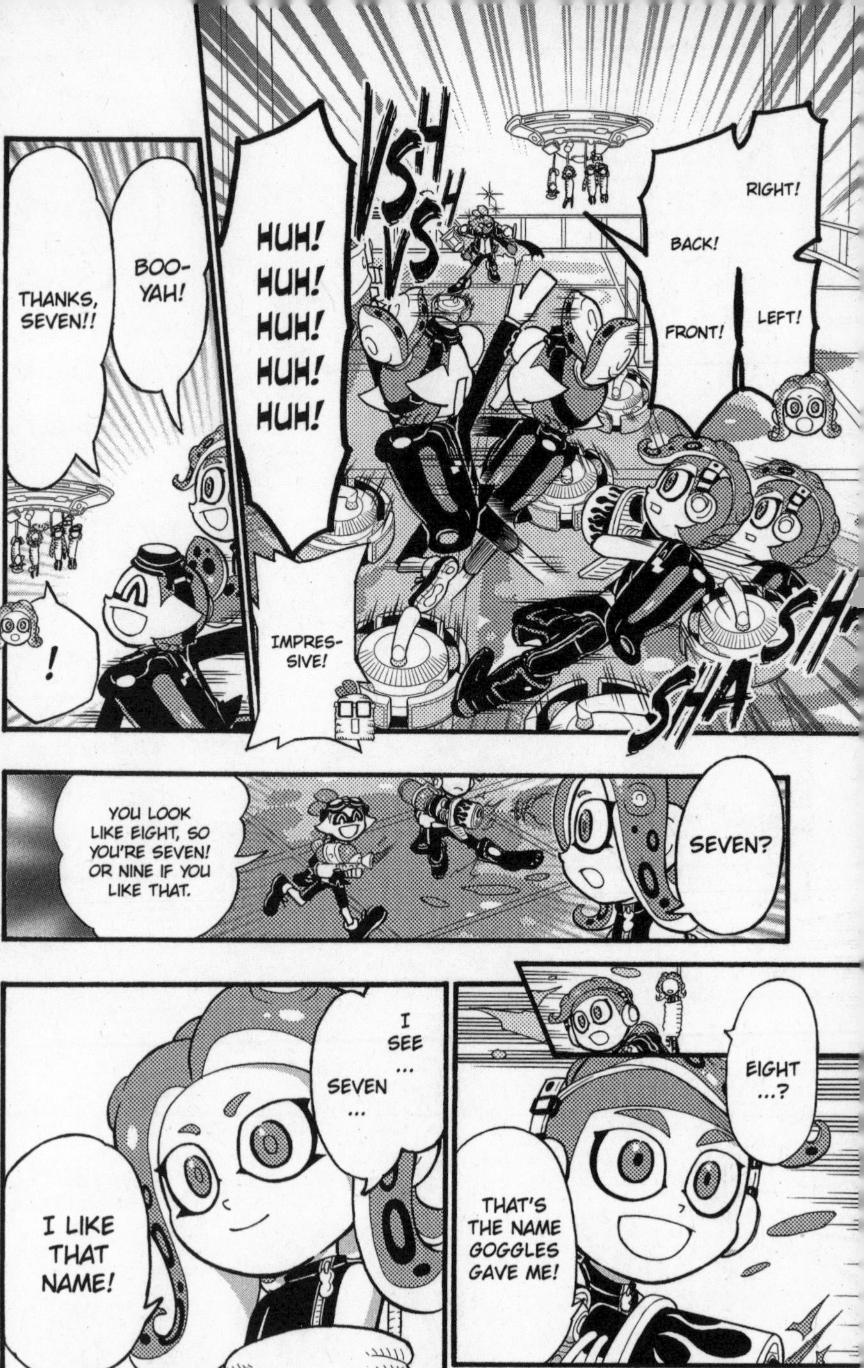
RIGHT! BACK! LEFT! FRONT!
VSH VSH
HUH! HUH! HUH! HUH! HUH!
SHA SHA
IMPRES-SIVE!
BOO-YAH!
THANKS, SEVEN!!
!
SEVEN?
YOU LOOK LIKE EIGHT, SO YOU'RE SEVEN! OR NINE IF YOU LIKE THAT.
EIGHT ...?
THAT'S THE NAME GOGGLES GAVE ME!
I SEE ... SEVEN ...
I LIKE THAT NAME!

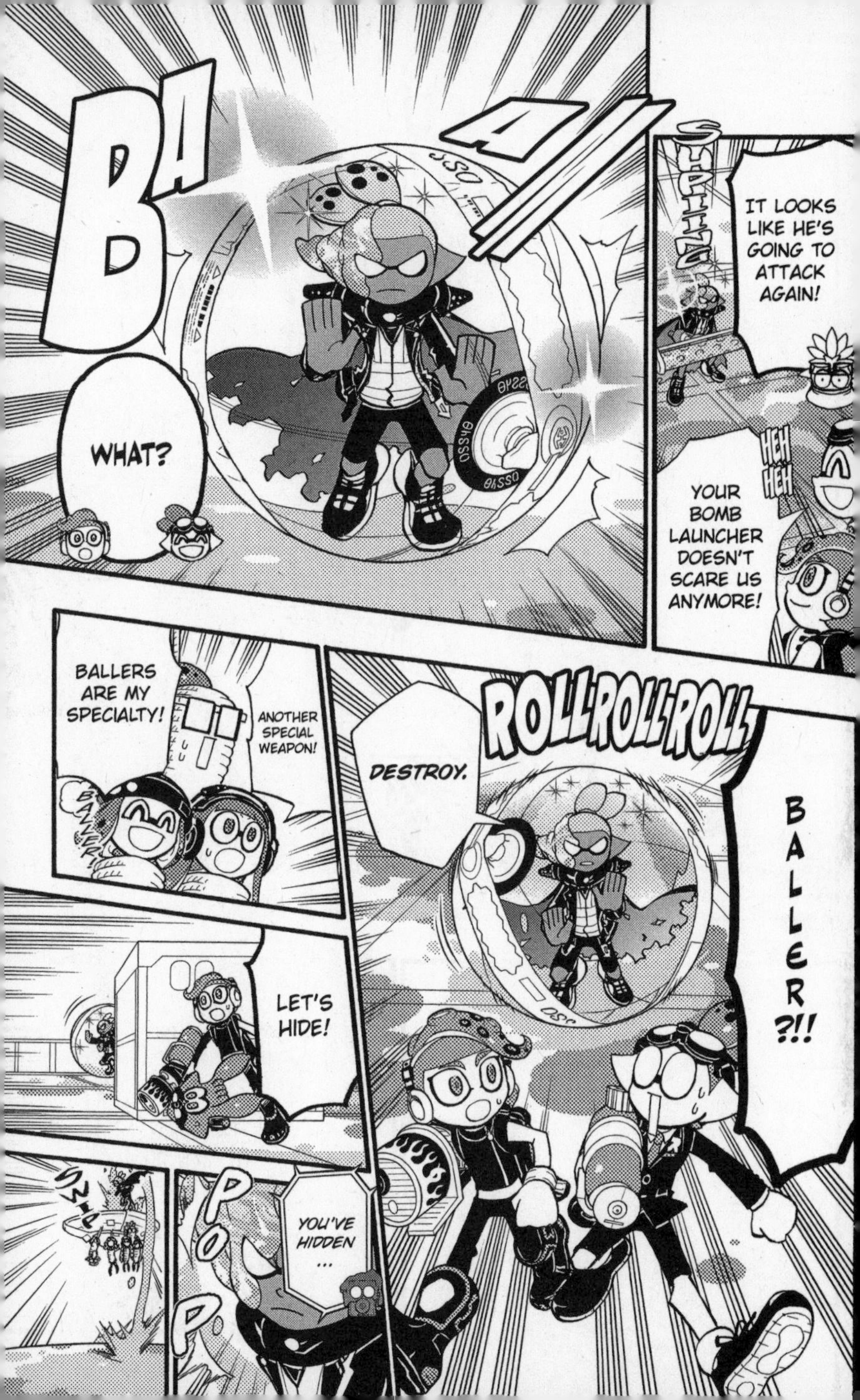
WHAT?
IT LOOKS LIKE HE'S GOING TO ATTACK AGAIN!
HEH HEH
YOUR BOMB LAUNCHER DOESN'T SCARE US ANYMORE!
BALLERS ARE MY SPECIALTY!
BALLER!
ANOTHER SPECIAL WEAPON!
ROLL ROLL ROLL
DESTROY.
BALLER?!!
LET'S HIDE!
POP
YOU'VE HIDDEN ...

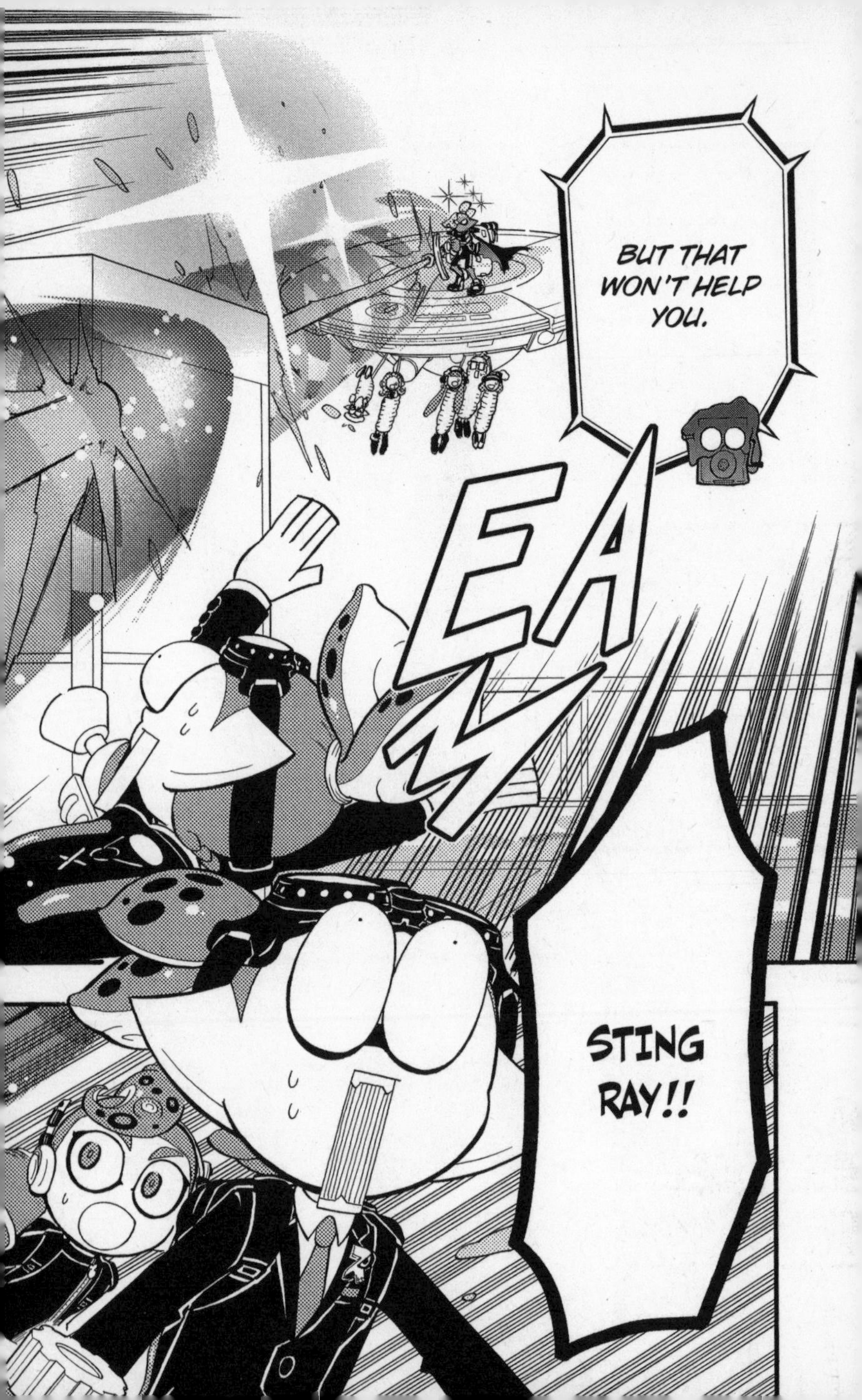
BUT THAT WON'T HELP YOU.
EAM
STING RAY!!

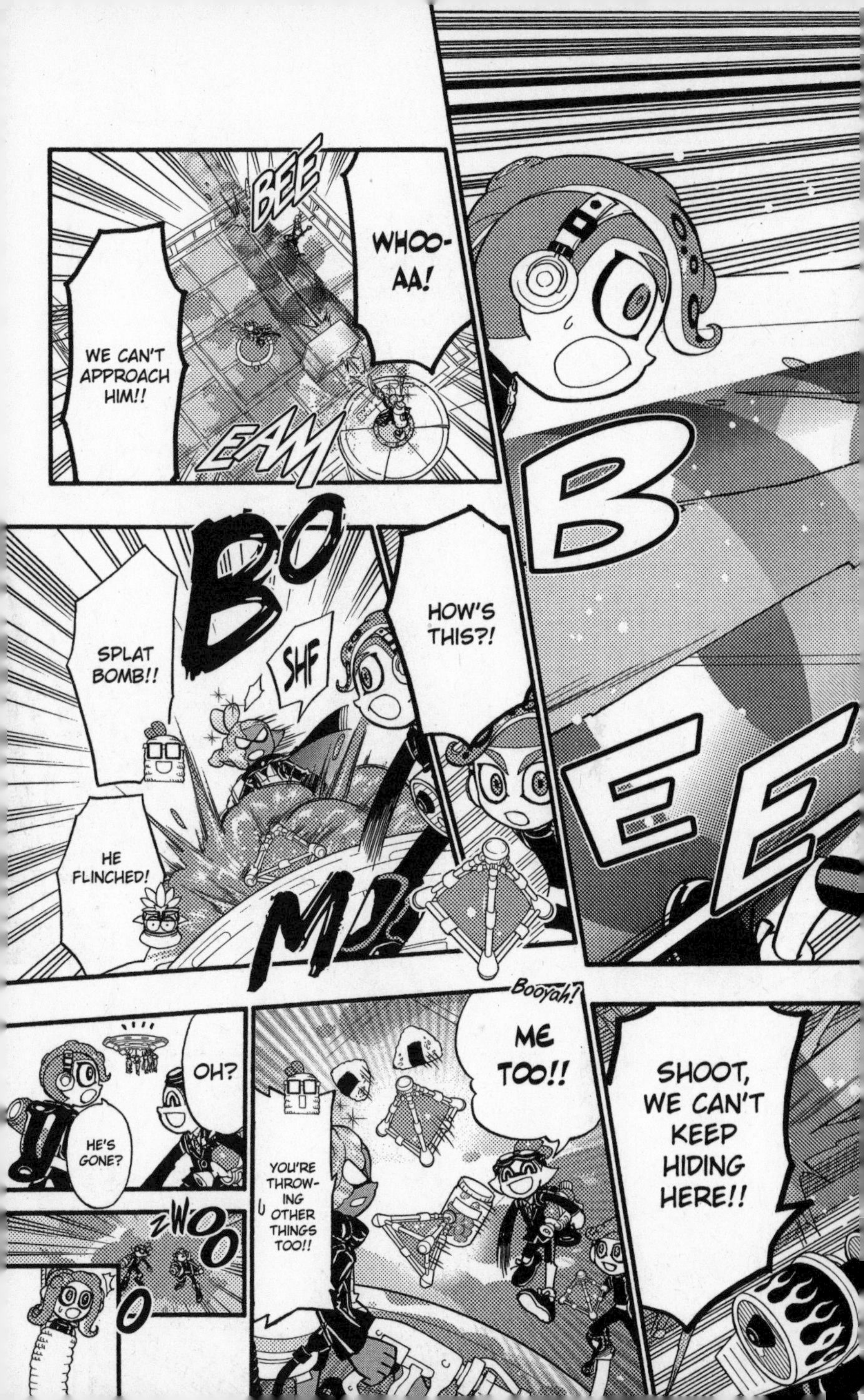
BEE
BEE
WHOO-AA!
WE CAN'T APPROACH HIM!!
EAM
BO
HOW'S THIS?!
SHF
SPLAT BOMB!!
HE FLINCHED!
M
SHOOT, WE CAN'T KEEP HIDING HERE!!
Booyah!
ME TOO!!
YOU'RE THROWING OTHER THINGS TOO!!
OH?
HE'S GONE?
ZWOO
O

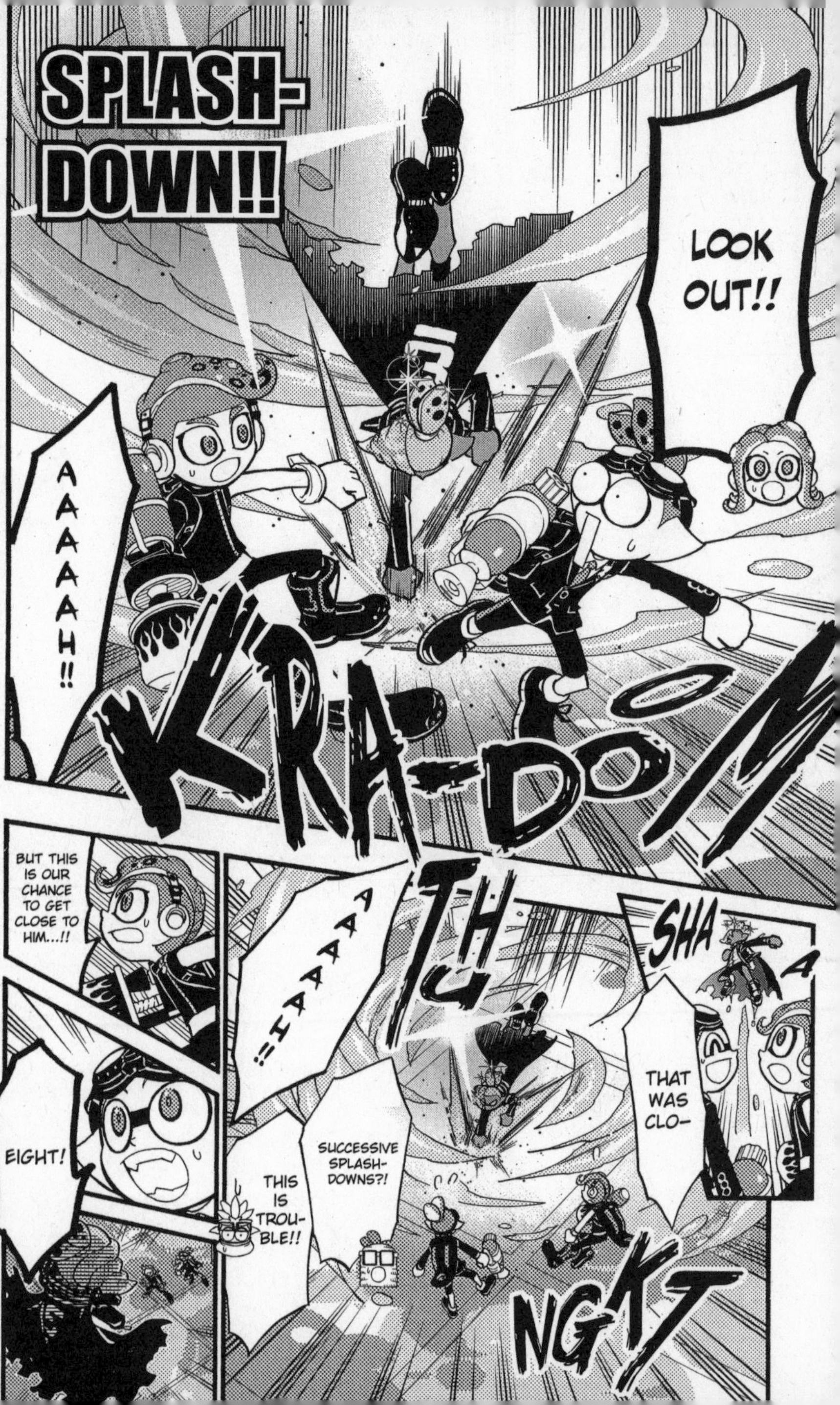
LOOK OUT!!
SPLASH-DOWN!!
AAAAAAAH!!
KRA-DOOM
SHAA
THAT WAS CLO-
AAAAAH!!
THU!
SUCCESSIVE SPLASH-DOWNS?!
THIS IS TROUBLE!!
NGKT
BUT THIS IS OUR CHANCE TO GET CLOSE TO HIM...!!
EIGHT!

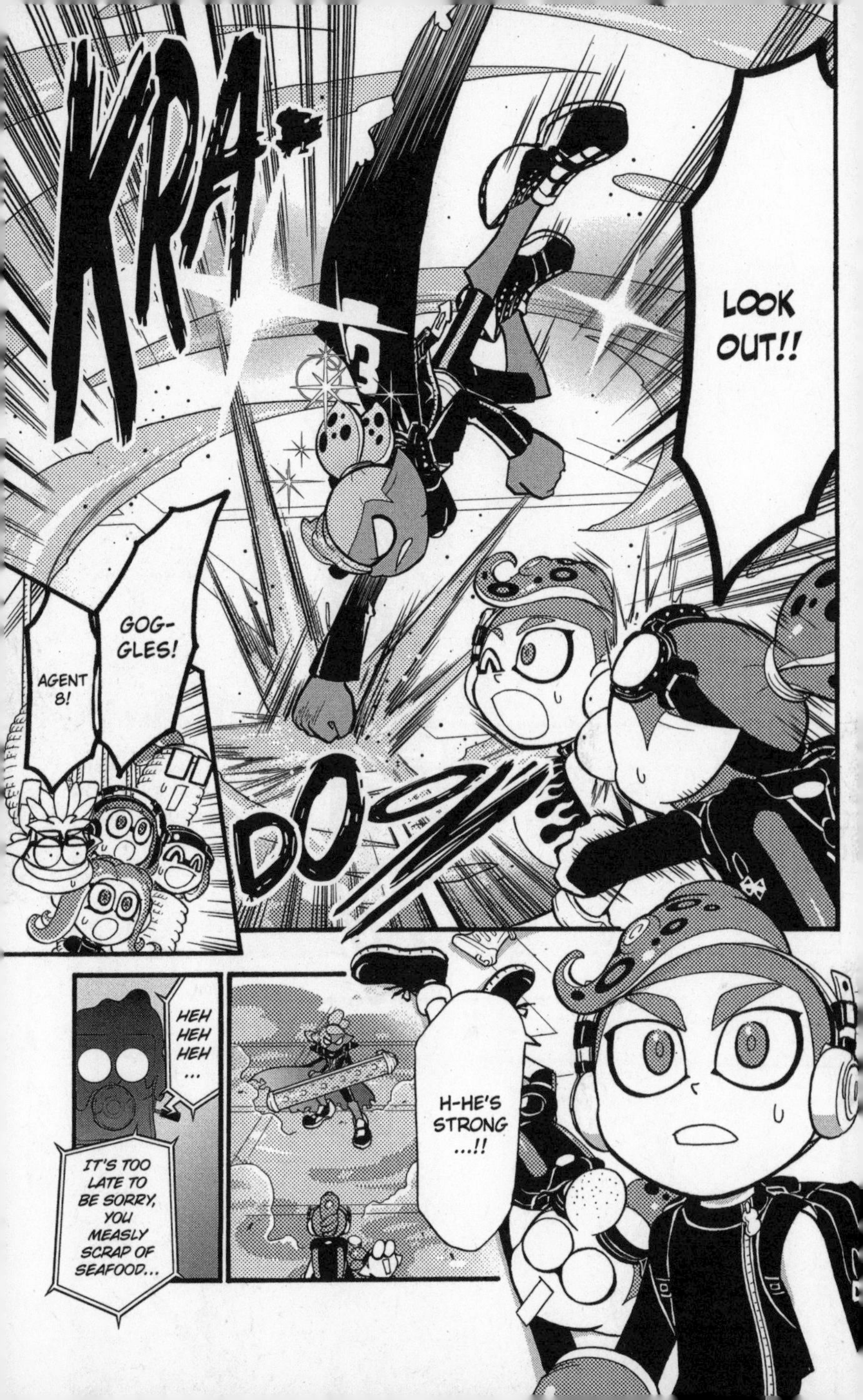
LOOK OUT!!
KRA
GOG-GLES!
AGENT 8!
DO
H-HE'S STRONG ...!!
HEH HEH HEH ...
IT'S TOO LATE TO BE SORRY, YOU MEASLY SCRAP OF SEAFOOD...

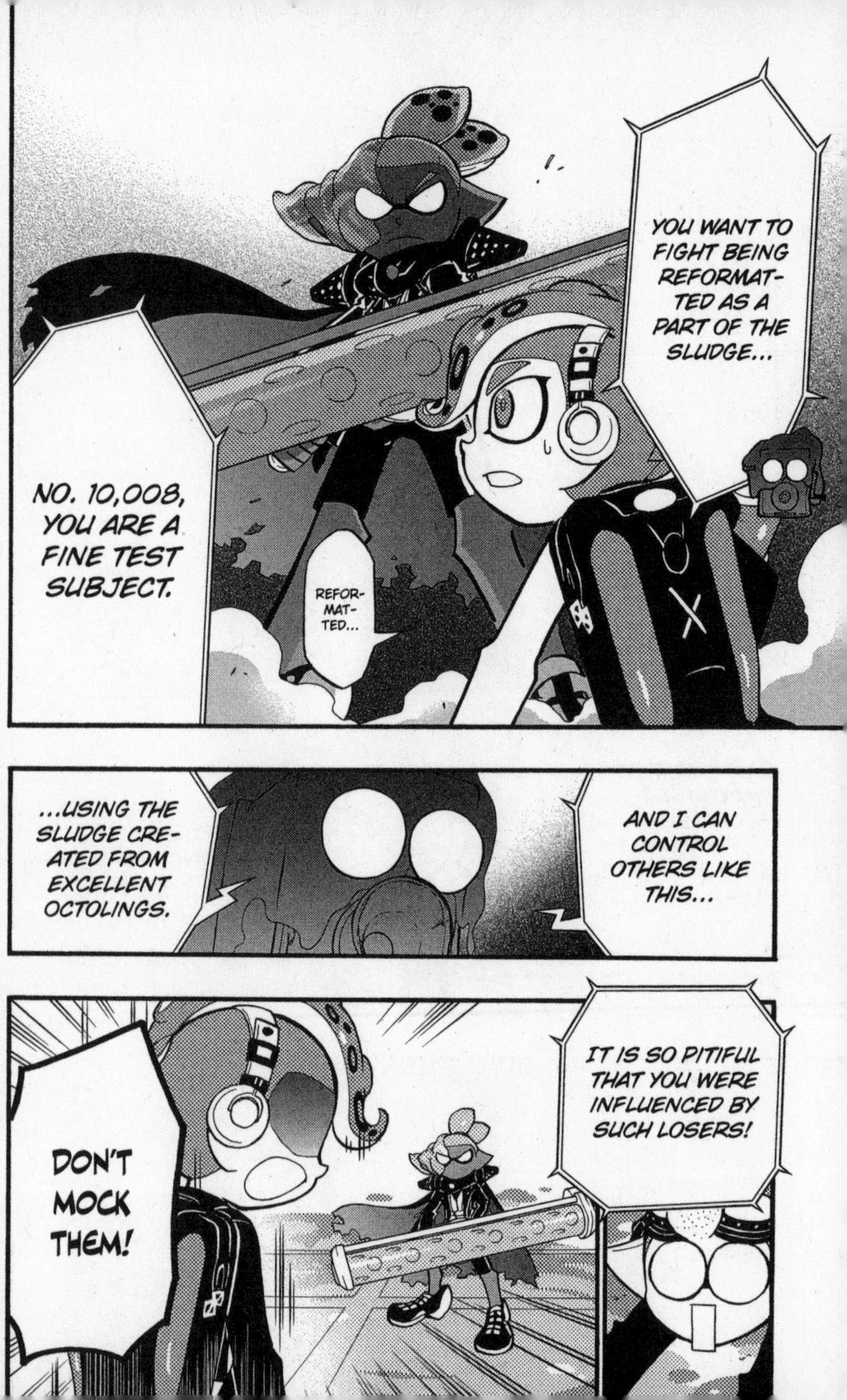
YOU WANT TO FIGHT BEING REFORMATTED AS A PART OF THE SLUDGE...
REFORMATTED...
NO. 10,008, YOU ARE A FINE TEST SUBJECT.
AND I CAN CONTROL OTHERS LIKE THIS...
...USING THE SLUDGE CREATED FROM EXCELLENT OCTOLINGS.
IT IS SO PITIFUL THAT YOU WERE INFLUENCED BY SUCH LOSERS!
DON'T MOCK THEM!

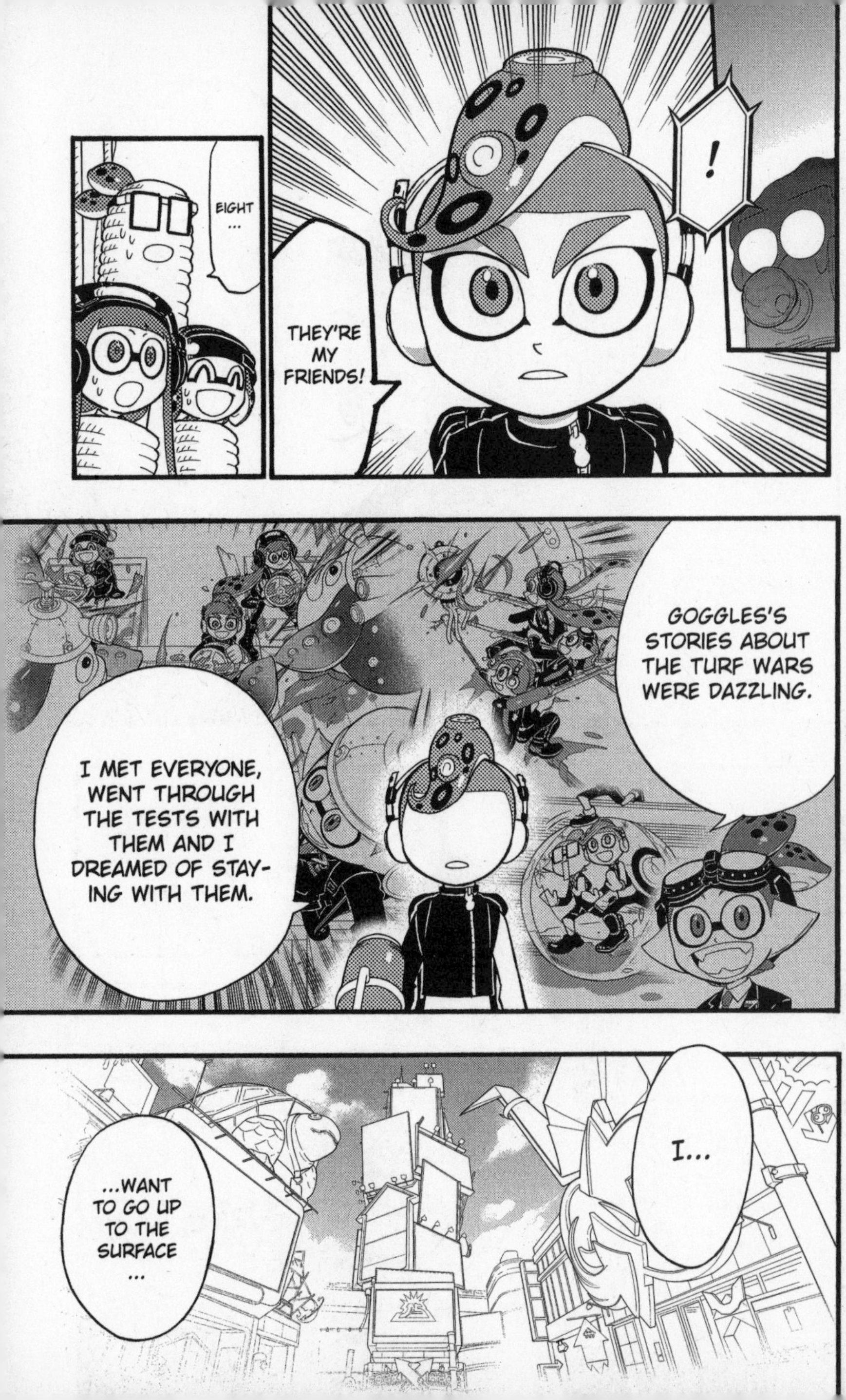
!
THEY'RE MY FRIENDS!
EIGHT ...
GOGGLES'S STORIES ABOUT THE TURF WARS WERE DAZZLING.
I MET EVERYONE, WENT THROUGH THE TESTS WITH THEM AND I DREAMED OF STAYING WITH THEM.
I...
...WANT TO GO UP TO THE SURFACE ...

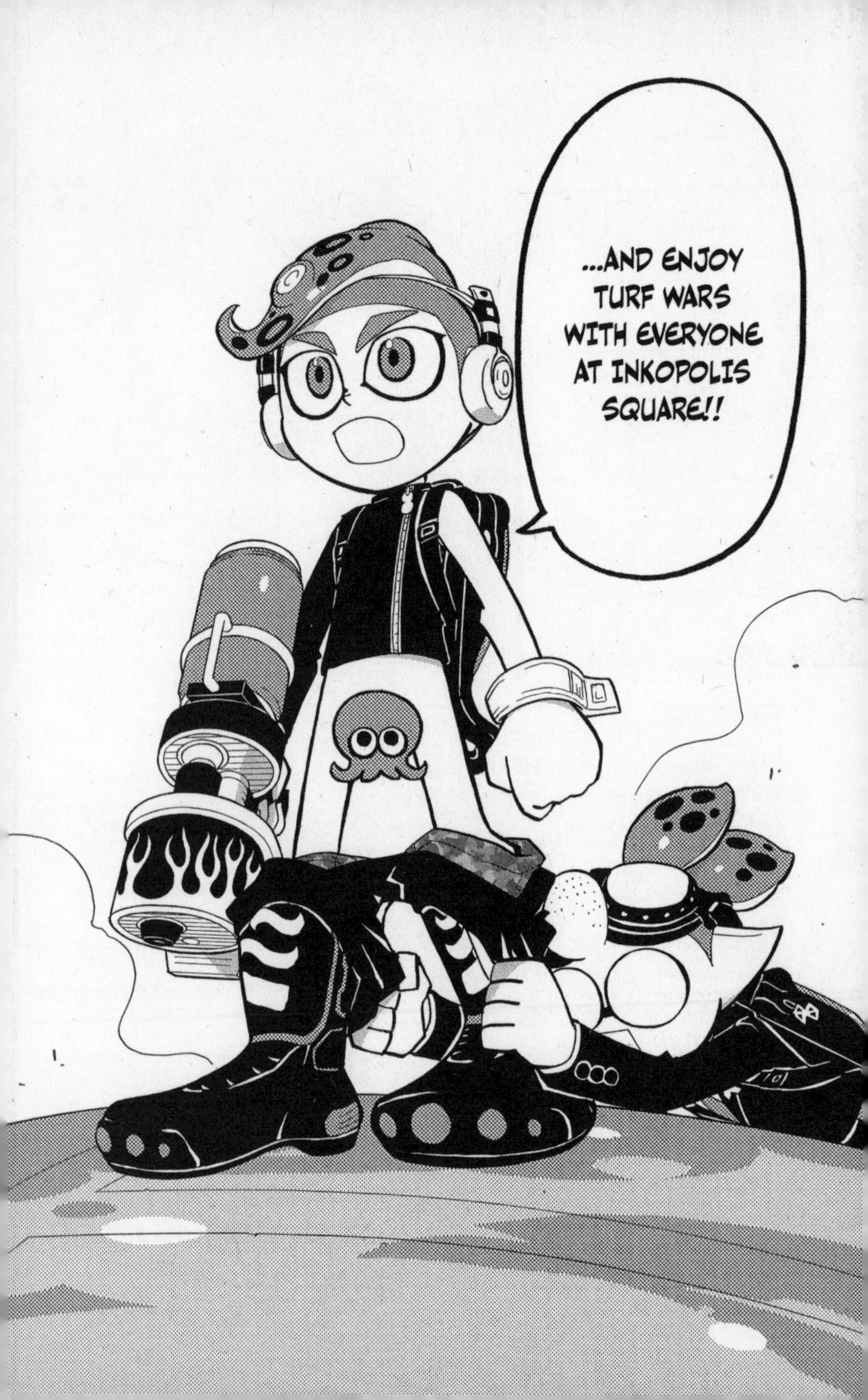
...AND ENJOY TURF WARS WITH EVERYONE AT INKOPOLIS SQUARE!!

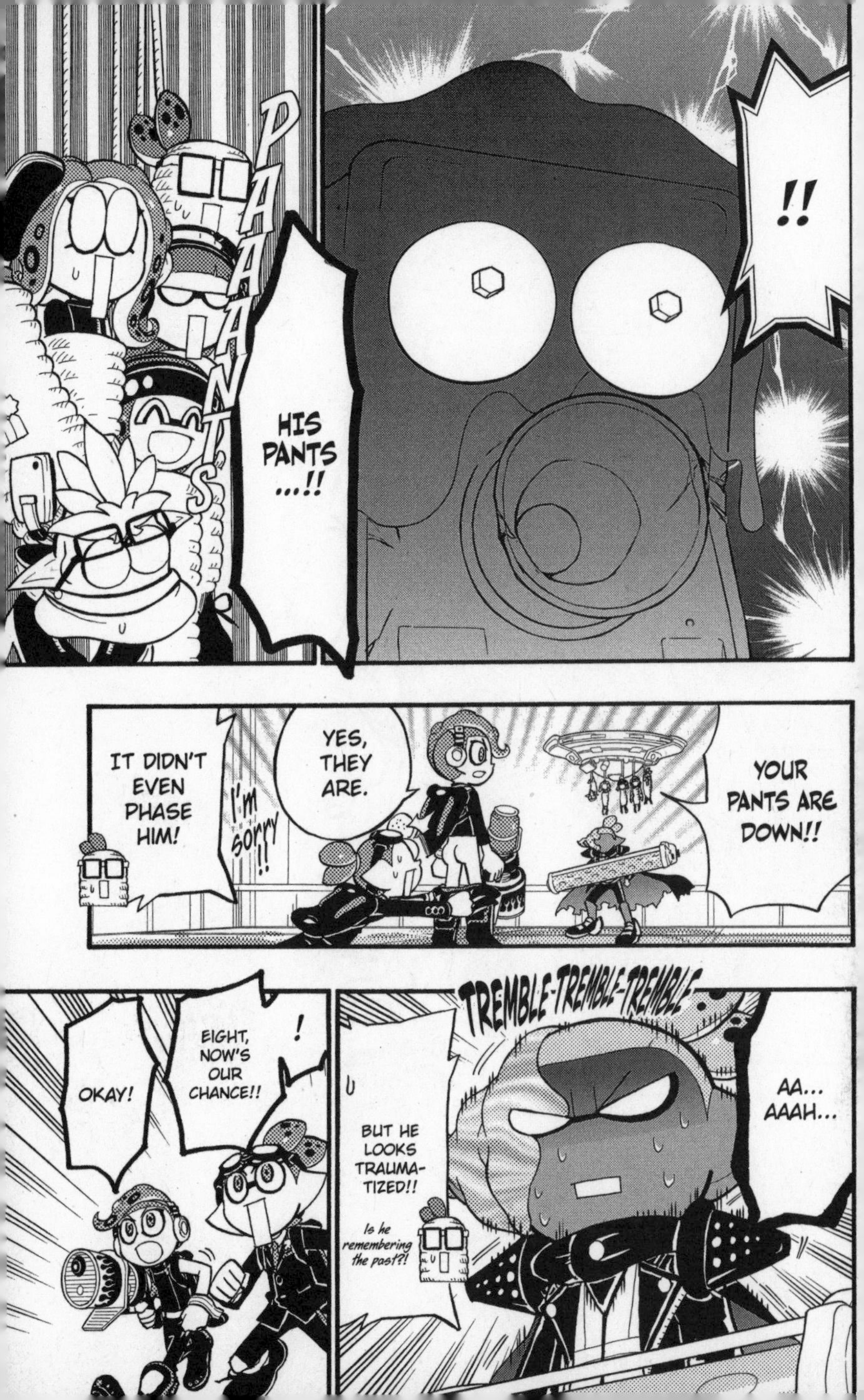
!!
PAAAANTS
HIS PANTS ...!!
YOUR PANTS ARE DOWN!!
YES, THEY ARE.
I'm sorry!!
IT DIDN'T EVEN PHASE HIM!
TREMBLE-TREMBLE-TREMBLE
AA... AAAH...
BUT HE LOOKS TRAUMA-TIZED!!
Is he remembering the past?!
!
EIGHT, NOW'S OUR CHANCE!!
OKAY!

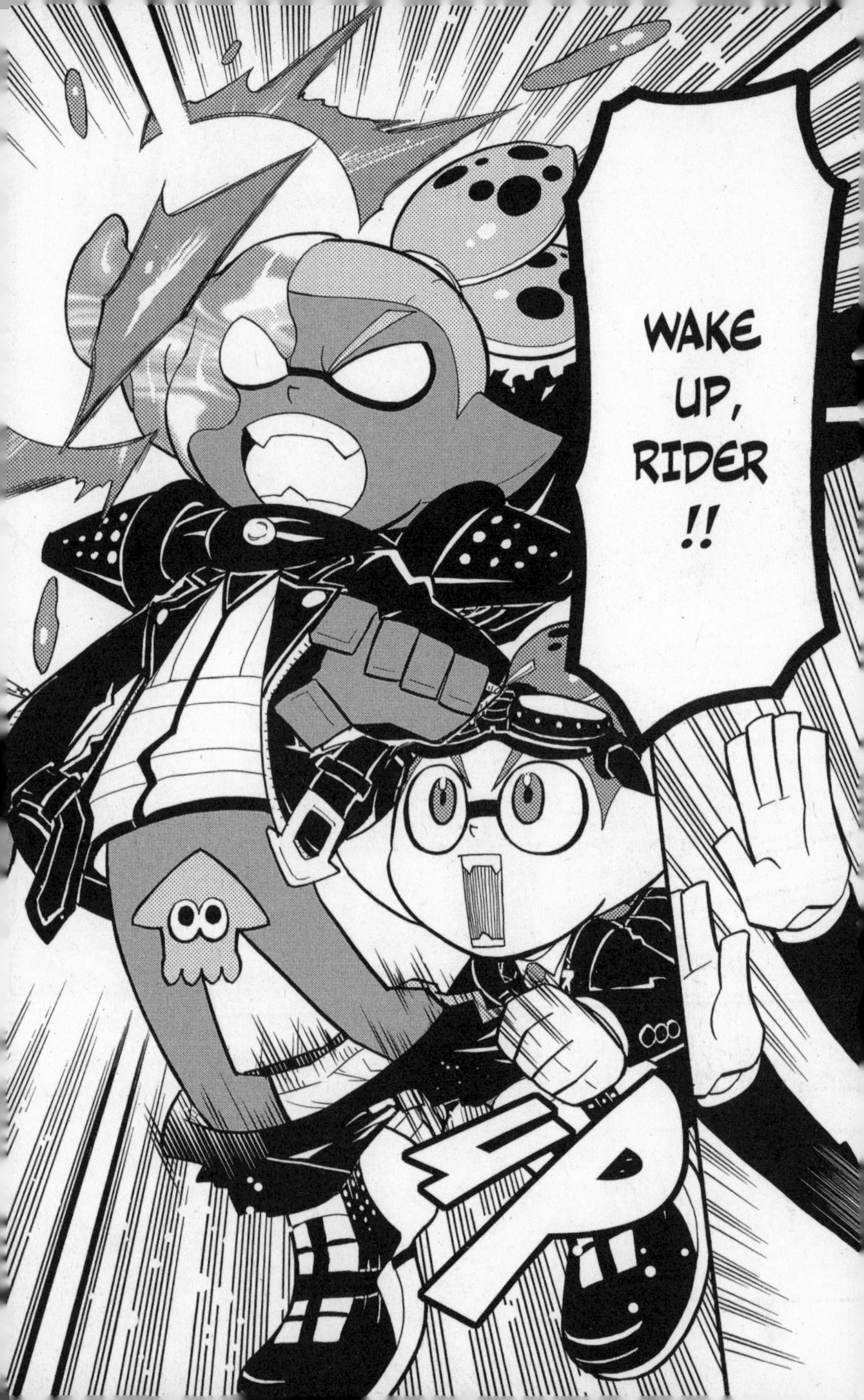
WAKE UP, RIDER!!

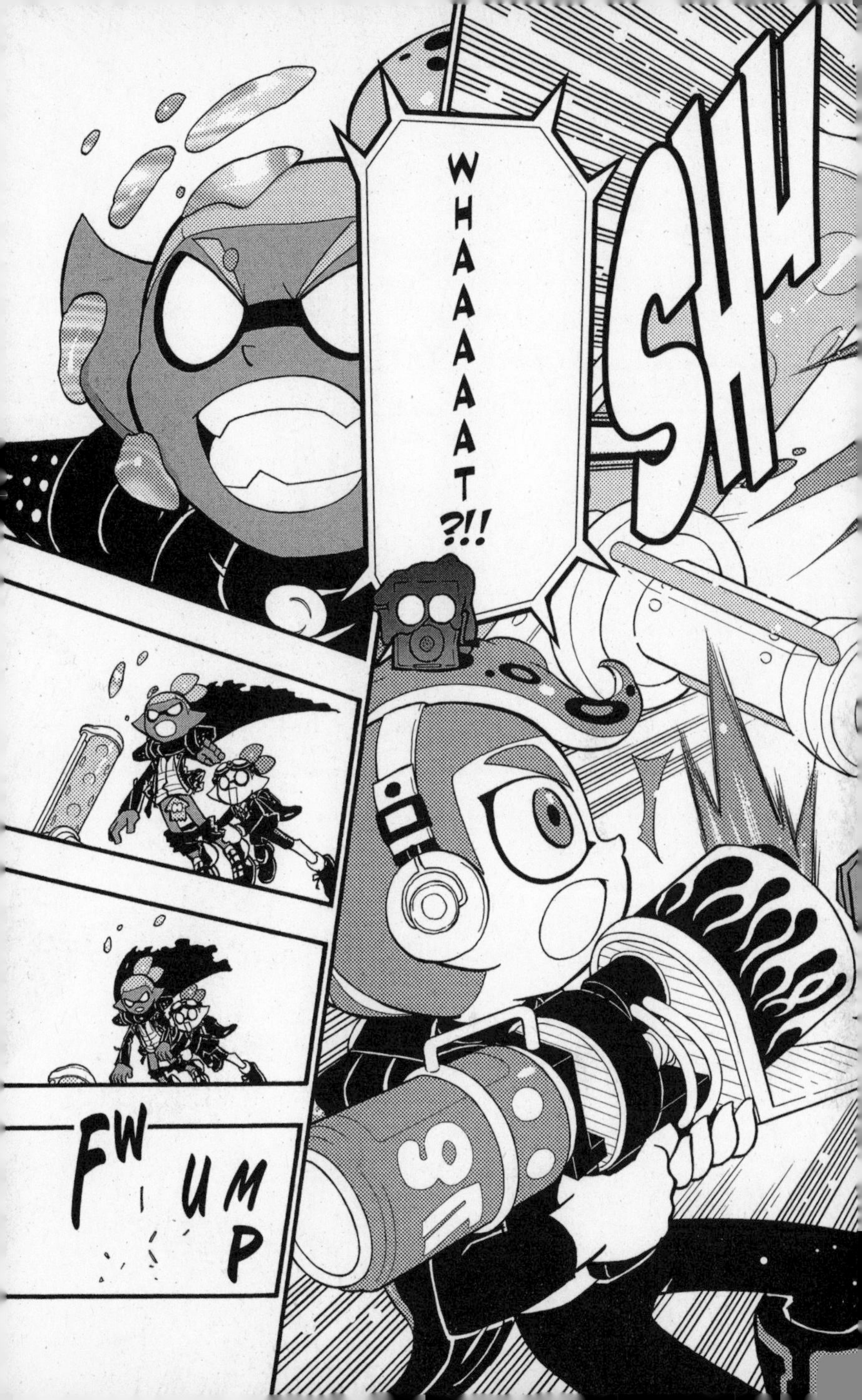
SH
WHAAAAAAT?!!
FWUMP

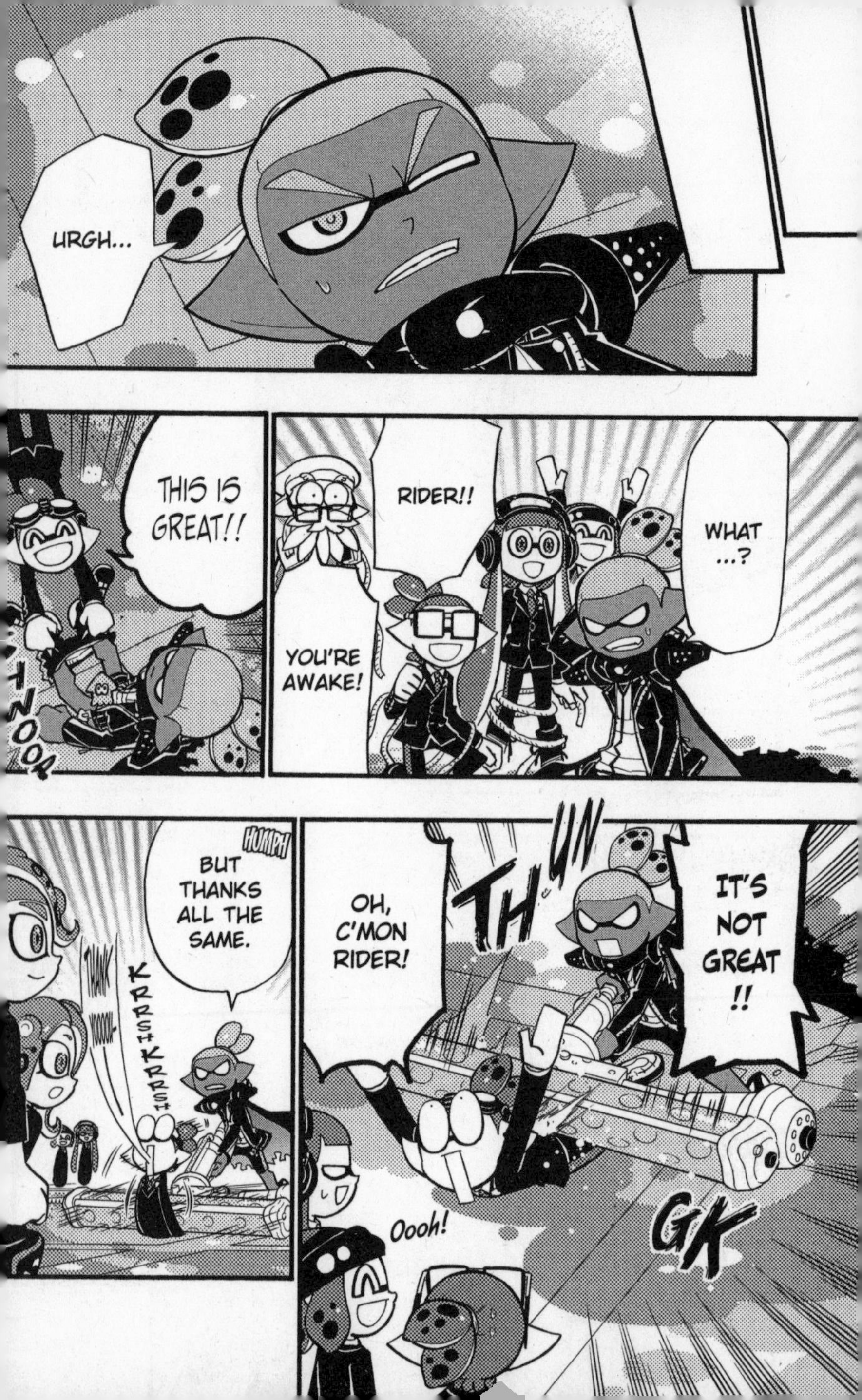
URGH...
WHAT ...?
RIDER!!
YOU'RE AWAKE!
THIS IS GREAT!!
THUN
IT'S NOT GREAT !!
OH, C'MON RIDER!
GK
Oooh!
HUMPH
BUT THANKS ALL THE SAME.
KRRSHKRRSH

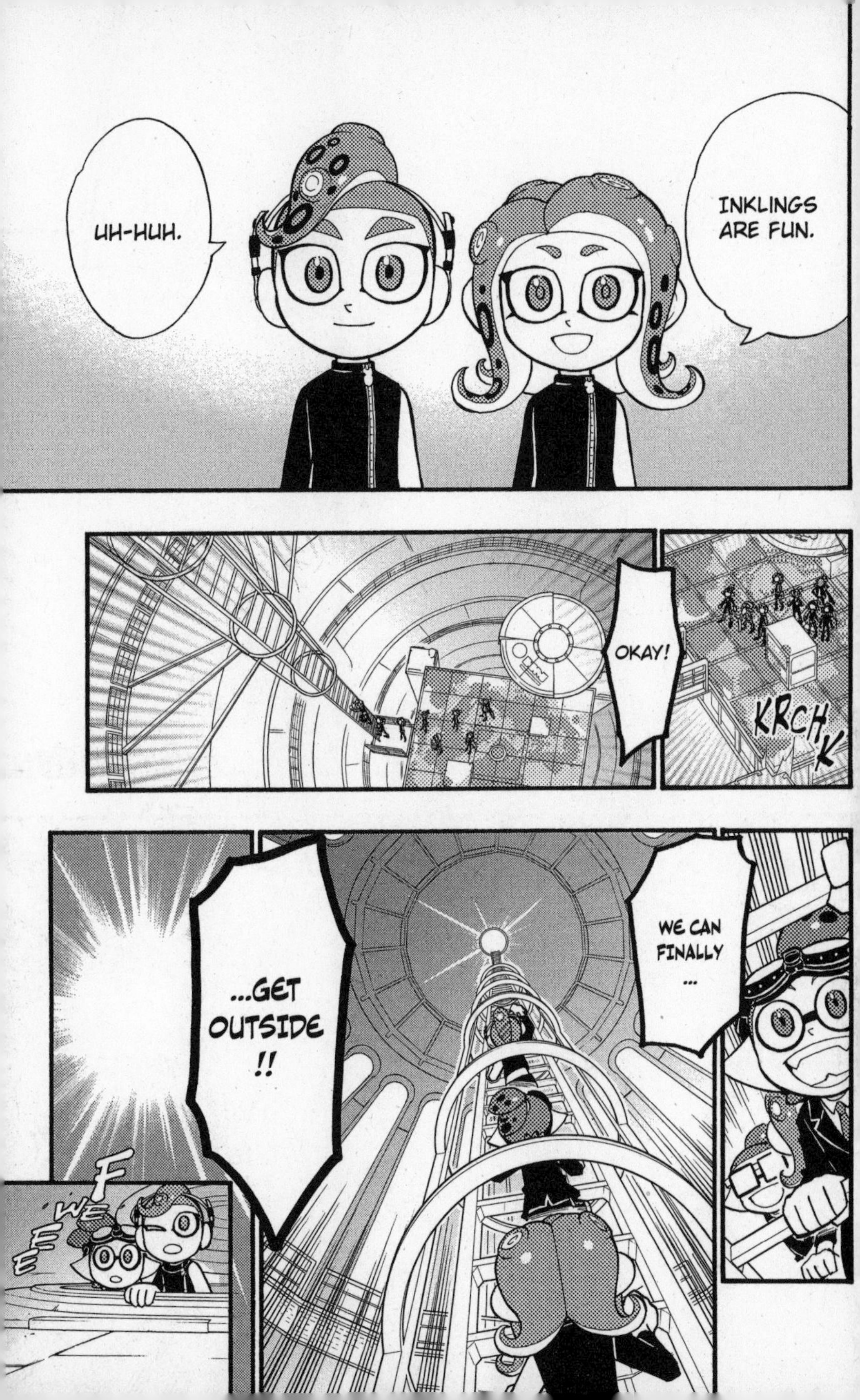
INKLINGS ARE FUN.
UH-HUH.
OKAY!
KRCHK
WE CAN FINALLY ...
...GET OUTSIDE !!
FWEEEE

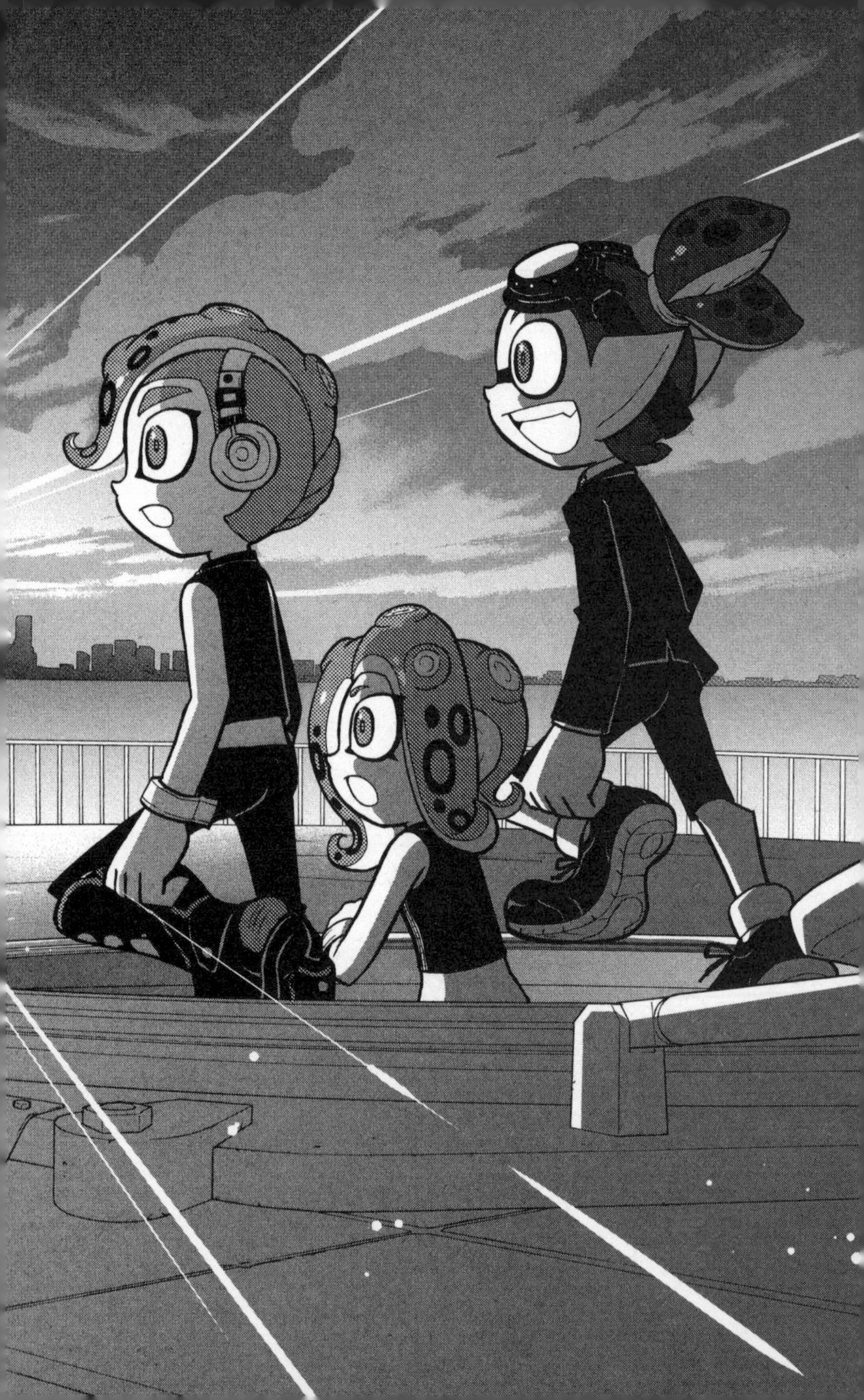

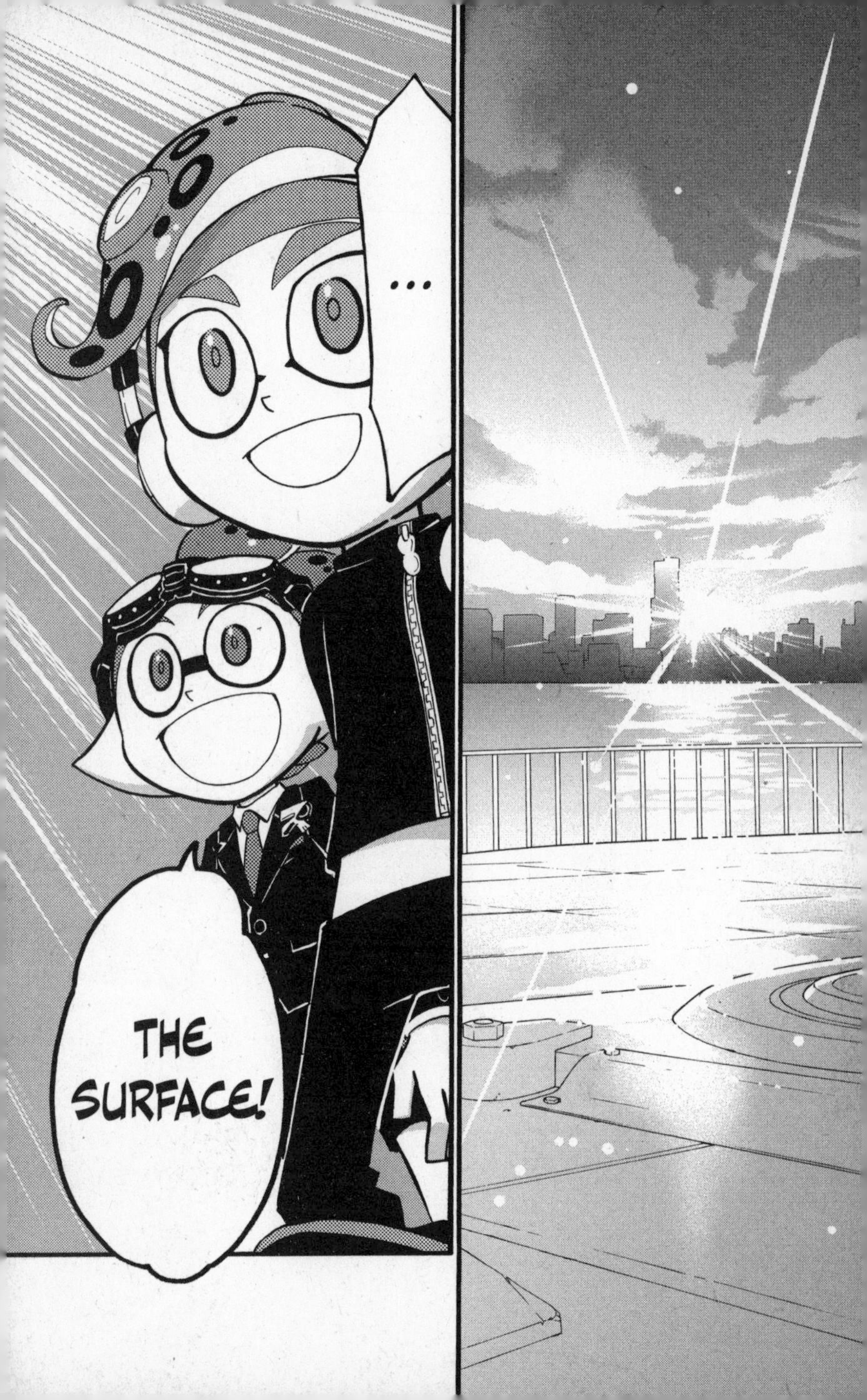
...
THE SURFACE!

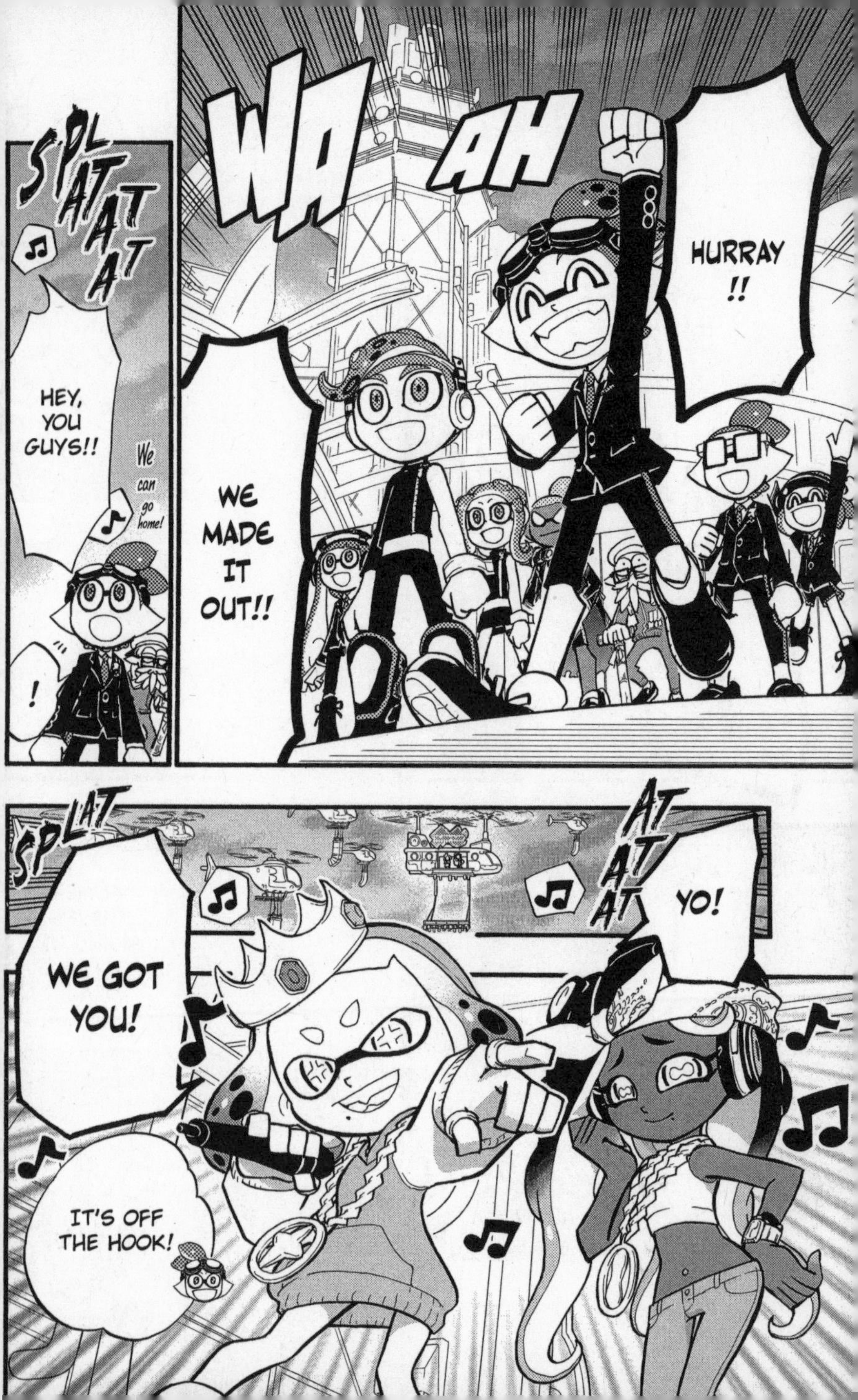
WA AH
HURRAY!!
WE MADE IT OUT!!
SPLAT AT AT AT
HEY, YOU GUYS!!
We can go home!
!
SPLAT AT AT AT
YO!
WE GOT YOU!
IT'S OFF THE HOOK!

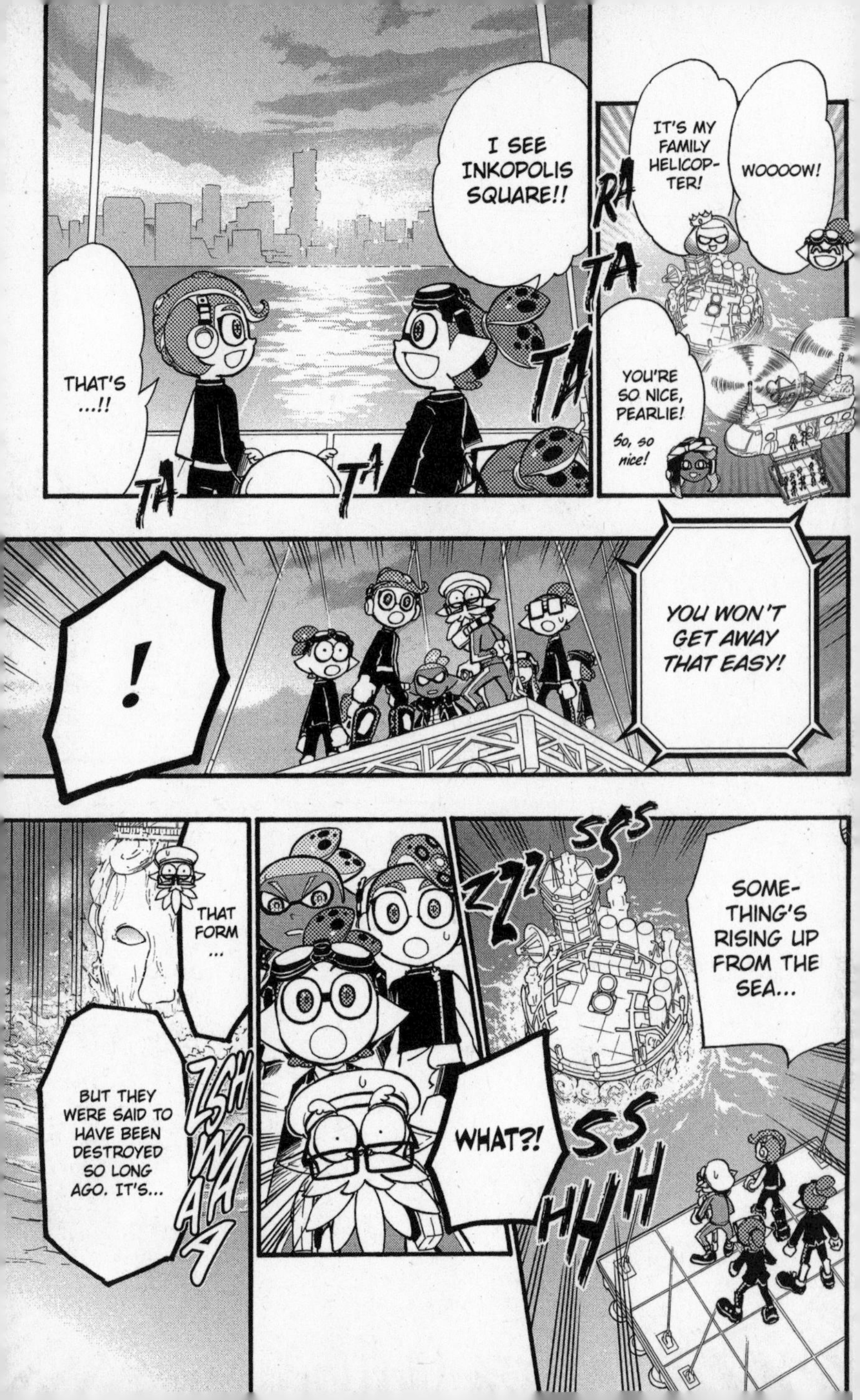
WOOOOW!
IT'S MY FAMILY HELICOPTER!
RA TA TA
YOU'RE SO NICE, PEARLIE!
So, so nice!
I SEE INKOPOLIS SQUARE!!
THAT'S ...!!
TA TA
YOU WON'T GET AWAY THAT EASY!
!
SOME-THING'S RISING UP FROM THE SEA...
SSS
ZZZ
SSHHH
WHAT?!
THAT FORM ...
BUT THEY WERE SAID TO HAVE BEEN DESTROYED SO LONG AGO. IT'S...
ZSHWAAAA

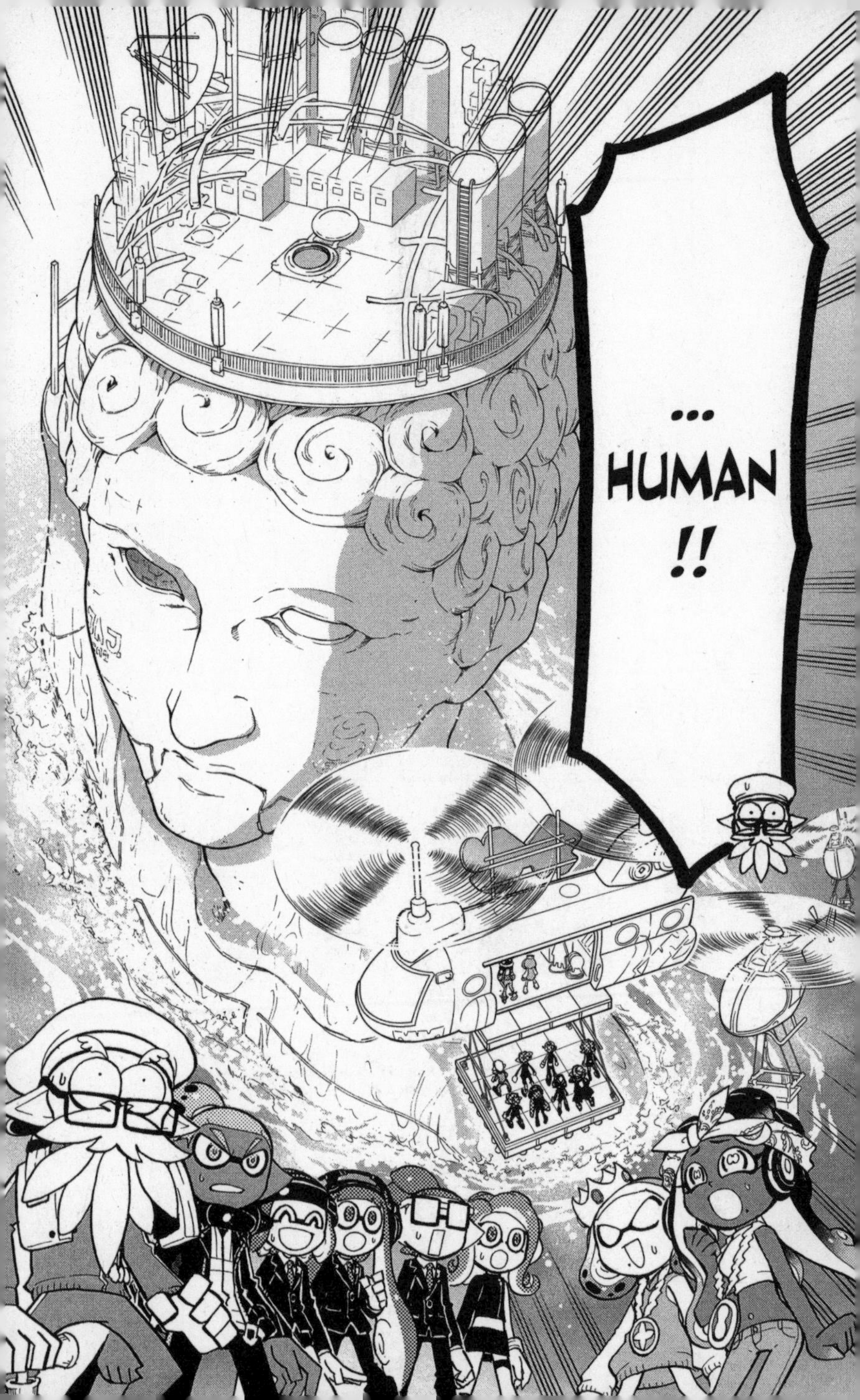
...HUMAN!!

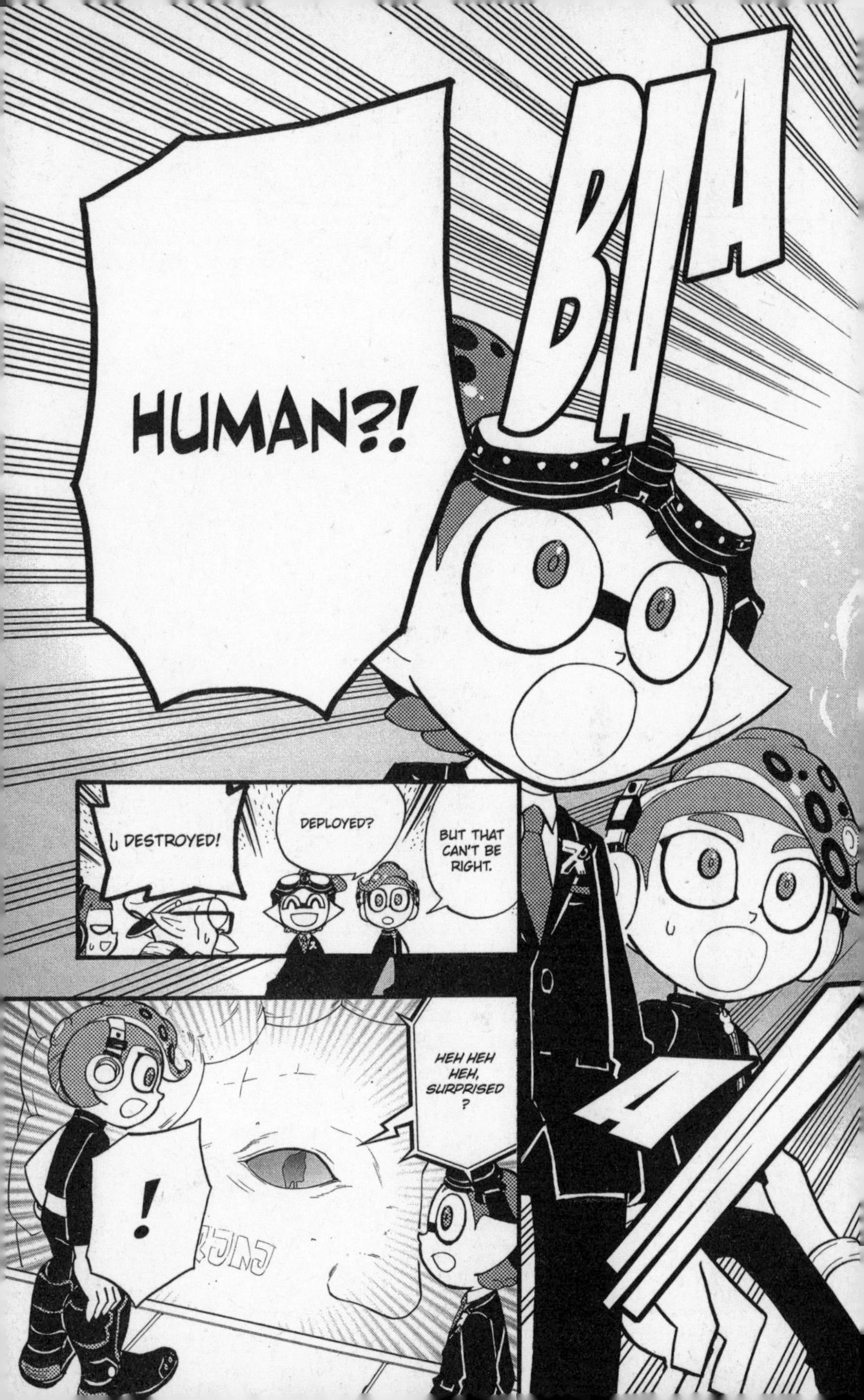
HUMAN?!
BUT THAT CAN'T BE RIGHT.
DEPLOYED?
DESTROYED!
HEH HEH HEH, SURPRISED?
!

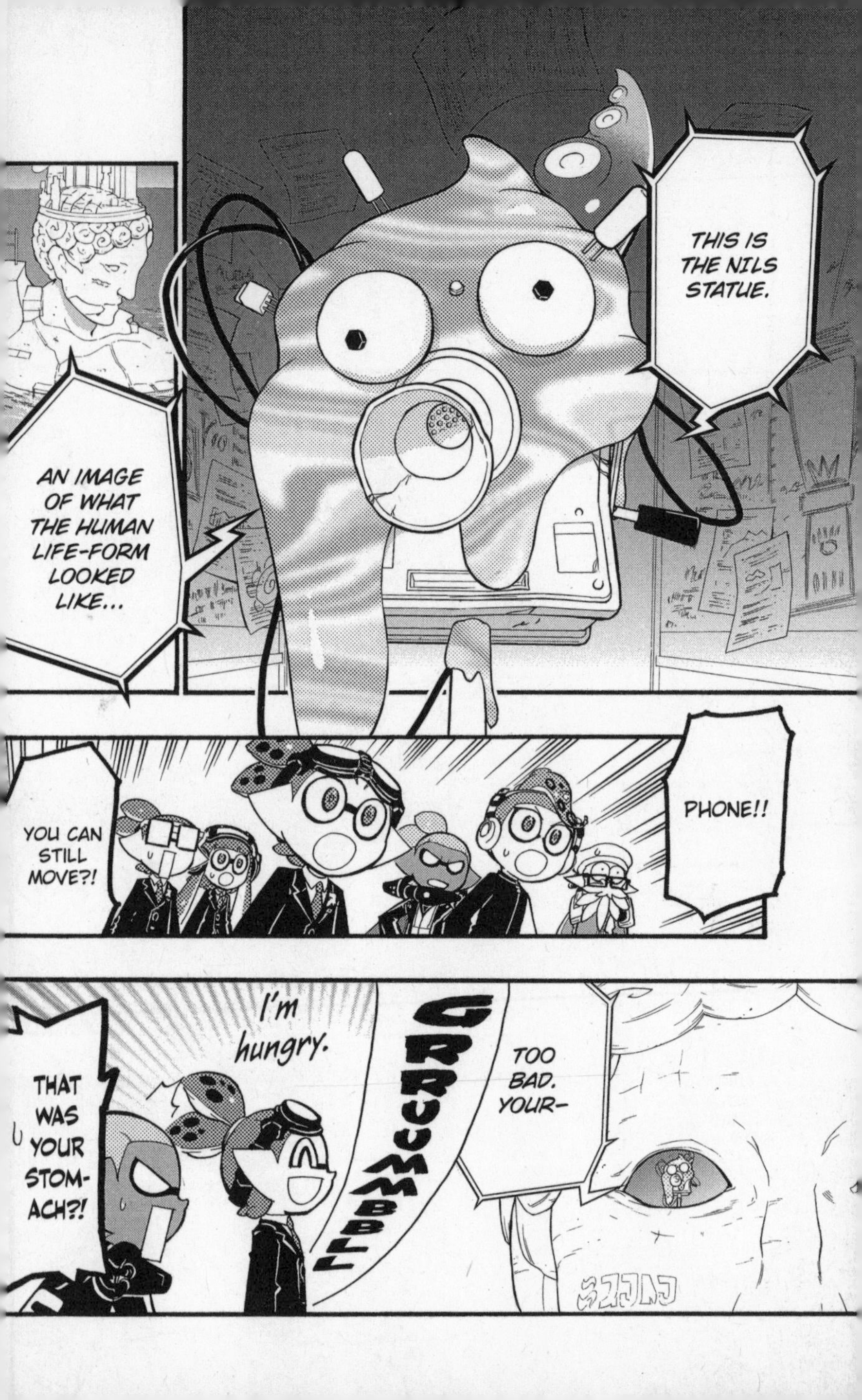
THIS IS THE NILS STATUE.
AN IMAGE OF WHAT THE HUMAN LIFE-FORM LOOKED LIKE...
PHONE!!
YOU CAN STILL MOVE?!
TOO BAD. YOUR-
GRRUUMMBBLL
I'm hungry.
THAT WAS YOUR STOMACH?!

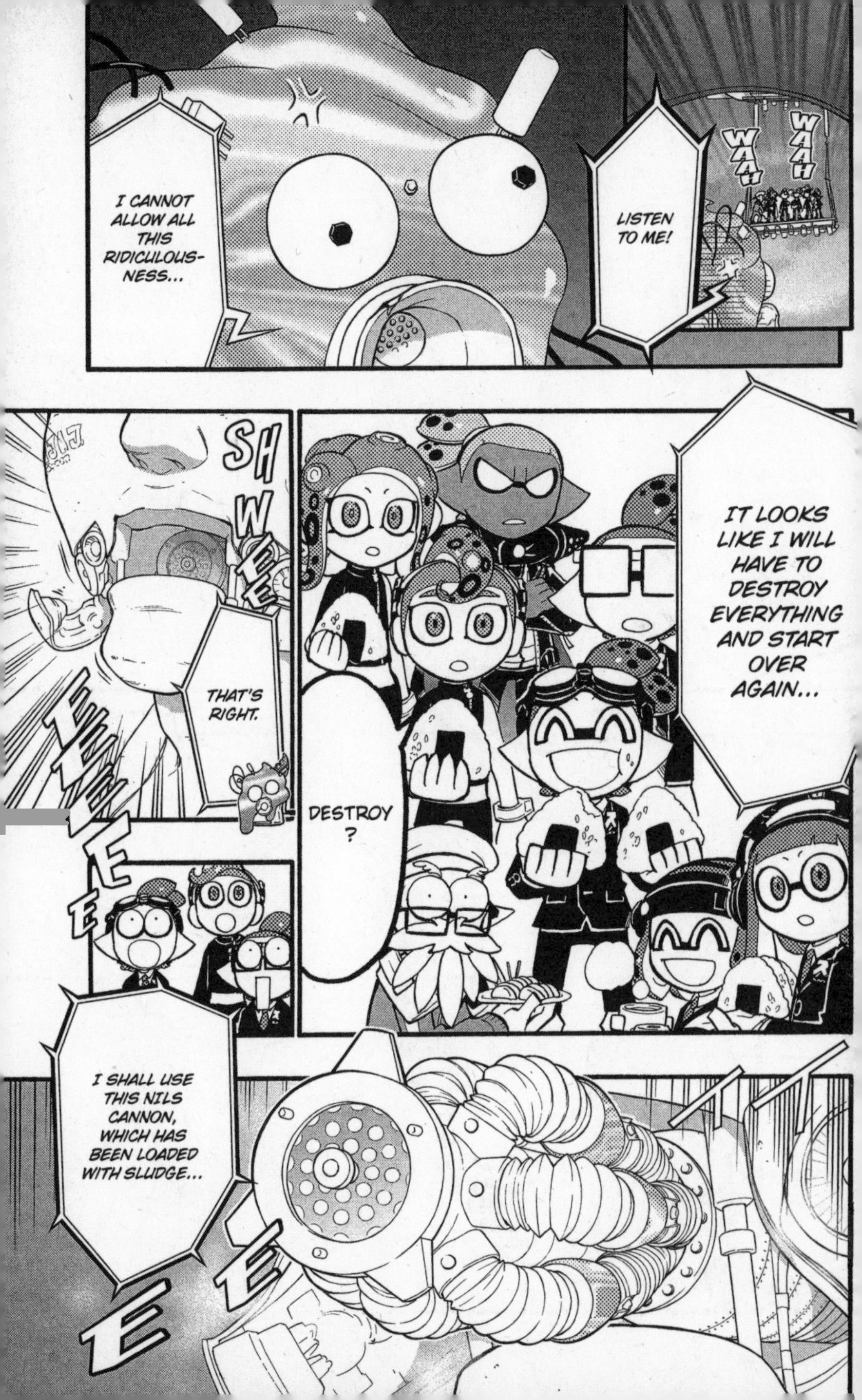
WAAH
WAAH
LISTEN TO ME!
I CANNOT ALLOW ALL THIS RIDICULOUSNESS...
IT LOOKS LIKE I WILL HAVE TO DESTROY EVERYTHING AND START OVER AGAIN...
DESTROY?
SHWEE
THAT'S RIGHT.
EEEEE
I SHALL USE THIS NILS CANNON, WHICH HAS BEEN LOADED WITH SLUDGE...
EEE

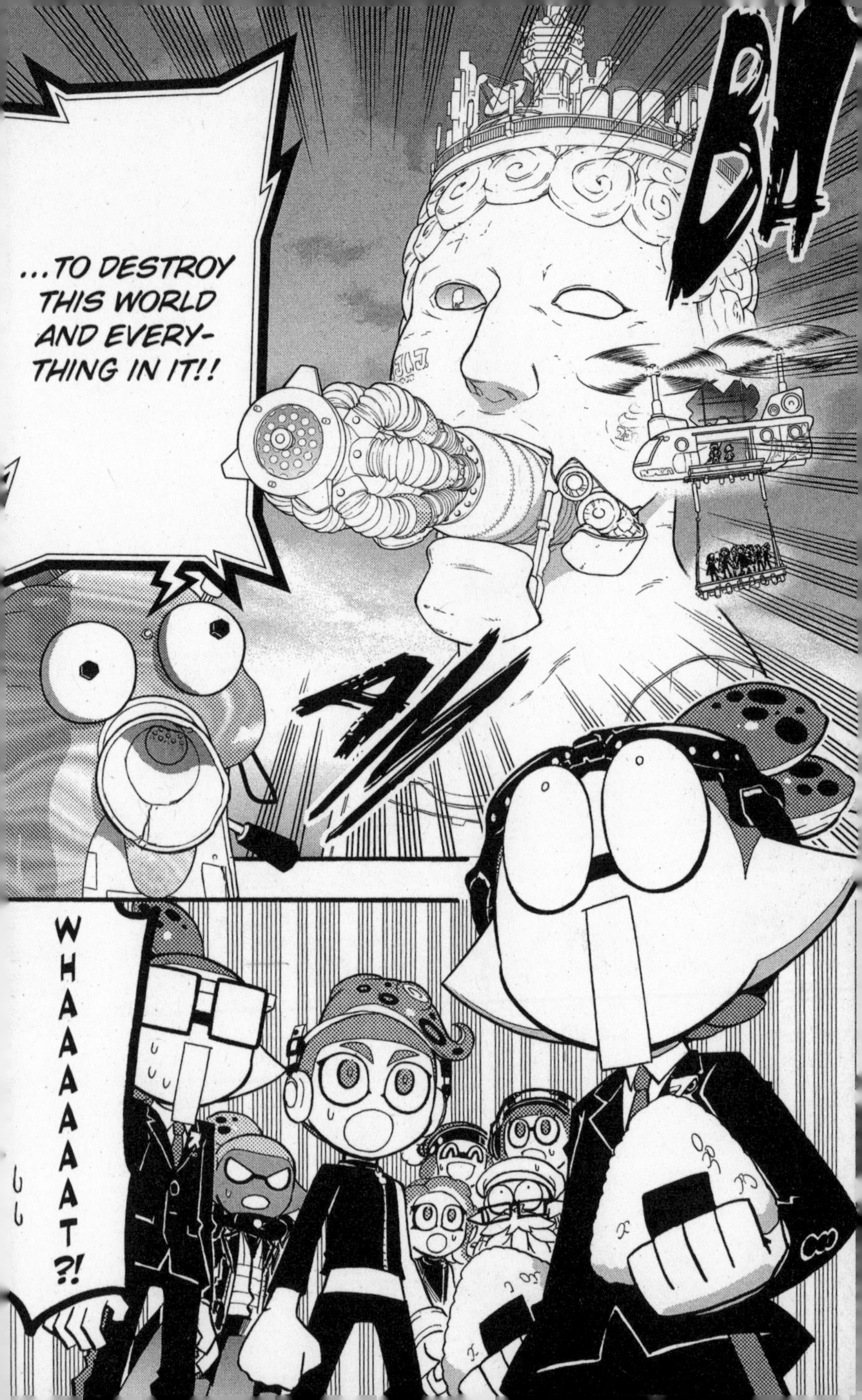
...TO DESTROY THIS WORLD AND EVERY-THING IN IT!!
WHAAAAAAAT?!

SPLATOON VOLUME 7 END / CONTINUED IN VOLUME 8

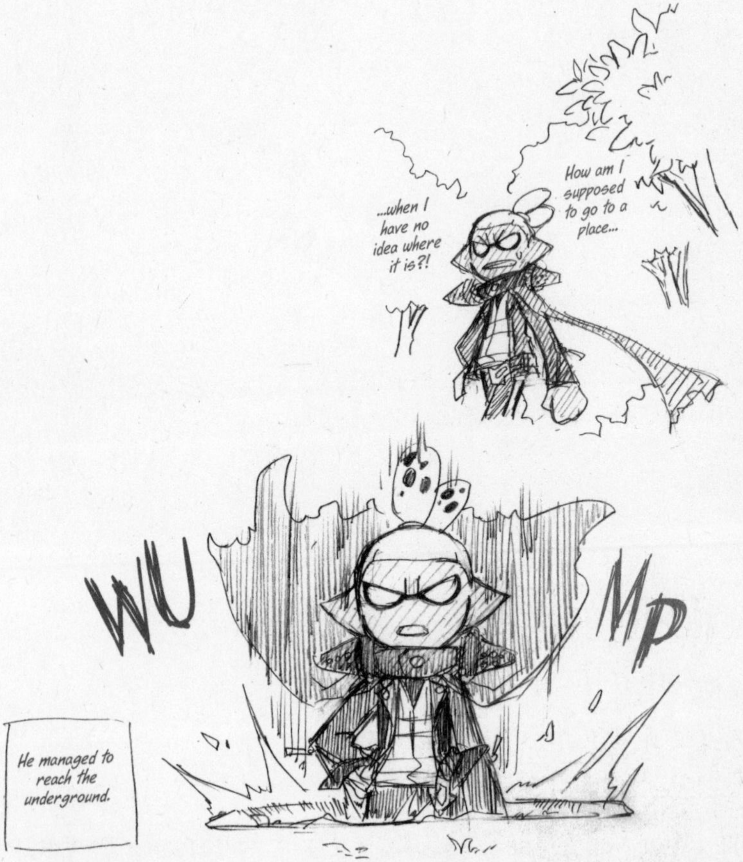
How am I supposed to go to a place...
...when I have no idea where it is?!
WUMP
He managed to reach the underground.

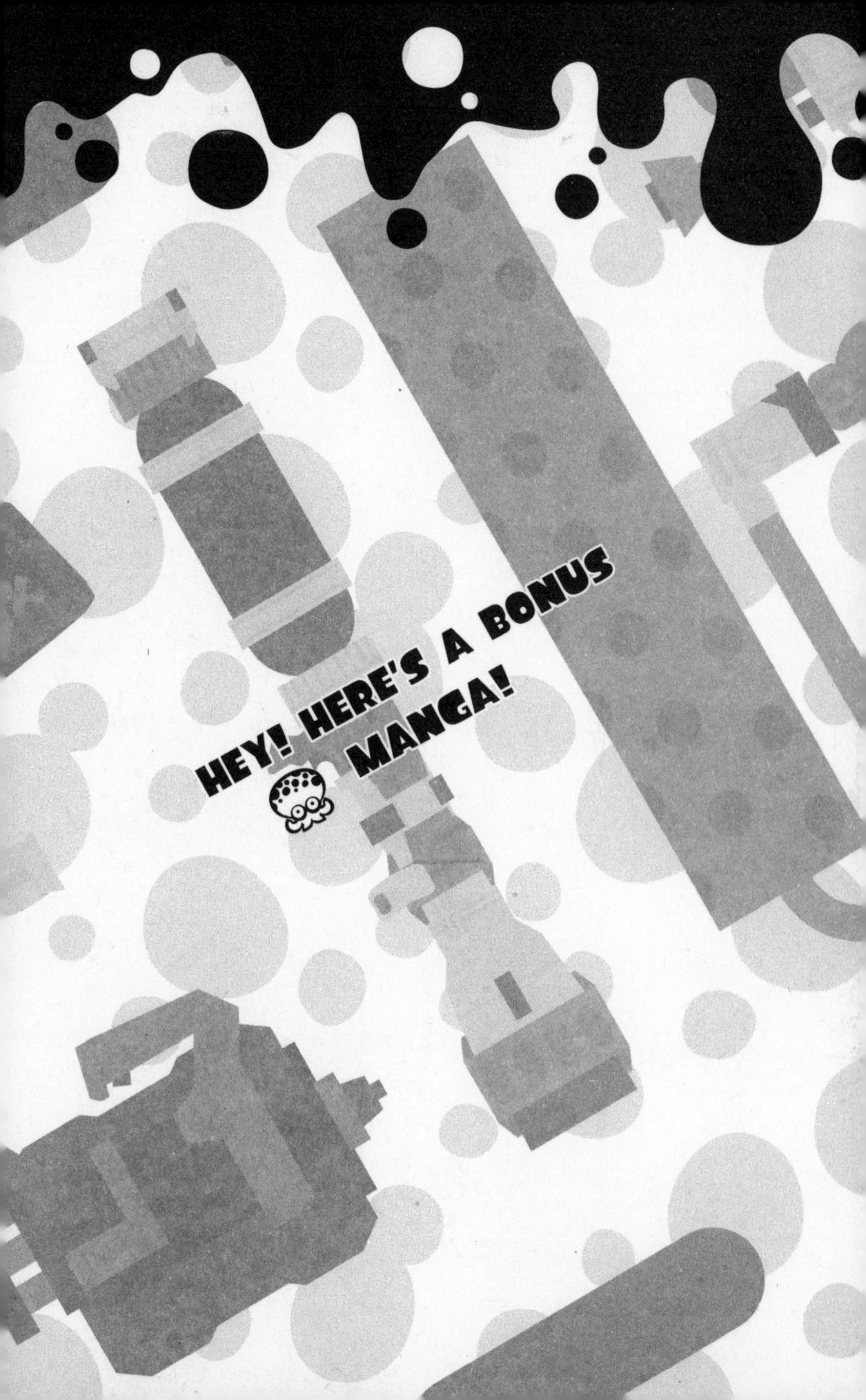
HEY! HERE'S A BONUS MANGA!

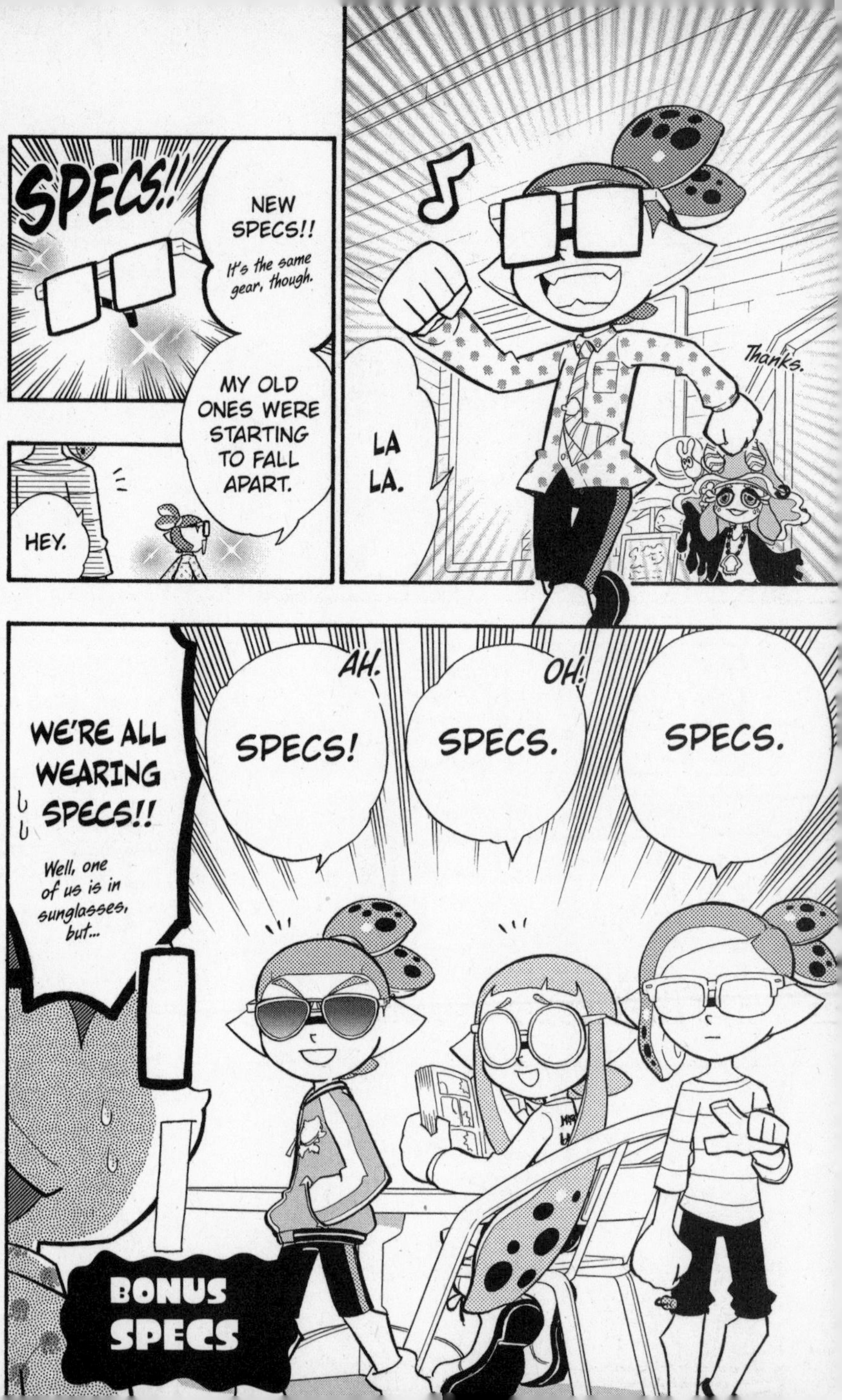
Thanks.
LA LA.
SPECS!!
NEW SPECS!!
It's the same gear, though.
MY OLD ONES WERE STARTING TO FALL APART.
HEY.
SPECS.
OH!
SPECS.
AH.
SPECS!
WE'RE ALL WEARING SPECS!!
Well, one of us is in sunglasses, but...
BONUS SPECS

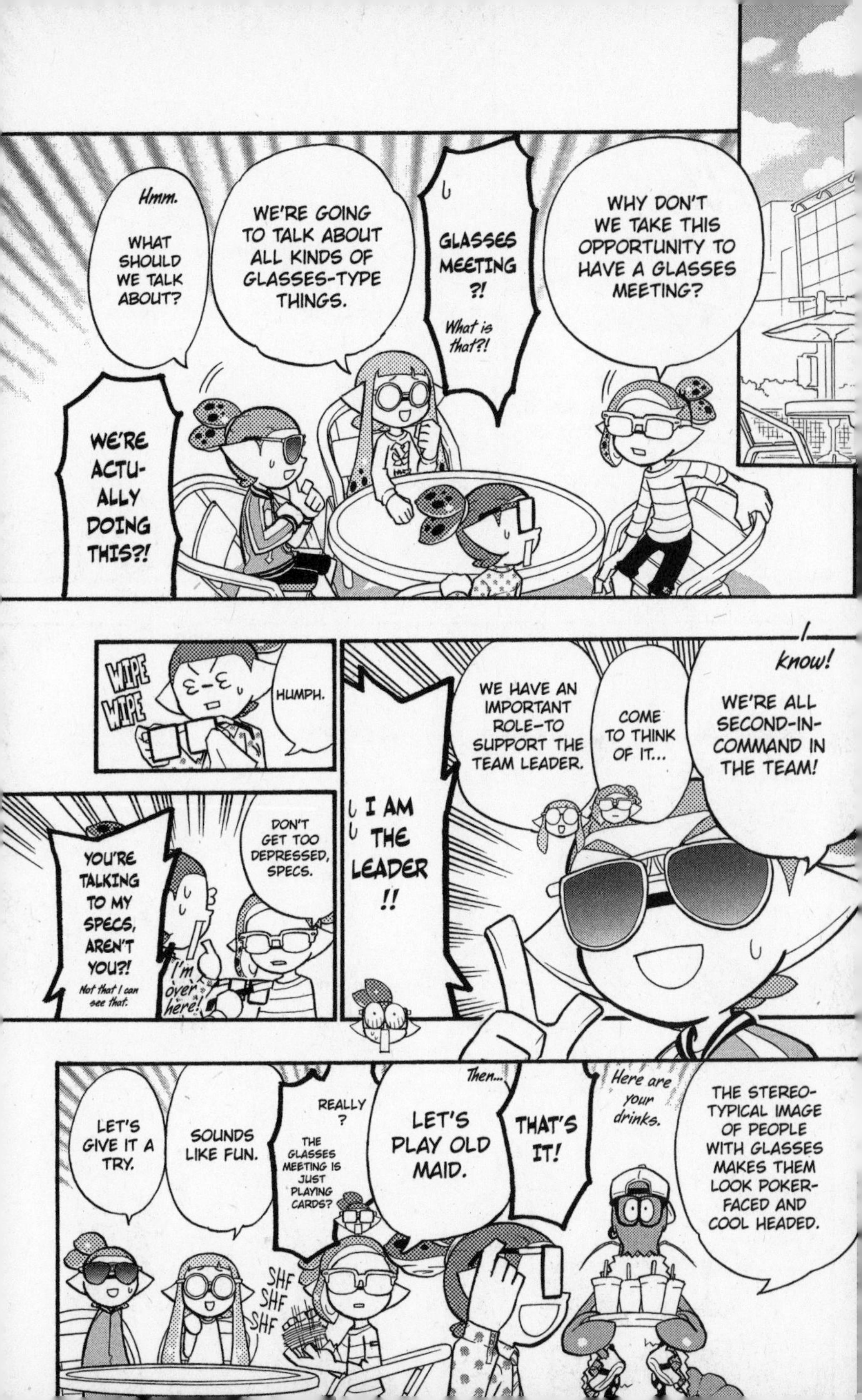
WHY DON'T WE TAKE THIS OPPORTUNITY TO HAVE A GLASSES MEETING?
GLASSES MEETING ?!
What is that?!
WE'RE GOING TO TALK ABOUT ALL KINDS OF GLASSES-TYPE THINGS.
Hmm.
WHAT SHOULD WE TALK ABOUT?
WE'RE ACTU-ALLY DOING THIS?!
I— know!
WE'RE ALL SECOND-IN-COMMAND IN THE TEAM!
COME TO THINK OF IT...
WE HAVE AN IMPORTANT ROLE—TO SUPPORT THE TEAM LEADER.
I AM THE LEADER !!
HUMPH.
WIPE WIPE
DON'T GET TOO DEPRESSED, SPECS.
YOU'RE TALKING TO MY SPECS, AREN'T YOU?!
Not that I can see that.
I'm over here!
Here are your drinks.
THE STEREO-TYPICAL IMAGE OF PEOPLE WITH GLASSES MAKES THEM LOOK POKER-FACED AND COOL HEADED.
THAT'S IT!
Then...
LET'S PLAY OLD MAID.
REALLY?
THE GLASSES MEETING IS JUST PLAYING CARDS?
SHF SHF SHF
SOUNDS LIKE FUN.
LET'S GIVE IT A TRY.

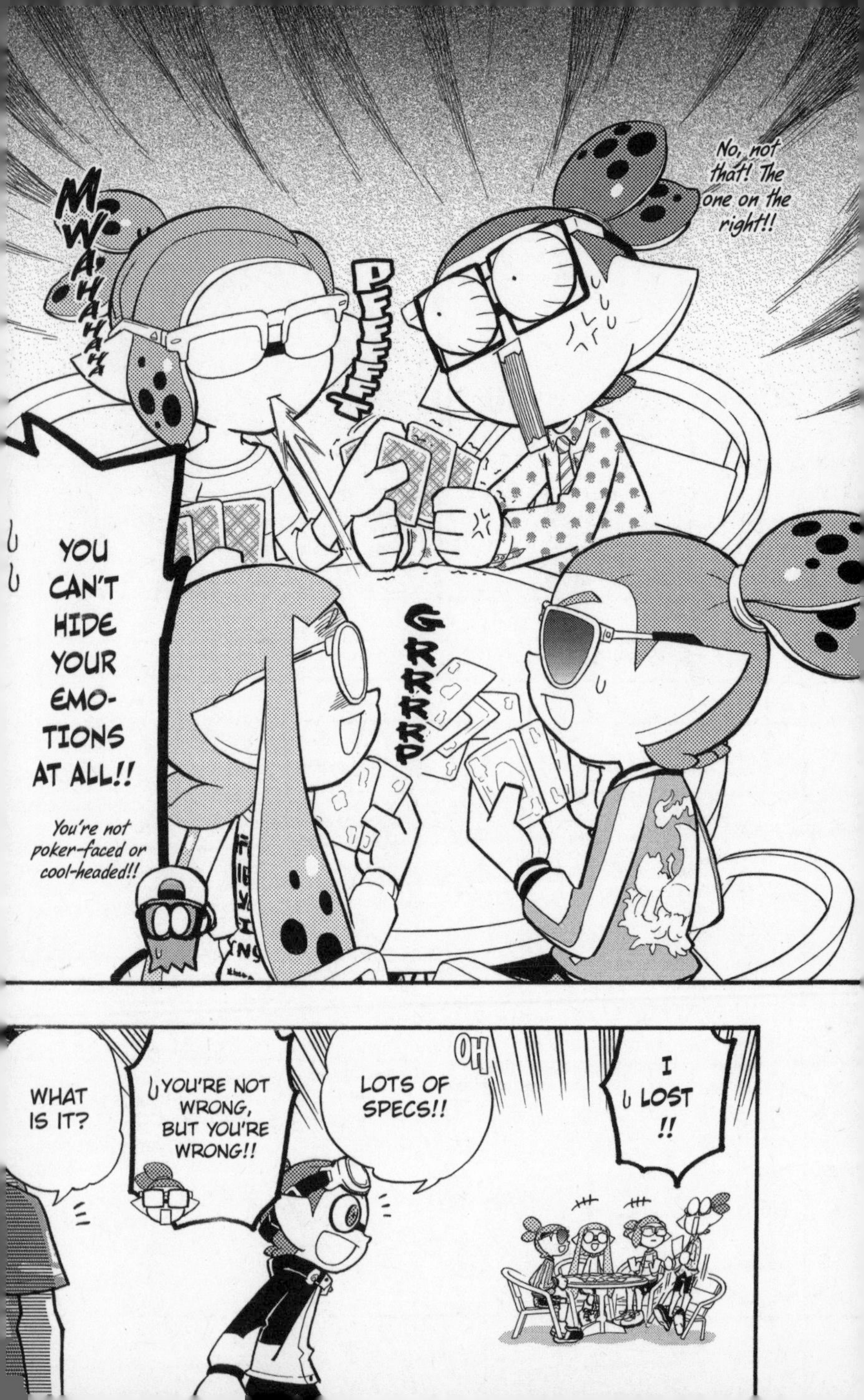
No, not that! The one on the right!!
PFFFFFT
MWAHAHAHAHA
GRRRRP
YOU CAN'T HIDE YOUR EMOTIONS AT ALL!!
You're not poker-faced or cool-headed!!
I LOST!!
OH
LOTS OF SPECS!!
YOU'RE NOT WRONG, BUT YOU'RE WRONG!!
WHAT IS IT?

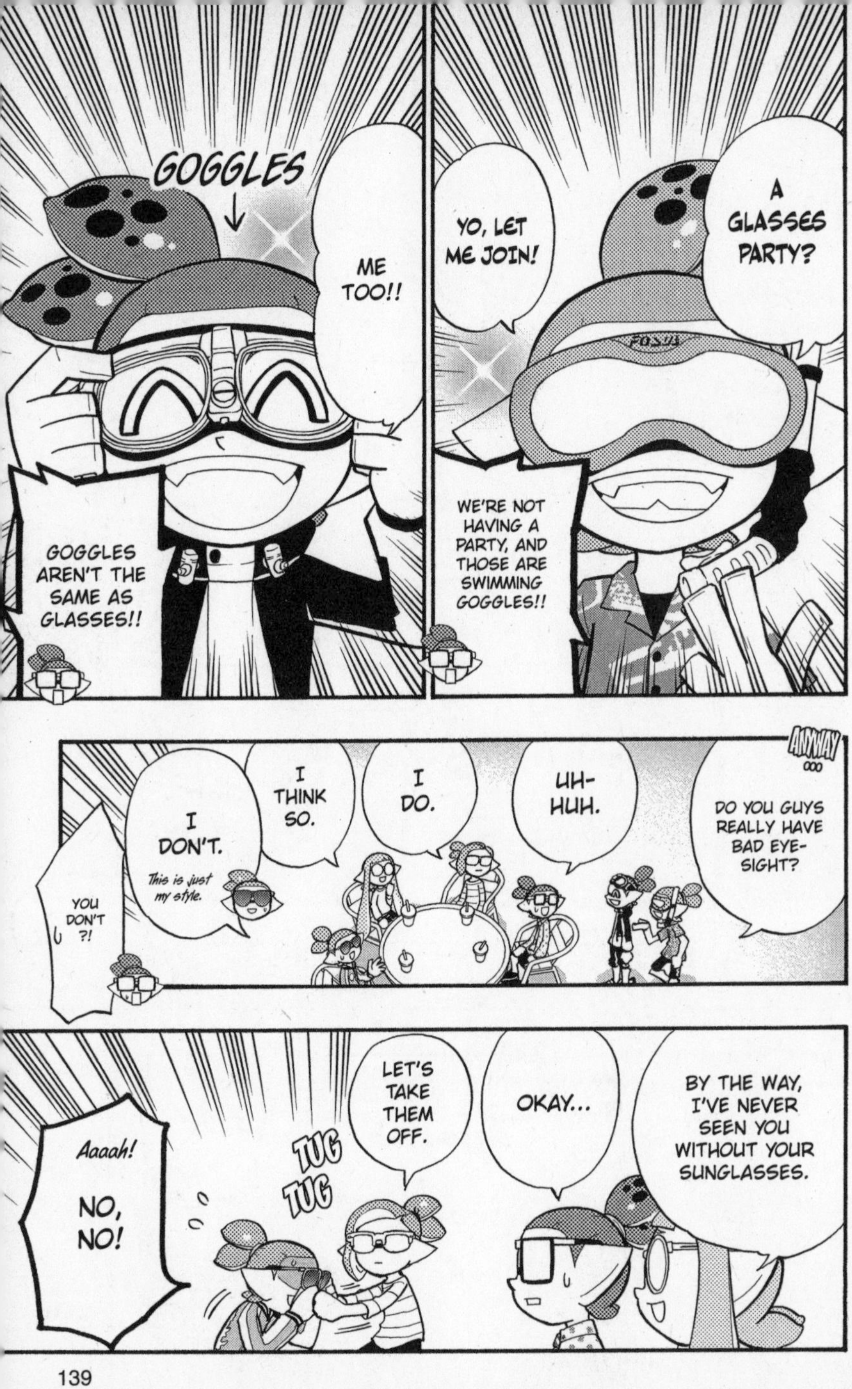
A GLASSES PARTY?
YO, LET ME JOIN!
WE'RE NOT HAVING A PARTY, AND THOSE ARE SWIMMING GOGGLES!!
ME TOO!!
GOGGLES
GOGGLES AREN'T THE SAME AS GLASSES!!
ANYWAY...
DO YOU GUYS REALLY HAVE BAD EYE-SIGHT?
UH-HUH.
I DO.
I THINK SO.
I DON'T.
This is just my style.
YOU DON'T?!
BY THE WAY, I'VE NEVER SEEN YOU WITHOUT YOUR SUNGLASSES.
OKAY...
LET'S TAKE THEM OFF.
TUG TUG
Aaaah!
NO, NO!

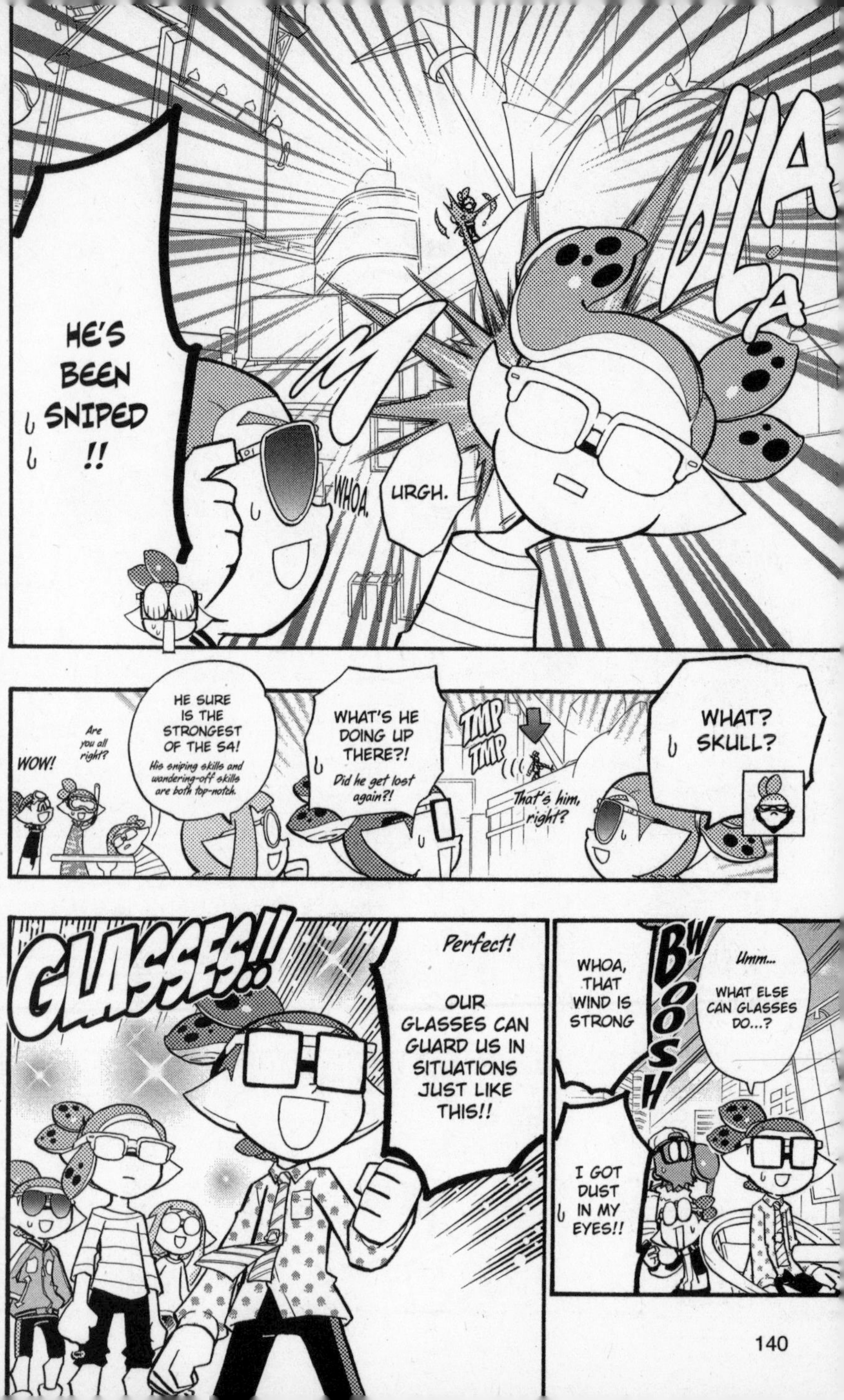
BLAM
URGH.
WHOA.
HE'S BEEN SNIPED!!
WHAT? SKULL?
That's him, right?
TMP TMP
WHAT'S HE DOING UP THERE?! Did he get lost again?!
HE SURE IS THE STRONGEST OF THE S4! His sniping skills and wandering-off skills are both top-notch.
Are you all right?
WOW!
Umm... WHAT ELSE CAN GLASSES DO...?
BWOOOSH
WHOA, THAT WIND IS STRONG
I GOT DUST IN MY EYES!!
Perfect!
OUR GLASSES CAN GUARD US IN SITUATIONS JUST LIKE THIS!!
GLASSES!!

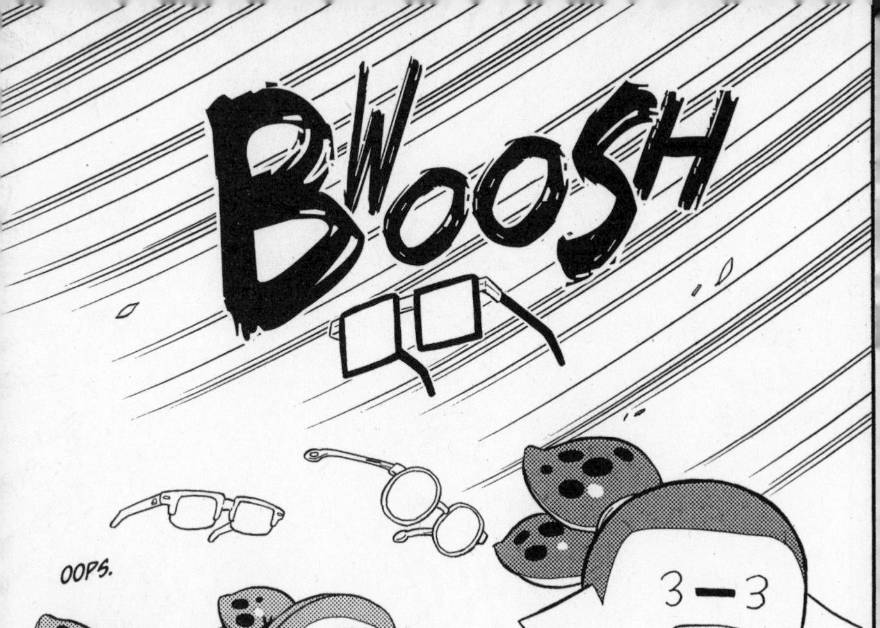
BWOOSH
OOPS.
SHFF

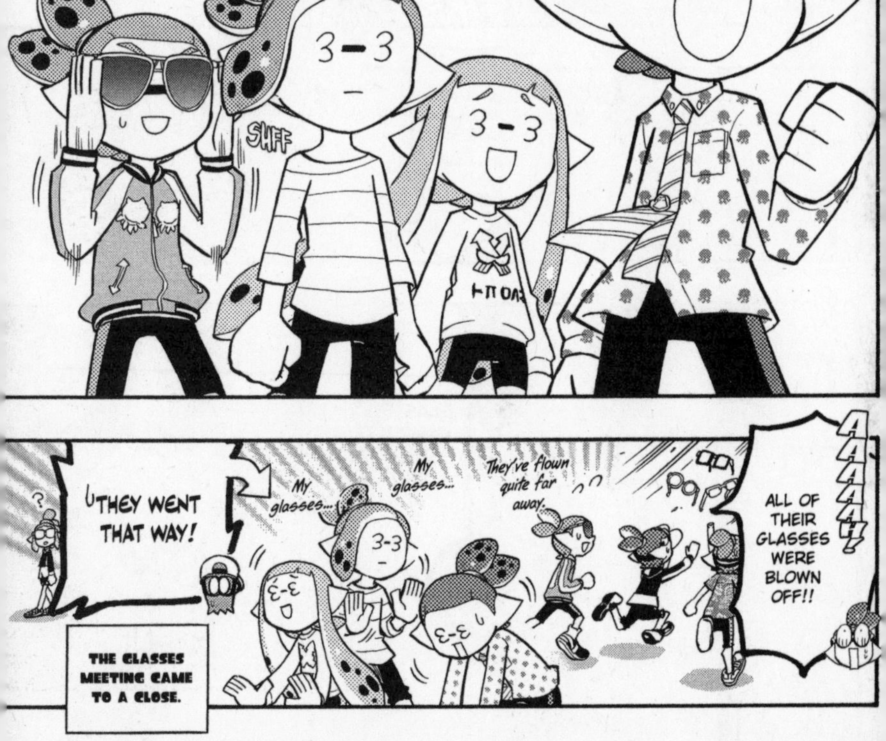
AAAAAAH!
ALL OF THEIR GLASSES WERE BLOWN OFF!!
They've flown quite far away.
My glasses...
My glasses...
THEY WENT THAT WAY!
?
THE GLASSES MEETING CAME TO A CLOSE.

ILLUSTRATION GALLERY

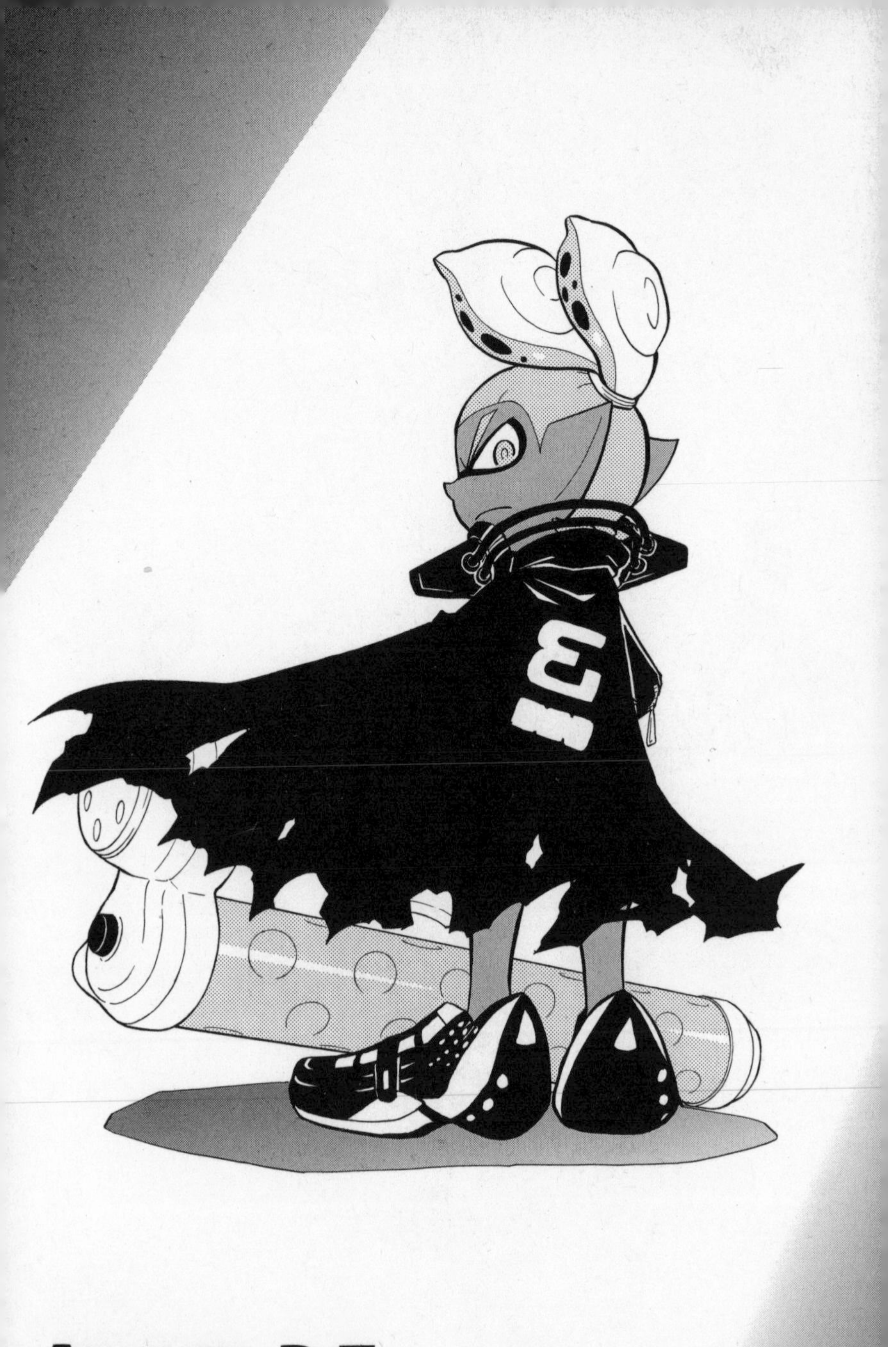

Agent 3.5

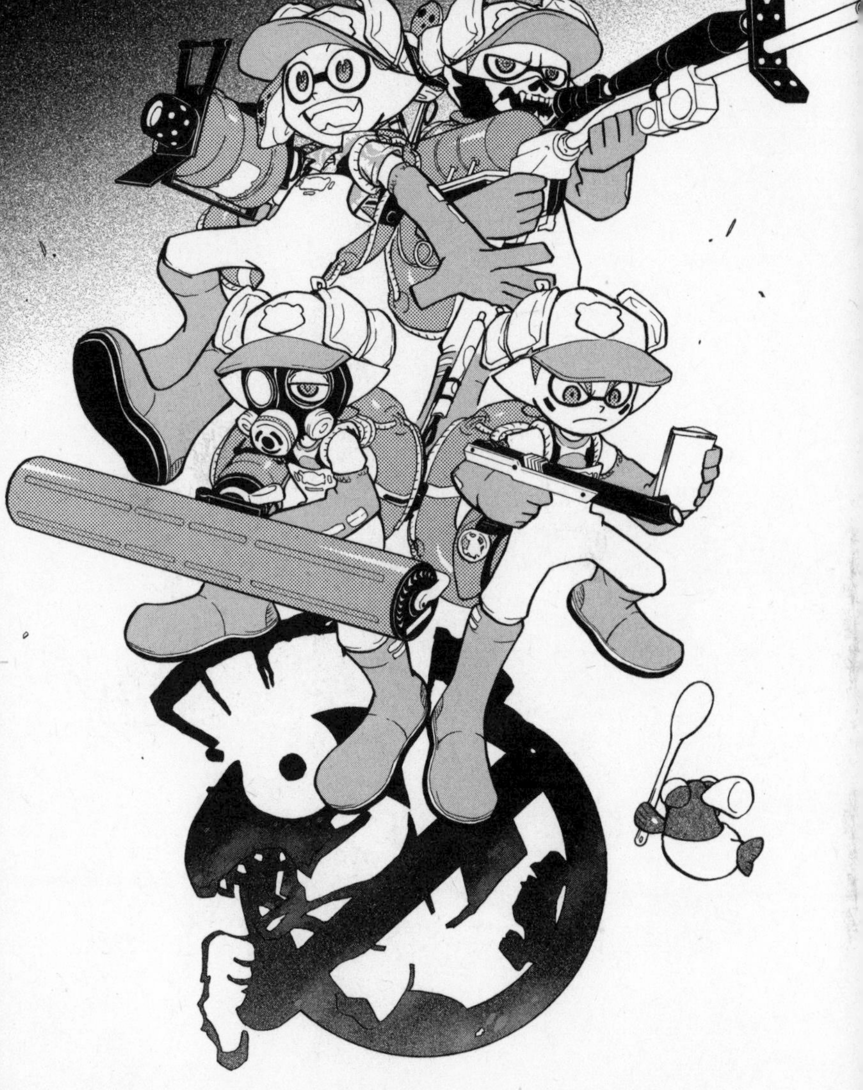

The S4 Salmon Run

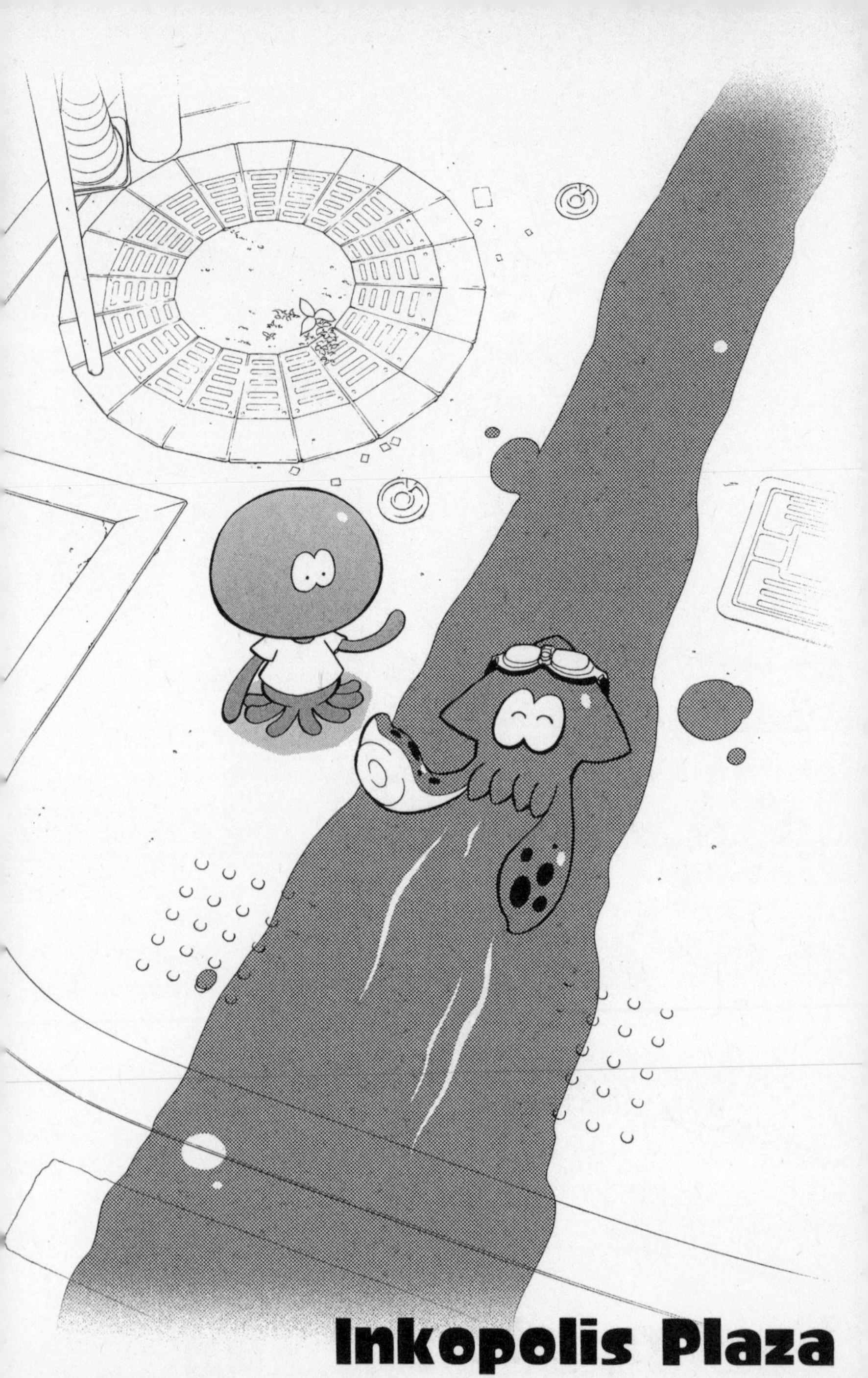

Inkopolis Plaza

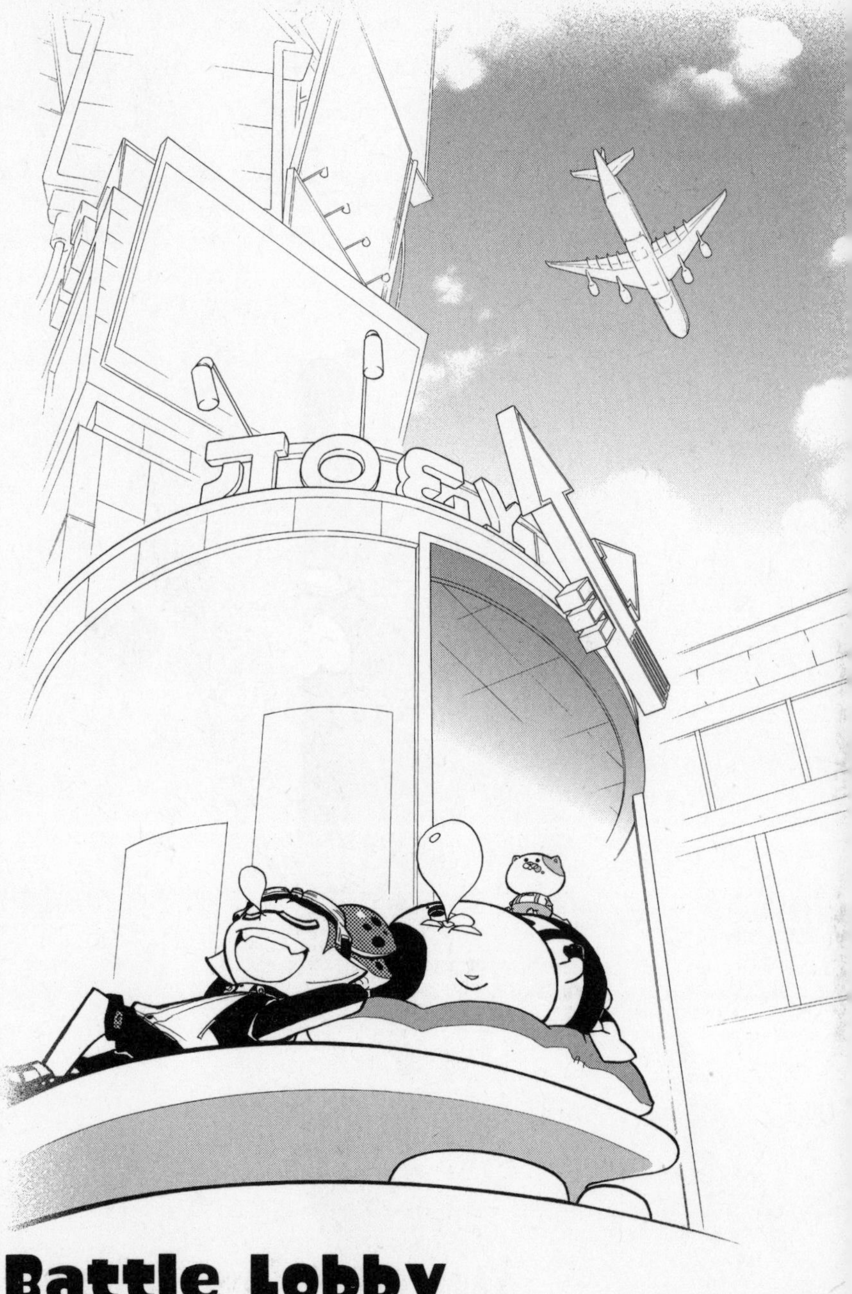

Battle Lobby

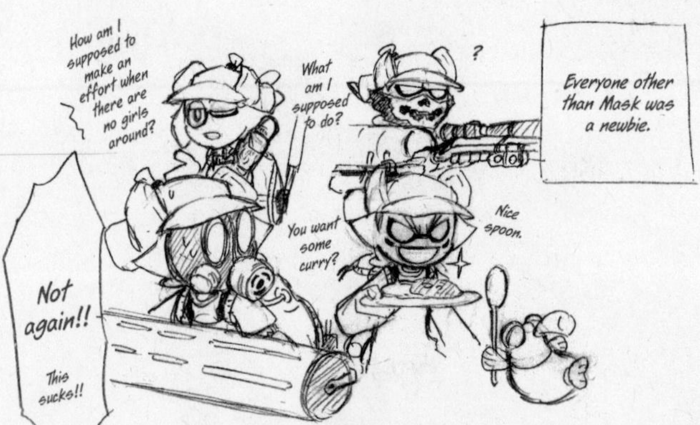
Everyone other than Mask was a newbie.
?
What am I supposed to do?
How am I supposed to make an effort when there are no girls around?
Nice spoon.
You want some curry?
Not again!!
This sucks!!

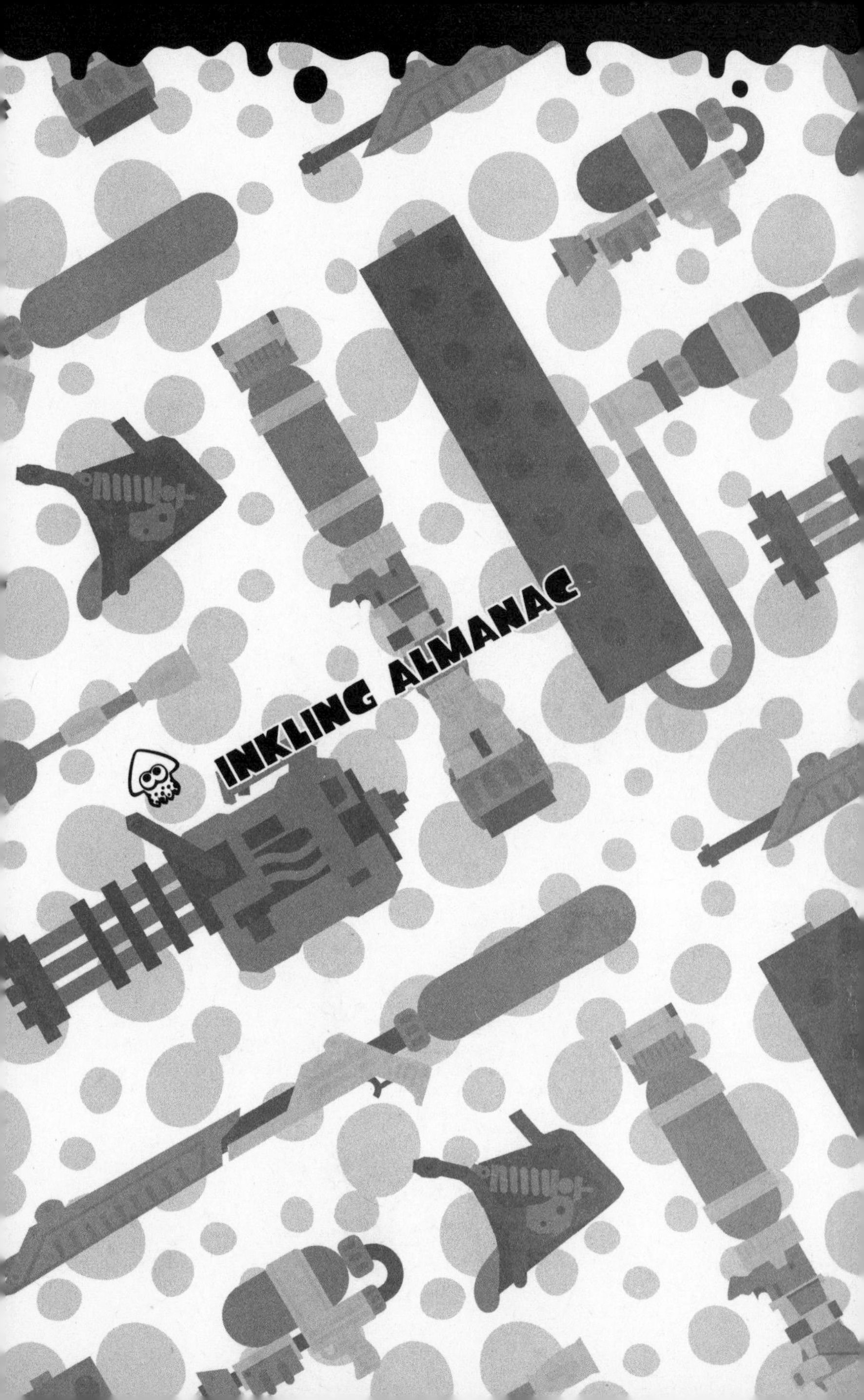
INKLING ALMANAC

ARC

Weapon: Splattershot, etc.
Headgear: Spy Goggles
Clothing: Spy Suit
Shoes: Spy Inksoles

GOGGLES

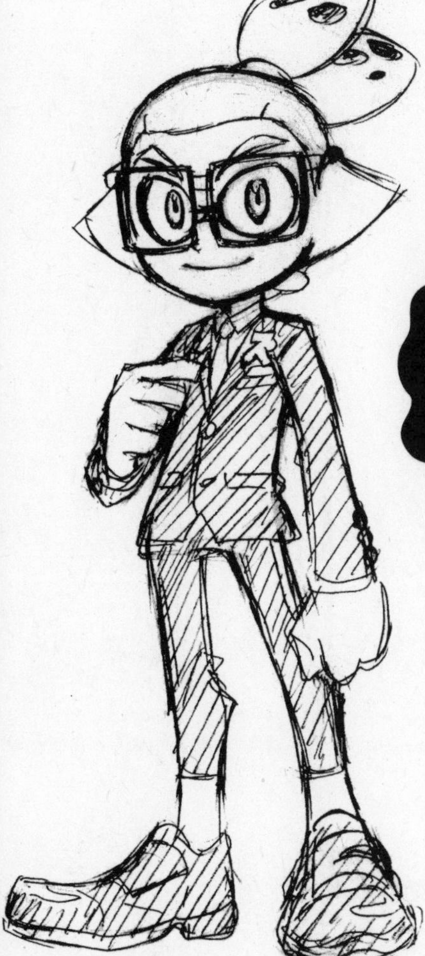

OCTO

Weapon: Undercover Brella, etc.
Headgear: Spy Specs
Clothing: Spy Suit
Shoes: Inky Kid Clams

SPECS

ARC

Weapon: Splat Charger, etc.
Headgear: Spy Headphones
Clothing: Spy Suit
Shoes: Punk Blacks

HEAD-
PHONES

OCTO

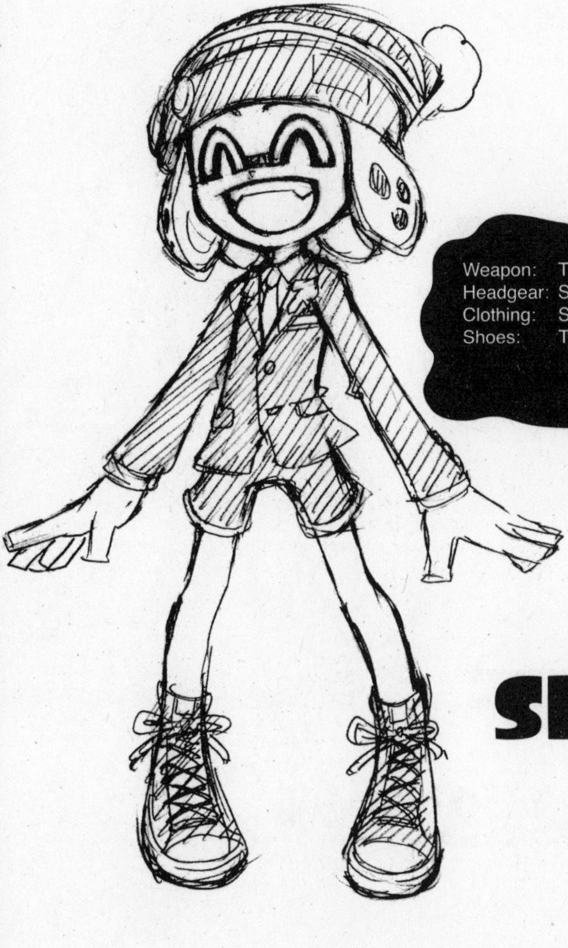

Weapon: Tri-Slosher, etc..
Headgear: Spy Bobble Hat
Clothing: Spy Suit
Shoes: Truffle Canvas Hi-Tops

SPECS

ARC

Weapon: Blaster, etc.

EIGHT

OCT

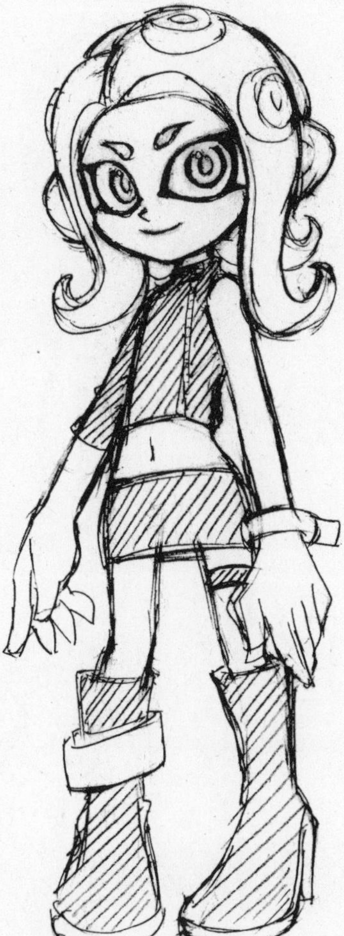

SEVEN

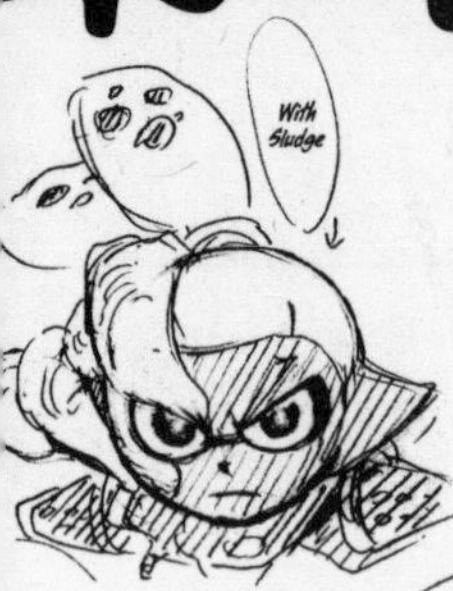
With Sludge

OCTO ARC

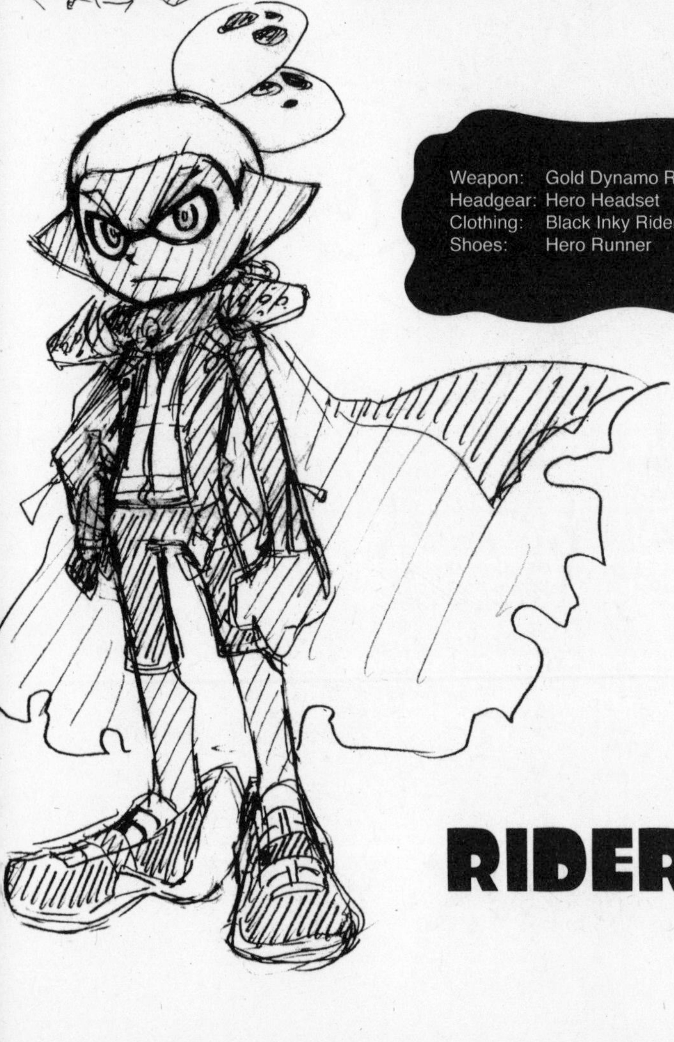

Weapon: Gold Dynamo Roller.
Headgear: Hero Headset
Clothing: Black Inky Rider + Hero Jacket
Shoes: Hero Runner

RIDER

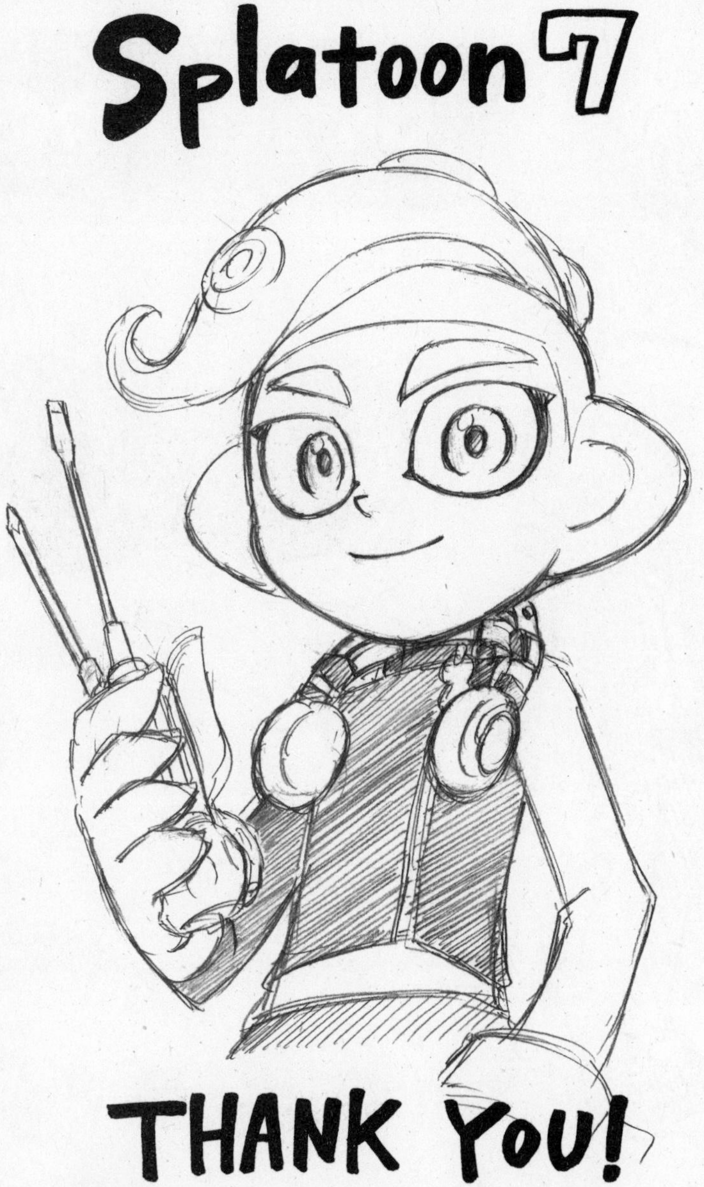
Splatoon 7
THANK YOU!

All aboard the Octo Arc!!

Sankichi Hinodeya

Splatoon™

Volume 7
VIZ Media Edition

Story and Art by
Sankichi Hinodeya

Translation **Tetsuichiro Miyaki**
English Adaptation **Jason A. Hurley**
Lettering **John Hunt**
Design **Shawn Carrico**
Editor **Joel Enos**

Original Japanese edition published by SHOGAKUKAN.
English translation rights in the United States of America, Canada, the United Kingdom, Ireland, Australia and New Zealand arranged with SHOGAKUKAN.

Original Design **100percent**

Printed in the U.S.A.

Published by VIZ Media, LLC
P.O. Box 77010
San Francisco, CA 94107

10 9 8 7 6 5 4 3 2 1
First printing, September 2019

VIZ MEDIA
viz.com

ratings.viz.com
RATED A ALL AGES

PARENTAL ADVISORY
SPLATOON is rated A and is suitable for readers of all ages.

Splatoon reads from right to left!

This is the end of this graphic novel.